WHOSE RAINBOW?

GOD'S GIFT OF SEXUALITY: A DIVINE CALLING

PETER JONES

 Ezra Press

Published by Ezra Press, a ministry of the Ezra Institute
for Contemporary Christianity
PO Box 9, Stn. Main.
Grimsby, ON
L3M 1M0.

Cover design by Sarah Sisco
Interior design by Rachel Eras

For volume pricing please contact the Ezra Institute:
info@ezrainstitute.ca

Whose Rainbow? God's Gift of Sexuality: A Divine Calling
ISBN: 978-1-989169-06-3

TABLE OF CONTENTS

FOREWORD
BY ROSARIA BUTTERFIELD

Only Peter Jones could write *Whose Rainbow?* Pastor, theologian, professor, prolific author, philosopher, husband, dad, granddad, old British guy (I mean this with all due respect), Peter Jones has lived through pivotal changes in Western culture and he knows how to catalog shattering worldview shifts better than any Christian writing today. This book is majestic, pastoral, insightful, disarming, easy to read and vital to digest.

A mere decade ago, a secular society registered homosexuality as one sexual variant among many. And before the *Obergefell* decision there was hope for Christian discourse to have a place in the public sphere. But this has all changed. Anything short of advocacy and celebration for the LGBTQ movement in the public sphere now implies bigotry, hatred, and immoralism. We Christians feel this. We know that we are becoming intolerable to our progressive, interfaith neighbors. The message that we need to leave our biblical Christianity at home and in the closet is made clear in every sensitivity training workshop where we learn to say, "Hi, my name is Rosaria; I identify as a woman and go by the pronouns she and her." How and why has this insanity come to us?

Whose Rainbow? explains why: because our society is not secular, but rather pagan. And in our pagan world, homosexuality has become the central religion. When homosexuality became the new religion, any rejection of any aspect of it is intolerable. Acceptance now comes with approval. No difference of opinion welcome. If Christians are to enjoy the ease of acceptance, the Bible must be rewritten according to the new rules of interfaith paganism. And progressive "Christians" have been more than willing to fill this bill.

Where did the religion of homosexuality get so much power?

LIFE PRE- AND POST-*OBERGEFELL*:

Obergefell vs. Hodges was the momentous June 2015 Supreme Court decision that legalized gay marriage in all 50 states. In addition to legalizing gay marriage, the *Obergefell* decision added a "dignitary harm" clause to the 14th Amendment. *Obergefell* thus functioned to do three things: 1). It codified the idea that sexual orientation is a category of personhood; 2). It expanded civil rights to include the harm done to one's dignity by anything that fails to respect and encourage LGBTQ identity (for example, failing to use "preferred pronouns" or failing to honor the perceived fixed truth of sexual orientation). This exceeds all other civil rights legislation to date as it creates a legal definition of harm based on the subjective feelings of perceived disrespect. 3). It put religious liberty on the firing line as it pits the teaching of the Bible against the teaching of the Supreme Court. After *Obergefell*, LGBTQ is "who" you are, not "how" you feel. And SOGI (sexual orientation gender identity) laws depend on the use of sexual identity orientation language and the world that it imagines. After *Obergefell*, the LGBTQ community became a political machine. And that political machine is not content to orbit in a parallel universe with the church. No, the biblical church's witness is itself a violation of dignitary harm.

ONEISM/TWOISM:

For decades, Dr. Jones has been working with cosmological concepts he identifies as oneism/twoism, a paradigm which offers profound insight into this pagan landslide. Simply put, oneism is pagan: it collapses God with the creation; twoism is theistic and biblical: it separates God from creation by honoring Him as the maker and sovereign King of heaven and earth and all that dwell therein. Our culture's exchange of twoism for oneism is a frightening word picture of Romans 1:25: "They exchanged the Truth for the lie…." What does this have to do with the growing LGBTQ rights movement within both the world and the church? Everything. Indeed, it puts everything that we have seen in the past two decades, but especially our post-*Obergefell* world, into biblical perspective.

- It explains how and why many denominations that were historically orthodox (two-ist) have normalized homosexuality and embraced it as a valid part of the life of the Church (one-ist).
- It reveals how foundational Biblical texts have been eliminated or rejected and replaced with one-ist views of sexuality.
- It unpacks the one-ist apostasy of interfaith, progressive, and gay Christianity.
- It anticipates how Christianity's decline produces paganism,

9

not secularism.

- It captures the way that the creation ordinance and Christ's redemption, Genesis 1:1-3 and Romans 1, is a Rosetta Stone for human identity, a blueprint of God's character, and a road map for which way is up.

Peter Jones handles with brilliance and insight both the Bible and a vast array of other theological and philosophical texts, seamlessly walking the reader through the labyrinth of chaos into the clear light of day. In addition to all of this, Peter Jones has a pastor's heart and a love for the lost. He knows grace. He knows that praying parents stand behind children presently lost to the LGBTQ world. He does not make into scapegoats people who proudly call themselves homosexual and live accordingly. He knows that the greatest testimony of God's righteousness is not the church lambasting the culture with the sword, but rather men and women who had once lived as homosexuals and who advocated for LGBTQ rights repenting and believing, committing their lives to Jesus and declaring victory over indwelling sexual sin, fleeing from false gospels and declaring them and their leaders wolves and villains as they become members in good standing in true biblical churches. Whose Rainbow? is the book for our times. May the Church heed the warning found within these pages. It is in the clear hope of seeing God's victory over the paganism of our culture, the apostasy of many churches, and the stubborn unbelief that rules many hearts that Peter Jones has written this, a book that must be read and heeded by every thinking Christian.

WHY THIS BOOK?

I humbly dare to tackle the controversial issue of homosexuality, even though myriad authors have already written volumes on the subject. As my readers know, I have been researching and pondering the rise of homosexuality in our culture for many years, but an experience I had prompted me to get this book out and finished. I was asked to speak at a Christian college where LGBT pressure on campus was growing and where rainbow flags were flying. I expected opposition from the student body, but when I lectured to 200 students, I was pleasantly surprised to have a standing ovation from about 80% of them. This is not the only time I have seen this enthusiastic response, which is noteworthy for the Millennial generation. Young people like to get to the heart of issues. For this reason, I am eager to explain the underlying worldview and theological issues that inspire the homosexual agenda to as many young readers as possible, since they represent the future of the culture and the church.

Our youth are being brainwashed by the LGBT movement in their schools, their libraries, their TV and movie content, their social media accounts, their families, and their friends. We must show our Christian children and young people the worldview basis for an evaluation of homosexuality and gender.

Our youth are not the only ones affected by the rush to approve the new gender identity theories. The Christian church at large is being deceived. If the next generation is to resist the cultural pressure in this area, they must be instructed in their homes, churches and Christian schools by leaders who stand firm for the right reasons, which are rooted in God himself and his nature as Creator and Redeemer. In order to do justice to the issues at hand, we need to get to the deepest possible level in our discussion. What we say about sexuality ultimately reflects what we think about God. In what follows I hope to demonstrate that a positive affirmation of homosexuality leads to a total rejection of the God revealed in the Bible and thus to a loss of the historic Christian faith. The stakes are enormous.

On this one issue of the LGBT agenda, human culture will divide in irremediable conflict. One simple example is the storm of protestors who crashed the opening of a Chick-Fil-A restaurant in Toronto. Years ago, owner Dan Cathy, an evangelical Christian, stated: "We are inviting God's judgment on our nation when we shake our fist at Him and say, 'We know better than you as to what constitutes marriage.'"[1] A pro-gay group, The 519s, through its spokesman Justin Khan, voiced its outrage: "We won't allow hateful rhetoric to be here. The fact that Chick-Fil-A is opening on the streets of Toronto is something that is quite alarming." Unfortunately, Chick-Fil-A has now caved under the pressure and has made it known that it will no longer give to ministries like the Fellowship of Christian Athletes and the Salvation Army because of their anti-LGBT stance. Such is the power of the LGBT movement.

This deep divide over sexuality is now also seen within the church. I feel a compulsion to warn the church about the deep theological implications of its decisions about sexual and gender issues, which have social and moral implications of the most crucial nature. How this problem is resolved will either affirm or destroy the traditions of Western democratic culture and of Christianity in particular. To speak truth about God the Creator will elicit opposition that will severely limit Christian freedom and doubtless lead to economic and even physical persecution.

I pray that this book will both shake you up and encourage you. The situation is far worse than you thought, but our God is far greater than you could ever imagine.

CHAPTER 1

HOPE IN THE RAINBOW?

In 1875, members of First Presbyterian Church in Columbia, South
Carolina stood in front of their church, stunned and dismayed.
In a chapter called "Many Coloured Rainbows," in a book on the
church's history, David Calhoun tells of a violent storm that brought
the church's magnificently tall steeple crashing to the ground. It "fell
its full length along the top of the building and rolled off on the
side...into the churchyard, breaking the tablets [gravestones dating
back to the Revolutionary War] which marked the resting places of
the dead." After the storm a grand sunset and a many-coloured rainbow appeared bringing encouragement and delight to the devastated
believers.[1]

Those Christian believers found assurance not simply in the
beauty of a rainbow, but in the God-infused hope it represents. In
Genesis 9, one of the earliest biblical texts, written thousands of

years ago, God declares the rainbow to be the work of the Creator of heaven and earth, recalling both his righteous judgment and his eventual blessing. Specifically, the rainbow reassures humanity that God will never again destroy the earth by flood:

> I establish my covenant with you, that never again shall all flesh be cut off by the waters of the flood, and never again shall there be a flood to destroy the earth. ... When the bow is in the clouds, I will see it and remember the everlasting covenant between God and every living creature of all flesh that is on the earth. (Gen. 9:8–17)

God's rainbow signifies a gracious promise of the divine Creator to be creation's caring Overseer and ultimate Savior. This principle is repeated at the end of the Bible: "[A]round the throne was a rainbow that had the appearance of an emerald" (Rev. 4:3). The prophet John's vision of the God of the cosmos is multi-coloured. In addition to green emerald, God's resplendent glory had the appearance of deep red precious stones of jasper and carnelian, and from the throne "came flashes of lightning, and rumblings and peals of thunder," and "burning seven torches of fire" (Rev. 4:3–5)—an amazingly colourful sight.

Once more, the colourful rainbow is associated with what God tells us from his throne of authority about the future of the earth. Here the rainbow again symbolizes the cosmic rule of the Creator, and of him the text affirms that he is the one "who lives forever and ever, who created heaven and what is in it, the earth and what is in it, and the sea and what is in it" (Rev. 10:6). Thus the 24 elders, symbolizing God's people in the Old and New Testament, "fall down before him who is seated on the throne and worship him who lives forever and ever. They cast their crowns before the throne, saying, 'Worthy are you, our Lord and God, to receive glory and honour and power, for you created all things, and by your will they existed and were created'" (Rev. 4:10–11).

In 1978, just over a century after the Columbia storm, at the request of city councillor Harvey Milk, Gilbert Baker designed the Rainbow flag, sometimes called the "gay pride flag" or "LGBT pride flag," in order to give visual identity to the diversity of the LGBT movement and to acknowledge the right of creatures to decide their fundamental sexual identity. Milk, the first openly avowed homosexual and pedophile[2] to be elected to public office in the United States, was for many years the most famous LGBT elected official. Regrettably, Milk was murdered that same year by a disgruntled fellow city supervisor. The Rainbow flag, however, quickly became a universally recognized symbol.[3] The homosexual movement has emerged from the closet, and the gay Rainbow is understood by all. In 2015, when the Supreme Court passed "same-sex marriage," the event was symbolically celebrated, as if on cue, by bathing the White House in multi-coloured floodlight.

"Whose Rainbow?" is not a trivial question of copyright on a representation of a meteorological phenomenon. Its use as a symbol of the celebration of homosexuality leads us to the ultimate question: Who defines reality—God, the eternal Creator, or human creatures?[4]

WHO OWNS THE RAINBOW?

So, we ask: Who owns the rainbow? The Apostle Paul asks this question in a different way: Should we worship the Creator or the creature (Rom. 1:25) as the author of reality? This, dear reader, is another form of the ultimate cosmological question this book tries to answer. The question is not one of a judgmental morality or hate speech that seeks to make people feel guilty about sins they may have committed. It is, rather, the decisive question of cosmic and human origins, of the ultimate meaning of existence, of the true source of our identity and of our hope. It is the question every human being must ask: "Who is God and who is man"? (Ps. 8:4).

Steven D. Smith, professor of law at the University of San Diego, raises this in a fresh way. His book *Pagans and Christians in the City: Culture Wars from the Tiber to the Potomac*[5] e shows how the pagan thinking of first-century Rome has returned to the West. He lays out the two worldview systems that faced off at the beginning of Western history—namely, pagan religion and early Christianity:

> [T]he pagan gods were actors (albeit powerful and immortal actors) of and within this world. The God of Judaism and Christianity, by contrast, is "the creator of the world...who dwells beyond time and space." ... Pagan religion locates the sacred within this world...[in a] religiosity relative to an immanent sacred. Judaism and Christianity, by contrast, reflect a transcendent religiosity; they place the sacred, ultimately, outside the world.[6]

Based on the observation of the French sociologist, Emil Durkheim (1858–1917), that "the religious nature of man...is an essential and permanent aspect of humanity,"[7] Smith concludes that "behind a façade of secularism...the old rivalry in the West between paganism and Christianity, or between immanent and transcendent religiosities, shows signs of becoming reinvigorated."[8] Smith notes that this rivalry also reinvigorated discussions about sexuality.

In the ancient world, "sexual passion reflects 'the indwelling presence of the gods.'...Sex was at the center of it all.... For Paul, the sexual disorder of Roman society was the single most powerful symbol of the world's alienation from God." This is why "early Christianity commonly equated fornication with idolatry. The confinement of sex to one partner within the sanctified bonds of matrimony was correlated with monotheism." In this case, marriage to one partner fit the belief in one God. In the other case, many partners of varying sexualities fit the belief in many gods.[9]

These observations make it clear that sexuality is not a subject unto itself but the expression of a deeply-held religious belief system, of which there are really only two. For some time now, I have called these two options Oneism and Twoism. Asking and answering the question about sexuality is neither an expression of bigotry nor an unhealthy preoccupation with sexual matters, but the recognition of the vitally important meaning of sexuality in the whole extent of human existence. It is asking, for the sake of human sanity, how the cosmos, and sexuality within it, has been and is put together.[10]

WORLDVIEW ARITHMETIC: COUNTING FROM 1 TO 2

If you can count from 1 to 2, you can be a theologian. Have you noticed the peculiar term that's popping up lately— "non-binary"? Now that I've mentioned it, you may start noticing it. You will see a demand for non-binary thinking for the culture of tomorrow. Now that's a peculiar way to describe human culture. The Google Dictionary defines binary as "relating to, composed of, or involving two things." Non-binary thinking rejects twoness, insisting on a kind of indivisibility of everything. Ultimately, you must choose either "one" (non-binary) or "two" (binary).

Contrary to what many major news outlets would tell you, the current frictions in the cultural ethos in the United States, as well as in the West in general, are not actually between bigots and progressives or between traditionalists and visionaries, as Steven Smith's book clearly demonstrates. The real debate touches the root question of how the world is put together and by whom. If you do not understand the profound worldview conflict that "non-binary versus binary" creates, you will not understand sexuality, God or the world. Let me explain.

We are confronted by two cosmologies, two descriptions of how the universe is put together: either a homocosmology, a world where everything is the same (homo in Greek means "same"); or a heterocosmology, in which difference is the key to meaning (hetero in Greek means "different"). The confrontation here is radical. Integration of these two views is impossible. There is no third way.

Progressive futurist theologian, Brian McLaren, once a conservative evangelical, calls for a new definition of God as "a bigger, non-dualistic, non-binary God."[11] He prefers a God who is "in the story, not outside of time and space like a prime mover or divine watchmaker."[12] McLaren's god is not different from us; he actually is us. Non-dualistic is another term for non-binary, since "dual" also means "two." These are broad, simplified ways of describing reality. Things are understood either through the rubric of oneness or twoness: non-binary or binary, non-dualistic or dualistic. This sounds ridiculously simple, but it is deeply theological.

In my book, *One or Two: Seeing a World of Difference*,[13] I show that binary and non-binary are the only two categories by which we can understand reality. These categories are biblical. The Apostle Paul states with outrageous simplicity that there are only two ways of being human: you either worship and serve creation or you worship and serve the Creator (Rom. 1:25). You cannot miss the either/or of these mutually exclusive options. If you worship creation, then created things are all that exist. There is no Creator. Everything has the same origin. I call this Oneism. You could also call it non-binary because "All Is One." All nature is self-creating and made up of the same stuff. Matter is supreme because it is ultimate and thus worthy of worship. Nothing is distinct from anything else. The organizing principle is oneness.

On the contrary, when you worship the Creator, you are recognizing that there is a reality outside of nature, a personal reality distinct from nature, namely God the Creator, who is nature's source. God is the only uncreated being. Everything else that exists is created by him. There are two very different kinds of existence that together give meaning to everything. In this sense, difference and distinction are fundamentally good and right. I call that Twoism: reality is organized around the binary principle of twoness.

A non-binary culture that worships only nature does not worship the Creator and is named as idolatry in the Bible. Worship of nature is the classic definition of paganism. So the non-binary, whether people realize it or not, is pagan Oneism. The other perspective, the world of the binary, is biblical Twoism. Our culture is eliminating binary distinctions wherever it can, especially in areas of spirituality and sexuality. In this way, ever since the 1960s revolution, Western culture has become steadily more pagan. The once marginal agenda for which the long-haired hippies clamored (radical freedom from God and especially from heterosexual morality) has been achieved and has become public policy, enshrined in law. With a society now so opposed to its Christian heritage, Christians must understand the binary character of life as the essence of the Christian faith. In fact, every human being must choose between these two options. The binary cosmos was not invented by mean-spirited conservative Christians. To understand the nature of the universe and our place within it does not imply a lack of love or a refusal to consider human justice. The theological data about the nature of existence precede any human opinions on the subject and define not only the difference between creatures and the Creator, but between males and females, right and wrong, or true and false. Behind the divisive current issue of sexual identity is the deepest of questions: Is there a personal Creator or does nature create itself?

THE CHURCH AT THE BRINK

Evangelical churches stand at the brink. If they accept and affirm the practice of homosexuality within the church, they will fall inevitably into liberalism and, finally, into non-binary paganism. When the Nashville Statement on Sexuality[14] was published in 2017, the Internet rocked with passionate responses from Christians denouncing the statement in righteous anger. Although it was written and endorsed by leading evangelical theologians (such as J. I. Packer and Al Mohler), the statement was dismissed by many Christian movements as a hateful attack on people with variant sexual identities.

Though the Nashville Statement deals with the seemingly peripheral question of sexual behaviour it raises crucial questions about the definition of God-honouring sexuality and of who is truly a Christian. The statement provokes Christians and the church to consider underlying issues of Christian orthodoxy and the nature of the cosmos.

As it was 500 years ago, at the birth of Protestantism, the church is once again asked to define orthodoxy. The sexuality issue in particular has led some Protestant churches to re-examine their commitment to the five solas of the Reformation: Scripture alone, faith alone, grace alone, Christ alone, to the glory of God alone. The cultural challenge to the gospel of Jesus Christ presents itself today as a different question than the one posed in the sixteenth century. At the Reformation, the essential question was: "Can I save myself by my good deeds"? Roman Catholics and emerging Protestants agreed on beliefs about God as Creator, the Trinity, and Christ's historical birth, death and resurrection, marriage and human sexuality. Current discussion does not begin with salvation, but with questions about the nature of personal identity and the relation between sexuality and the heart of the gospel.

Because these questions are so essential and the subject so culturally volatile, many pastors, even well-meaning orthodox pastors, do not dare—or perhaps do not know how—to deal with the issue. Afraid of upsetting members who might have sexual temptations, they choose to ignore these sensitive subjects. But silence is deadly. The flames of this current apostasy are raging through our churches.

In such a crucial issue, we must find a discourse that avoids emotionalism, moralism, hatred, bigotry, or mere traditionalism. Our response must go to the heart of the question. Many Millennial Christians, who are now becoming the church's leaders, need a clear and profound statement of the truth, for they are leaving the church in droves because of its perceived mistreatment of homosexuals. If we are to understand sexuality, we need to hear a holistic, binary account of what the Bible says about it.

TWO WORDS OF CAUTION

As we deal with the volatile issue of alternate sexuality (homosexuality, lesbianism, transgenderism, transvestism, agenderism, drag, etc.) and its relationship to biblical faith, we need to remember two important principles:

First, there must be no contempt for gay individuals. Christians may never show contempt for anyone, for we are all made in God's image. We must not demonize homosexuals, show them bigotry or "righteous anger." The problem is much bigger than any one person. On a personal level, many who claim an alternate sexual identity have known suffering and rejection, whether from abuse by sexual predators or from heartless treatment by believers who have judged and dismissed them. Jeffrey Satinover, a recognized authority on homosexual experience, notes that while the present normalization of homosexuality increases the likelihood that a young person will adopt a homosexual lifestyle, "ridicule, rejection, and harsh punitive condemnation...will be just as likely to drive him to the same position."[15]

A Christian discussion of the issue must avoid moralism. All human beings are noble, yet fallen, creatures. No one can speak from a position of moral superiority. A Christian, better than anyone else, knows how deep and wide is the vileness of his sin and the mercy of his God. The forgiven Christian will communicate God's forgiving love, which each of us needs. If God is rich in "kindness, forbearance and patience...that lead to repentance" (Rom. 2:4), so must be God's people. We cannot begin with accusations of deliberate sin. Many homosexuals have known sexual desire for their own gender since childhood. Before treating the question of sin, we must deal with the question of a fallen world, and of homosexuality as out of step with original creation—as "unnatural," as Paul says in Romans 1:26.

Second, we need a clear definition of "gay Christianity." The issue is confusing. The Gay Christian Network, founded in 2001 by Justin Lee, states: "[The Gay Christian Network] is designed to be a haven for all gay Christians. Our membership includes both those on Side A and on Side B." For those who may not be familiar with this terminology, Side A refers to those who have abandoned the historic Christian teaching about sexuality and marriage and now affirm, as good and right, same-sex relationships and same-sex "marriage." Those who hold this position generally associate with liberal Protestant denominations. Side B refers to those who affirm Christian teaching, even the traditional Christian ethic on sexuality and marriage, yet identify as LGBT. Both Side A and Side B are against the promiscuity and sexual looseness that are often a part of the secular world.[16]

Side B stirred up news in 2018 when it organized a self-proclaimed evangelical Revoice conference, which took place in a Presbyterian Church in America facility. This conference sought to develop a future Christianity

> where LGBT people can be open and transparent in their faith communities about their orientation and/or experience of gender dysphoria without feeling inferior to their straight, cisgender[17] brothers and sisters; where churches not only utilize but also celebrate the unique opportunities that life-long celibate LGBT people have to serve others; where Christian leaders boast about the faith of LGBT people who are living a sacrificial obedience for the sake of the Kingdom; and where LGBT people are welcomed into families so they, too, can experience the joys, challenges, and benefits of kinship.[18]

These are certainly issues that have needed to be discussed for a long time. Unfortunately, even this approach fails to do justice to Scripture. Side B argues that non-realized homosexual orientation can be pleasing to God since, according to them, relationships in creation before the Fall were not all necessarily heterosexual in orientation. Same-sex "aesthetic orientation," they claim, is not sinful since it is not necessarily erotic. Such orientation can be celebrated as male-to-male aesthetic and relational friendship.

Some of the main Side B organizers and speakers gladly join in common efforts with Side A advocates because they share a common "identity."[19] Moreover, the language of "sexual minorities" implies permanent and unchangeable identity and is thus a demand for recognition as a normative cultural category. Revoice seeks to redeem

"Queer culture," but same-sex attraction and effeminacy,[20] not only physical homosexual behaviour, are sinful, and we are called to repent both of sin and of any inner desire to sin (Rom. 8:12–13, Jas. 1:13–15).

Certainly, the church and individual Christians should regret the way homosexuals have often been treated. We have failed to understand the suffering and brokenness of our brothers and sisters who fight strong homosexual desires, but we cannot adopt the ideology of Revoice as a biblical way to love fellow sinners. To do so would deny our love for God by considering the possibility that the image of God (Gen. 1:27–8) revealed in the male/female distinction includes some third kind of androgynous human being.

Temptation, which comes to us from the outside, is not a sin. Temptation is part of the human lot, but it takes root because of our sinful nature. Jesus was tempted by the devil, yet without sin. Scripture is very clear: "For we do not have a high priest who is unable to sympathize with our weaknesses, but one who in every respect has been tempted as we are, yet without sin" (Heb. 4:15; see also Luke 4:13; 1 Cor. 10:13.). The "gay Christian" worldview that I analyze in these pages as having no place in the Christian church is Side A, which justifies intentional commission in bodily action of homosexual sex as in line with Christian teaching. Side B is made up of those who feel that homosexual acts are a temptation to be resisted, because they rightly believe that Scripture is opposed to homosexual acts.[21] Side B seeks to maintain the biblical teaching concerning the refusal of same-sex practice and takes up a rightful defence of celibacy. However, by claiming homosexuality as a valid orientation that God accepts—indeed creates—Side B undermines the binary image of male and female taught in the Scripture as reflecting the person of God. Side B people should resist the temptation to consid-

28

er nonpracticing homosexuality as pleasing to God. Homosexuality (including homosexual thoughts and desires) is the result of the Fall and, in itself, expresses Oneism, even in its celibate form. Side B gives passive approval of homosexuality as something normal.[22]

The fact that a discussion of this nature between Christians in Christian churches has gotten to this point shows how successful was the movement that started in the Sixties and has educated Christian leaders of today. In so many ways, that generation has often been a destructive generation, which we will consider in the next chapter.

CHAPTER 2

THE CULTURAL DOMINATRIX

DESTRUCTIVE GENERATION

I am a historical artifact; I admit it. As my faithful readers are no doubt tired of hearing, I played music with my school chum, John Lennon. Strange, but true. Yet something even stranger happened during my lifetime: the arrival of the Sixties Cultural Revolution. Ken Myers explains that "*The Sixties* is a phrase that happens to have a numerical form, but it is a phrase that is more like *The Reformation* or *The Enlightenment*, summarizing a range of ideas, social and cultural realignments, and changes in popular consciousness."[1] As I settled into seminary life in New England, a young atheist Marxist named David Horowitz was in Berkeley, California editing a left-wing magazine called *Ramparts* and promoting student revolution against all authorities. Horowitz knew the leaders of the Sixties revolution, particularly those associated with a small, violent underground group called the Weathermen.

AYERS AND DOHRN

In that group was a couple, Bill Ayers and Bernadine Dohrn, who blew up buildings and killed policemen. David Horowitz heard Bernadine's foul-mouthed and determined vow to "smash monogamy" and to "produce a world revolution."[2] That revolution has highly influenced the current culture of the United States. Ayers and Dohrn later befriended future President Barack Obama in Chicago and helped him prepare for his presidency, though he was no doubt better served by the charm of another cultural revolutionary, Saul Alinsky, who suggested more subtle subterfuges for taking over a culture.[3]

Much later Horowitz abandoned Marxism and came to understand what the Sixties Cultural Revolution was all about, as the title of his book says: *Destructive Generation*. He declared "the radical future [proposed by revolutionaries to be] an illusion, and the American present worth defending."[4] And the beat goes on. In November, 2019, cop-killer Dohrn's and Ayers' adopted son, Chesa Boudin, equally as radical as his parents, won the election to become San Francisco's next district attorney. According to Boudin, "The people of San Francisco have sent a powerful and clear message. It's time for radical change to how we envision justice."[5]

FOX-GENOVESE

Another influential witness to the Sixties upheaval is Elizabeth Fox-Genovese, who—like Horowitz—was a radical, hippy Leftist. Later, as a Harvard historian, she concluded that the Sixties Cultural Revolution that she helped foment was "a cataclysmic transformation of the very nature of our society."[6] Western culture was shattered by an invasion of both ancient Eastern paganism and pre-Christian sexual practice. These changes transformed a world influenced for a millennium and a half by Western Christian traditions into one with many of the accoutrements of the ancient and pagan Roman Empire.[7] The speed with which this cultural shift has transpired is stunning. The golden rule of the new morality goes like this: "The deepest moral law is to be true to oneself." "Follow the desires of your heart." "Do not judge others." "To love is to accept all—no discriminations, no distinctions." "There is no law outside of us because there is no God outside of us."

APOSTASY: SEXUAL AND SPIRITUAL

This ideological apostasy occurs in the West at two essential levels of human existence: the sexual and the spiritual. For discussion they may be separated, but as an ideology they belong together. This is a biblical theme, as Jesus warns the church in Thyatira (Rev. 2:20): "Beware of the woman Jezebel, who calls herself a prophetess and is teaching and seducing my servants to practice sexual immorality [sexuality] and to eat food sacrificed to idols [spirituality]." The text calls this amalgam "the deep things of Satan" (Rev. 2:24).

The current integration of homosexuality into the life of the culture and the church is portrayed as a harmless personal orientation, to be celebrated along with all other personal orientations. But we must evaluate the deep spiritual implications of such a radical redefinition of sexuality. Both sexuality and spirituality get to the essence of who we are. The subtitle of a book I wrote, *The God of Sex*,[8] says it well: *How Spirituality Defines Your Sexuality*. Even Christian De La Huerta, an openly homosexual author and Oneist radical thinker, recognizes the integral relationship between spirituality and sexuality in his powerful book about the history of homosexuality, *Coming*

33

Out Spiritually: "Sexuality without spirituality becomes boring and addictive and even cynical; spirituality without sexuality becomes disengaged and diseased, that is, disincarnated."[9]

The point is essential—sexuality and spirituality cannot be separated. The question then becomes: What sexuality and what spirituality? The two kinds of sexuality, homo or hetero, are integrally linked to the two kinds of spirituality, pagan worship, or worship of the Creator. Sexuality and spirituality must be seen as building either an integrated hetero- or homo-cosmological vision for the future of the world.

In this chapter and the next, we will examine the huge changes that have taken place in Western culture since the Sixties—first to sexuality, and then to spirituality.

A New View of Marriage and Gender

As Kristin Luker, professor of law and sociology at the University of California, Berkeley, explains:

> Men and women of a certain age have lived through a revolution as disorienting and historically important as any of the revolutions we routinely recognize as such…. That revolution questioned a whole set of assumptions about what were the right ways for men and women to relate to one another sexually, how sex was and should be related to maleness and femaleness, and how and where marriage and sex should coincide. The opening up of what had been taken-for-granted truths has changed the world.[10]

The revolution in marriage is not imaginary: from the 1960s to 2009, out-of-wedlock births in the United States rose from 7% to 40%. In Europe it is close to 60%.[11] Following the Obergefell decision to legalize same-sex "marriage" in the United States, Paul

Kengor, a contemporary specialist in the study of Marxism, stated with shock: "[T]his is the only time that a majority of everyday Americans have agreed with communists in one of their sharp, atheistic stances against marriage and the family.... It is a breath-taking development to behold."[12] The American majority, he goes on to say, "no longer holds fast to the traditional-religious boundaries that navigated the lives of their ancestors."[13]

During my boyhood, no one mentioned homosexuality. How is it that, two generations later, barbaric Dionysian sex orgies are normal fare for university students? The 2018 annual "Sex Week" at Northwestern University featured a Chicago-based dominatrix named "Lady Sophia" who taught the students various BDSM (bondage, discipline, and sadomasochism) practices. Says the advertising: "What better way can you learn about the basics of BDSM than from a professional domme in Chicago?" No one bothers to ask *why* students need to know the basics of BDSM. This very same Sophia is the dominatrix who runs Chicago Dungeon Rentals and is a "well-respected sex educator."[14] What happened?

Under the mystical sway of the cultural dominatrix, we dismiss God's glorious plan for sexuality as a tired religious platitude and consider as imaginary Scripture's teaching about creational and biological differences between men and women, on whom is imprinted the image of God (Gen. 1:26–27). Contemporary cultural sensibilities incline many Christians to truncate their Christian activity to "caring for the least, or being the merciful Samaritan, or welcoming the outsider or washing people's feet."[15] While these attitudes are essential to a life lived for Jesus, "progressive" Christians who dismiss the Bible's teaching on sexuality unwittingly adopt a form of creation-denying Gnosticism. They cannot truly care for people if they invite them to adopt the ancient Gnostic heresy, which threw God the Creator into Hell.[16] Our culture has made into a human rights value what Paul describes as unnatural (Rom. 1:26). For Paul, homosexuality is unnatural not only for believers but for everyone, because it is out of order with the physical cosmos as God the Creator made it. Engaging in homosexual activity is thus both a rejection of the real, natural world and of God himself, who is both moral judge and intelligent Creator of all things. To deny the authority and goodness of God's created design is serious heresy, and the eviscerated "message of love" will not help to bring the neighbour into a true relationship with the God of love. In fact, denying God as Creator and Lord may push one down the path that leads to destruction, as Paul shows in Romans 1.

Behind the warm, fuzzy calls to unity and the can't-we-all-get-along tolerance, there is a profoundly anti-biblical agenda, committed to silencing God's truth about the world and resisting the good news that genuine love, God's love, is accessible. Any pastor or church leader who, in the name of love for neighbour, seeks to normalize as Christian all the bizarre sexual options in the LGBTQiAPK+ paradigm (as people vainly seek to create their own identity) fails to realize the deep level of ideological apostasy now on offer.

Catholic theologian Benjamin Wiker, with anguish, well understands the situation in his church:

> As Christianity slowly evangelized the pagan Roman Empire, the widespread acceptance of men having sex with boys was replaced by widespread moral revulsion (and the appearance of anti-pedophilia laws that followed upon it). The same is true as well for homosexuality, sexual slavery, abortion, infanticide and euthanasia. They became moral issues, rather than accepted pagan social practices, only because of Christian evangelization…. The sole reason that there are still secular

laws on the books that prohibit and punish pedophilia is that Christianity came to dominate culture in the West through evangelization. The only reason that we have accepted homosexuality in culture and in law is the increasing de-Christianization or paganization of the culture in the West.

Wiker sees a horrible irony:

The recent sexual scandals in the Roman church where the very men most authoritatively charged with the evangelization of all the nations are full-steam ahead bringing about the devangelization of the nations. In doing so, these priests, bishops, and cardinals at the very heart of the Catholic Church are acting as willing agents of repaganization, undoing 2,000 years of Church History.[17]

TWO INFLUENTIAL FATHERS OF THE SIXTIES

Originally, the Sixties sexual revolution was a heterosexual revolution. I remember a deep conversation in a Harvard Divinity School dorm with my fellow students in 1968. We noted the remarkable amount of free sex on campus, but it never crossed our minds to mention homosexuality or transgenderism. Free "hetero" sex was encouraged due to the popular self-defined sex researcher, Alfred Kinsey,[18] and also to the creator of *Playboy* magazine, Hugh Hefner.[19] Both of these influential architects of our sexual culture were sexual perverts in deep reaction against their Christian backgrounds.

ALFRED KINSEY

Kinsey was born in 1894 into a strict Methodist home in Hoboken, New Jersey, in which dancing, tobacco, alcohol, and dating were all forbidden. He eventually severed all ties with his parents—and their religion—and lived the rest of his life as an avowed atheist. As the first major figure in American "sexology," he published *Sexual*

Behaviour in the Human Male (1948)[20] and *Sexual Behaviour in the Human Female* (1953),[21] both of which topped the bestseller lists and turned Kinsey into a celebrity. The Kinsey reports, which led to a storm of controversy, are regarded by many as a precursor to the sexual revolution. His work was deliberately controversial and arguably dishonest, since he interviewed volunteers who were not representative of the general population. Kinsey reported that American women were either sexually repressed (married) or highly promiscuous.[22] Kinsey shook the nation with his books, claiming that between 30% and 45% of men have affairs; that 85% of men have sex prior to marriage; that a staggering 70% of men have slept with prostitutes; and that between 10% and 37% of men had engaged in homosexual behaviour.

In *Kinsey, Sex and Fraud*, Judith Reisman and Edward Eichel unmasked the Kinsey studies. The UK-based medical journal *The Lancet* evaluated Reisman's and Eichel's findings: "[T]he important allegations from the scientific viewpoint are imperfections in the [Kinsey] sample and unethical, possibly criminal, observations on children. ... Dr. Judith A. Reisman and her colleagues demolish the foundations of the two [Kinsey] reports.[23]

Kinsey was, by all accounts, a sexual pervert. As summarized by Susan Brinkmann, "He was a pederast who enjoyed public nudity, made explicit sex films and eventually developed such an extreme sadomasochistic form of autoeroticism that some believe it caused his untimely death in 1956."[24] Judith Reisman notes:

> Kinsey solicited and encouraged pedophiles, at home and abroad, to sexually violate from 317 to 2,035 infants and children for his alleged data on normal "child sexuality." Many of the crimes against children (oral and anal sodomy, genital intercourse and manual abuse) committed for Kinsey's research are quantified in his own graphs and charts.[25]

This father of the sexual revolution was a sadomasochistic bisexual sex criminal who facilitated the sexual torture of infants and children. He was not engaged in scientific research to see where the data took him, but to launch a crusade that would undermine traditional sexual morality.[26]

HUGH HEFNER

Hefner's religious upbringing was similar to that of Kinsey. He grew up in a "conservative Midwestern Methodist" home of "guilt-ridden Puritanism, an environment and lifestyle he rejected and that caused him to become the 'pamphleteer' of the sexual revolution."[27] As for his beliefs about God and traditional religion, he considered himself agnostic and believed that religion was a myth. Marking Hefner's death in September 2017, a journalist stated: "The Great Depression and World War II were over and America was ready to get undressed."[28] Such was the legacy of Hefner, whose son tries to define his father's life as the realization of noble values: "My father [was] a leading voice…advocating free speech, civil rights and sexual freedom."[29] That is not exactly how British journalist Piers Morgan describes an evening at the Playboy mansion: "It was the nearest thing to a Caligula-style Roman orgy I have ever experienced."[30]

Dr. Michael Brown concludes: "These men were rebels and sex-addicts, spreading a message and lifestyle that has brought bondage rather than freedom to untold millions."[31] These are not the kind of men we should trust in building a culture and a worldview for our children and a morality for our churches. They openly celebrated and marketed unlimited sex as a human right for personal health. Thanks to them and to the broader Sixties revolution, this unrestrained view of sexual morals is now systematically promoted and given pride of place in our culture and in our children's education.

Today, their sad legacy has combined with powerful internet technology, bearing vile fruit that makes *Playboy* magazine seem so tame that it is now out of business. Currently, "online porn is now standard operating procedure for a near-majority of men."[32] Internet pornography is merely the logical (and ongoing) progression of Kinsey's and Hefner's promotion of sex as a god and pleasure as an idol, a way of life that also dehumanizes women and celebrates infidelity. Not without cost.

A Catastrophic Transformation

Ironically, the same week that Hefner died, the United States Center for Disease Control and Prevention (CDC) reported that there were roughly "20 million new STDs in the United States each year, and half of these are among young people ages 15 to 24."[33] The CDC also said that "Across the nation, at any given time, there are more than 110 million total (new and existing) infections." They added: "More than two million cases of chlamydia, gonorrhea and syphilis were reported in the United States in 2016, the highest number ever."[34] What a price to pay for sexual liberation! How could our Western culture, so strongly influenced by the Christian faith, allow these men a determining role in establishing normative sexual practice?

In light of these facts, Elizabeth Fox-Genovese, mentioned earlier, is not the only one to describe the Sixties as "a catastrophic transformation."[35] Another observer, a Jewish journalist in Britain, Melanie Phillips, sees the same thing: "the real agenda [of]... 'the attack on Western civilization' has been to use sexuality as a battering ram against the fundamental tenets of Western culture in order to destroy it and replace it with a new type of society altogether."[36] The Sixties sexual revolution moved the culture not only into heterosexual libertinism, but on into homosexuality and beyond, in an attempt to destroy the very foundation of God-created sexuality.

Enter the brilliant Gabriele Kuby,[37] another once-radical Sixties feminist. Kuby provides unrelenting documentation of the Cultural Revolution's remorseless hyper-sexualization of Western culture. The significance of the rise of this powerful and seductive ideology within the last one or two generations, with no connection to Christian history or biblical teaching, makes one wonder how the churches do not see this as they justify sanctifying homosexuality in their midst, claiming the culture is wisely way ahead of the church and that the church will one day inevitably have to catch up. Why would churches naïvely conform to this recent anti-Christian agenda that eventually will silence the gospel?

Gabriele Kuby has come to see the vast implications of this mysteriously powerful cultural transformation that "started with student rebellions… [and] now is the revolutionary cultural agenda of the world's power elites."[38] She further describes this revolution as a spiritual transformation that rejects any standards of sexual morality but "attempt[s] to create a new human being."[39] Kuby defines the power of the movement not as an outward imposition of a political structure but as an attack "aimed at the person's innermost moral [and spiritual] structure.… A person, sexualized from childhood, is taught: 'It is right to live out all of your instincts without reflection. It is wrong for you to set boundaries for them.'"[40] This is essentially what evangelical pro-homosexuals are now advocating, whether they realize it or not.

A WORLDVIEW FOR THE SEXUALLY LIBERATED

Already in 1966, secular sociologist Philip Rieff wrote that "the West was rapidly re-paganizing around sensuality," and that "sexual liberation was a powerful sign of Christianity's demise."[41] In 1993, this repaganization was reaffirmed by a cover story in *The Nation*, noting that if the gay-rights cause, which was then still "a small and despised sexual minority," was to survive and eventually succeed, it needed to invent for itself "a complete cosmology." The term "cosmology" is not referring to peripheral personal rights or individual choices but to an all-consuming worldview reinterpretation of the elements of human society inscribed in law.[42]

Such a worldview is now well-developed. Homosexuality was first presented blandly as an issue of individual civil rights, the exercise of which would not disturb the peace of the dominant heterosexual culture. Surprise! For those who saw clearly, the intent was not to remain undisturbed in the closet but to challenge the philosophical norms of Western culture and to change the presumption of its heteronormativity. Thus, the movement would redefine the meaning of existence for everyone. As early as 1970, the *Gay Revolution Party Manifesto* said: "The gay revolution will produce a world in which all social and sensual relationships will be gay and in which homo- and heterosexuality will be incomprehensible terms." This is none other than a revived and re-interpreted egalitarian Marxism for the twenty-first century.[43]

It is inevitable that we should now see these radical and destructive ideas brought into the nation's schools via the LGBT notions of a "comprehensive sexuality" agenda. In Texas, parents involved with the organization MassResistance[44] sponsored an evaluation of the "Welcoming Schools" program (issued by the Human Rights Campaign) for the benefit of parents. They showed that teachers are encouraged to "integrate the LGBT propaganda throughout the classroom experience, and…into the youngest grades."[45] As part of this indoctrination, pornographic terms and images are introduced to young children, and elementary school teachers are being told not

42

to use the terms "girl" and "boy," in order to be more ideologically inclusive. That is, be more non-binary.

THE RISE OF THE NON-BINARY

On January 1, 2019, here in my home state of California, Senate Bill 179 went into effect, offering a third gender option (non-binary) on its state identification documents. In a sense, California state documents now exhibit in readable form the rejection of God's created differentiation between male and female, as emphasized in Romans 1:25. The logic of refusing God the Creator and worshipping creation ends up, as the Apostle Paul shows, in a blurring of created genders.

For the same non-binary ends, transgender ideology is being imposed on unsuspecting schools, parents and children as a scientific and biological reality despite obvious and scholarly evidence to the contrary. Children are used as pawns in an ever-broadening ideological campaign for a "genderless" culture, creating a generation of adults convinced of the pure subjectivity of gender.[46] We have descended into cultural irrationality: God placed maleness and femaleness into the creation to give us an obvious sense of difference, but those holding political power are legislating that feelings are more reliable than facts.

Couched in language of "civil rights" and "inclusiveness," this destructive philosophical/religious approach opens the door for any and all sexual choices. In spite of assurances that such changes would not affect the general population, our suppression of the creational binary of male and female has major implications for the way ordinary people think and act. For instance, legal research shows that in Canada, the concept of "family" is now "thoroughly unmoored from presumptions about marriage, gender, sexual orientation, reproduction, and childrearing; the notion that romantic relationships—whether casual, cohabiting or connubial— must be limited to two persons at one time may be the next focal point of change."[47] This same study affirms that "data currently available on polyamorous relationships suggest that the number of people involved in such families is not insignificant and may be increasing."[48] Sociologists suggest that the rise of the "bromance" (a close, emotionally intense, platonic bond between two men) and the decline in homophobia in Western societies is helping to make male-male-female or other threesomes more acceptable. "Younger guys engaging in threesomes are shifting along with society toward being less homophobic… This is allowing them to have threesomes with other men without it challenging their sexuality."[49]

Such changes in sexual practice have religious implications, both in the secular culture and in the church. In the United States, 75% of the Millennial generation accept the LGBT agenda.[50] The Pew Trust found that 61% of Republicans aged 18 to 29 approve of gay marriage, and 43% of those aged 30 to 49.[51] It is only a matter of time before Western culture ages into a majoritarian pro-homosexual populace.[52] Already, same-sex "marriage" is supported by a margin of nearly two-to-one. As for evangelicals, the Pew study continues: "Evangelical Protestants who are Millennials (those born from 1981 to 1996) are considerably more likely than older evangelical Protestants to support same-sex marriage and to say homosexuality should be accepted by society."[53]

NEW GENDER THEORIES

Since the Sixties this non-binary sexual movement has become increasingly radical. Some sexual theorists are seeking ways to prove that there are no biological "men" and "women."[54] Postmodern feminist Judith Butler, for example, in her books *Gender Trouble: Feminism and the Subversion of Identity*[55] and *Undoing Gender*,[56] sees gender as "performativity theory." Being a woman or a man is not something that one is but something that one *decides* to do. There is no pre-determining divine creation; only self-creation. As one of the early feminists, Simone de Beauvoir, stated in 1949: "On ne naît pas femme: on le devient"—"one is not born a woman; one becomes one."[57] Gender is a constructed status, radically independent from biology or bodily traits, "a free floating artifice, with the consequence that man and masculine might just as easily signify a female body as a male one, and woman and feminine a male body as easily as a female one."[58] This is the ultimate denial of binary sexuality.

Transgender is no longer a cultural oddity creating difficulties for a minuscule percentage of the population. Transgender theory has become the final argument in the contemporary project for the destruction of Western culture. If one accepts that sexual identity is self-created, biology becomes meaningless and can be manipulated to fit one's chosen gender.

As the famous phrase goes, "Ideas have consequences." The culture reflects the ideas of its best-known thinkers. A "new" view of open sexuality came in through the Sixties in the popularization of old school pornography. Once the domain of shady red-light districts and just as shady "adult bookstores," pornography now arrives packaged and ready to use at the click of a mouse.

The *Huffington Post* grants that we live in "a society that is deeply immersed in and obsessed with pornography."[59] Such widespread use of pornography can be "associated with more permissive sexual attitudes… [and a] greater experience with casual sex behaviour," stemming from the vast change in thinking.[60] Technology is only the servant to the mindset of the culture, which profits thousands in this

$13-billion-a-year industry. This perverted greed has helped expose 90% of young boys and 60% of young girls to pornography before the age of 18.[61] One website demonstrates the social crisis caused by pornography in a list of 121 articles, broadcasts, radio shows, and podcasts that involve sexual experts who confirm the existence of porn-induced sexual dysfunctions.[62] Too much imaginary and artificial sex turns people away from real sex.

Christian believers who understand the gospel and are engaged in a worshipping body of faithful believers must not remain aloof from what Gabriele Kuby calls the "global sexual revolution." It threatens not only Western Christianity but the advance of Christianity in general. There is a spiritual-sexual agenda in our Jungian, post-theistic, postmodern, pro-choice, nonjudgmental culture. As we naïvely crossed the bridge into the third millennium to the tune of Lennon's "Imagine," full of hope for a new world order of unity and love, respect and democracy, we brought over that bridge the androgynous, sexually unfettered "new man" of pagan spirituality. At the very moment that the New Age gurus declared the imminent arrival of the Age of Aquarius, the eighteenth-century theosophist Franz Xaver von Baader's[63] prophecy seems to be appearing—the return of the original androgyne. This androgynous idealism shaped the eschatological view of Jungian psychologist June Singer (1920–2004), who called for a "new sexuality" of androgyny. Are we on the verge of witnessing the construction of an eschatological Sodom and Gomorrah, as the title of a pro-gay book, *Reclaiming Sodom*,[64] suggests? June Singer asks, "Can the human psyche realize its own creative potential through building its own cosmology and supplying it with its own gods?"[65] In other words, based on the notion of sexual androgyny, she calls for a coherent, all-encompassing, attractive and religiously pagan account of the nature of existence, that is, a new "progressive" cosmology for the post-Sixties Age of Aquarius.

One final witness, from another brilliant female scholar, Mary Eberstadt, shows the extent to which the sexual morals of Western culture have imploded since the Sixties. She states that "illegitimacy is not only no longer stigmatized: across the West, it is so widespread as to be unremarkable...out of wedlock births are the new normal."[66] The facts back her up. Citing a report from *Child Trends*, she notes that "Between 1970 and 2009...the percentage of all births that took place outside of marriage increased from 11% to 41%."[67] She notes the same kinds of statistics with divorce and broken homes. Her book defends the thesis that our culture's loss of God is deeply tied to the destruction of the natural family. This of course shows also the full extent of the Sixties sexual revolution.

The elimination of the biblical God and of biblical sexuality as a philosophical and ideological program is already deeply embedded in our collective unconscious and has already wreaked havoc on our culture. This is why the clear-thinking ex-radicals of the Sixties, all of them unbelievers, now describe the nature of the Sixties as "a cataclysmic transformation of the very nature of our society" (Fox-Genovese),[68] a "destructive" event (Horowitz),[69] a "battering ram" (Phillips),[70] radically "disorienting" (Luker), and a "loss of faith in God" (Eberstadt).[71]

The spiritual revolution that we will discuss in the next chapter is rendered possible and largely successful by the accompanying sexual revolution, though influence goes in both directions. Without controlling parameters for sex, anything goes. The same is true for the spirit, which is why it is natural that polytheism leads to poly-sexuality and *vice versa*. Christian believers must understand the spiritual changes that have occurred if we are to make wise and principled assessments about the present cultural ideology of sexual liberation.

Chapter 3

Go East, Young Man

My favorite "picture worth a thousand words" was in the *Huffington Post*: twenty Canadian policemen in official uniform, sitting on prayer stools in a Buddhist temple, deep in meditative mode. These officers, from Ontario's Peel Regional Police Force were in the temple for a lecture on Mindfulness Meditation and Buddhist philosophy. The deputy abbot, Bhante Saranapala, observed with satisfaction: "They were very nice and they liked it and they think it should be part of their daily practice."[1] These law-enforcement professionals are trained in binary, right/wrong Western laws on which their police work depends. Did they realize that the principles behind Buddhist spirituality are all non-binary (Oneist) principles? Can they put their new spiritual training into practice by issuing a parking ticket marked "guilty and not guilty"? This photo is a poignant snapshot of the present spiritual situation of our Western culture, in which we have trouble identifying what is right and what is wrong.[2]

THE NEW MYSTICISM

This spiritual change also has its roots in the Sixties Cultural Revolution, which was not only sexual in nature, but also spiritual.[3] It brought to the West a new kind of mysticism. Pagan spirituality and pagan sexuality arrived in the West at the same time. While one might attribute a change in sexual choices to identity issues or civil rights, the accompanying spiritual upheaval places the Sixties revolution in a deeper, religious domain. The hippies sought not only free sex, but a free search for the divine self, based on an Eastern belief in the god within, and thus a "religious" morality that allowed free sex. That is why hippies went east and gurus came west, giving rise to the so-called New Age phenomenon. Though the term New Age is passé, it has gone viral under the rubric of the New Spirituality that emerged from it. No longer seeking a revealed religion, people now say they are "spiritual but not religious." They get inner revelation not through revealed doctrine but by engaging in Hindu yoga, Buddhist Mindfulness Meditation, and Eastern-inspired contemplative mysticism. Their concerns are personal transformation and stress reduction.

Some claim the name "progressive"—in both a cultural and spiritual meaning—assuring us that they are on the right side of history, a history moving forward to a new world of rights for all. Of course, human beings have made legitimate progress in all kinds of cultural areas. But here is a progressivism that proposes abolishing any and all of our truth anchors in favor of a Oneist utopian vision of sophisticated progress. These progressives perhaps do not realize that the Oneness they propose has tempted humanity in the past, with less than stellar results. They are not progressing but rather regressing.

After two thousand years of Christian influence in the West, who would have thought that contemporary Western civilization would see the reappearance of the Oneist, Creator-denying thinking that was so widespread in pre-Christian times? The reason is simple. Throughout history, there have been only two possible spiritual options: Oneism or Twoism.[4]

Professor John Oswalt, an expert in Near Eastern religions from the period contemporary with the Old Testament, explains the essence of this Oneist myth:

> [W]hen we talk about the common worldview of myth, we are not talking about a quaint, outgrown idea without relevance to the present. Myth is not the thought of primitives who cannot think of reality in abstract terms. It is simply a way of thinking about reality different from the one that shaped Western thought [Twoism].... [T]his understanding of reality is increasingly common in the modern, technological world.... [I]t is the same...as that which has existed for thousands of years.[5]

Douglas Groothuis, a Christian philosopher and specialist in New Age thinking, described the Sixties as a "revolution in consciousness," taking place in Western society as a meta-movement, which he calls "the One."[6] A new worldview is proposed: All is one—both good and evil; both divine and human.

In 1974, an anthropologist wrote about the Sixties with appropriate academic reserve: "A change in the conception of God is a cultural event of some magnitude."[7] *Some magnitude*! This change of gods is part of the "cataclysmic transformation," which occurred in two stages. The first was the New Age, which emphasized an individual search for the inner, divine self. Its wild success led to a second stage, in which gurus developed a thorough-going pagan worldview,

hoping to create a transformed global humanity—a "new humanism." In the first half of the twentieth century, Carl Jung, a major
architect of Sixties' thinking, believed that his "Depth Psychology"
would become "the world's final, unitary religion."[8] Jung's American
disciple, June Singer, understood the revolutionary character of her
mentor's vision, and took up his call. She declared programmatically: "We have at hand…all the ingredients we will need to perform
our own new alchemical opus…to fuse the opposites within us."[9]
In her 1977 book, *Androgyny*, Singer predicted that "the androgyne
participates consciously in the evolutionary process, redesigning the
individual,…the society and…the planet."[10] Since 1991, when I
returned to the United States, I have been following the work and
writings of many influential cultural leaders. I have attended pagan
conferences, listened to online courses, and read the work of others
who have done similar research. These seemingly abstract views of
humanity bring together thousands of speakers, political leaders,
businessmen and attendees of all sorts in major global meetings and
organizations, some of which are passionately committed to a kind
of takeover of the culture based on a cogent, broad cosmology that
will silence objectors and make falsehood look perfectly acceptable—
they seem to be making progress on this front.

Non-binary Spirituality

Acceptance of non-binary spirituality is all of a piece with the acceptance of non-binary sexuality, which we examined in the previous
chapter. Both areas have abandoned a biblical sense of right and
wrong, true and false. A stunning example would be the normalization of the Drag Queen Story Hour, in which sexually perverted
males, dressed as sexually attractive women, read gay-oriented books
to children in public libraries, with the approval of many librarians,

parents and local officials. At an event in Chula Vista, California, close to my home, in September 2019, there were as many supporters of the event, including parents, as those opposing it, including many Christian parents. One supportive parent said she felt it was important to turn out to support the LGBT community in response to the opposition. And with regard to her child, whom she brought, she stated: "I'm not going to let her grow up thinking that it's OK to be hateful like these people [the protestors] outside."[11] This blurring of both sexuality and spirituality has taken place because of a major change of worldview (as this parent above demonstrates), which has gone wider and deeper than we have doubtless imagined. Clearly it is a cultural revolution that affects all areas of our contemporary world and all kinds of people.

Robert Knight notes that "beginning in the 1950s, America began changing rapidly from a Christian-based culture—one defined by pursuit of virtue informed by religious values—into a 'sensate' culture, in which individuals seek pleasure at the expense of family, community and, ultimately, country."[12] The acceptance of normalized homosexual practice, while often driven by concern for those who are suffering, occurs within this radical ideological context, which drowns out any notion of moral and spiritual purity. This ideology redefines human sexuality as the freedom to express any and all sexual options. In a redefinition of civil rights, we are sweeping aside Christian definitions of nation, family, church, and normative personal identity. By the same token, such a culture also undermines the deep meaning of the gospel, by rejecting the person and being of God the Creator.

New Age mysticism, brought to the West in the process of this spiritual revolution, as one author named it,[13] undermined what Samuel Huntington (professor at Harvard for fifty years) calls "the

Anglo-Protestant culture, traditions, and values that for three and a half centuries had been embraced by Americans of all races, ethnicities, and religions."[14]

The 1965 Immigration Act removed racial and national barriers and significantly altered the demographic mix in the United States. There is nothing wrong with welcoming immigrants from a variety of ethnicities and nations as long as the founding principles of the United States are taught to and embraced by new arrivals. However, the promotion of multiculturalism challenged what was considered to be "narrow Eurocentric concepts of American democratic principles, culture, and identity."[15]

The spiritual turn to Eastern religions has fostered a cultural movement that is, as Huntington puts it, "an anti-Western ideology."[16] The results are pervasive. It is not only immigrants who do not know or accept the founding principles of the nation. The ideological revolution has taken place in our educational system, especially our universities. Campuses are hostile to old-fashioned Enlightenment views held by a dwindling majority. Western Civilization courses and American History courses are a rarity.[17] At the beginning of the twenty-first century, "none of the fifty top American colleges and universities, including Stanford, required a course in American history."[18]

In truth, one lays down Huntington's book, *Who Are We?* persuaded that citizens no longer know who they are or how they can regain a sturdy sense of national identity. Huntington's suggestions for restoring American identity now seem quite improbable: promotion of the English language and the Christian religion, for example. Alas, Huntington's sociological approach never sufficiently took into account the massive sexual and spiritual revolution of our time.

A Hindu Great Awakening?

Two recent, well-researched sociological studies, not written from a Christian perspective, independently demonstrate a significant Western conversion to Eastern spirituality.

One study is by Colin Campbell in *The Easternization of the West*, who argues that:

> there is a process of Easternization currently occurring in the West... quite unlike anything previously experienced..... [I]t concerns fundamental changes in the dominant worldview...in all areas of life, including religion...medicine, the arts, political thought and even science.... [I]t also concerns what has been lost"—namely, faith in Christianity and in "the power of reason to usher in a better world."[19]

The expression "quite unlike anything previously experienced," fits with Fox-Genovese's evaluation of changes that are a "cataclysmic transformation."

The second is a study by Philip Goldberg, a Western Jewish convert to Hinduism, who published *American Veda* in 2010,[20] in which he states that "large numbers of Americans have arrived at the worldview of Hinduism, a reconfiguration comparable in power to the Christian Great Awakenings of the eighteenth century."[21] In particular, he points to the seminal Hindu notion of *advaita* ("not-two") as non-dogmatic and a religious nonnegotiable. Although not-two or non-binary are necessarily in radical opposition to the Christian faith, Goldberg believes that the notion is the "Christian" West's future spiritual destiny.[22]

Goldberg's comparison to the Christian Great Awakenings of the eighteenth century captures the immensity of that event. Samuel Huntington described the nature of the First Great Awakening: "for the first time" people from all the colonies shared a "social, emotion-

al, and religious experience. It was a truly American movement…
whose themes…were subsequently transferred from a religious to a
political context."[23] Huntington describes a deep blend of religion
and politics. One can only imagine what the great new pagan spiritual awakening will do to both our religious and our political scene.

The Hindu non-binary excludes any ultimate Other. God is
not separate from us: God is us. Goldberg claims that America has
become Hindu, since so many now believe that "all is one," and defi-
nitely not two. Through this belief in Oneism, Eastern religions like
Hinduism, Sikhism, Buddhism and Taoism have invaded the West.
Later Oneist religions like Sufism, Neoplatonism,[24] Gnosticism, and
Kabbalah are also commonly disseminated.

A Hindu expert, Dr. Madan Lal Goel, professor at the University of West Florida, gives a clear definition of Hindu One-ness:

> Hindus worship God as One Reality, One Consciousness. Behind the
> diversity of existence, there is Unity; behind individual souls, there
> is the Self. All beings are unified in that One Self. As God contains
> all, the creation is more accurately described as a manifestation. God
> becomes the creation.[25]

In other words, there is no biblical distinction between Creator and
creature, for all is one, and all is made up of the same divine substance. All is non-dual.

In her autobiography *Enthralled,*[26] Christine Chandler describes
her experience as a thirty-year disciple of non-binary Tibetan Buddhism. She is an academically trained psychotherapist who practiced
Mindfulness Meditation for hours each day. Mindfulness Meditation
is offered to the Western beginner as a means of quieting the mind
from its constant search for right and wrong as well as living in the
moment in order to lessen stress. According to Chandler, the serious

practitioner finally concludes that "the world is just an illusion....
[T]he self and the other must be destroyed"[27] via the "esoteric
logic of non-duality."[28] The practice is self-hypnotic Oneism. As a
non-Christian, Chandler does not see that the classic Buddhist goal
of denying the objectivity of created reality and its role as witness to
God, is a denial of God the Creator.

Chandler left the group after thirty years, convinced she was
losing her mind. She came to consider Mindfulness Meditation as
mind control, and concludes that "if you can diminish the ability to
reason and think objectively...you can eventually weaken the foundation of Western civilization."[29] This, she believes, is the present
intention of Eastern Buddhism.

Gnostics, We Welcome You in the Name of Jesus

The invasion of Eastern religions in the Sixties affected not only
the general culture, but also liberal Christianity. Within a year of
returning to the States in 1991, after 17 years of Christian service in
France, I published a book with the title *The Gnostic Empire Strikes
Back: An Old Heresy for the New Age*.[30] I couldn't help noticing that
New Age spirituality, so popular in the Sixties, was not a minor
deviation in Western spiritual practice but a major apostasy from
the classic Christian faith. In that short book I compared New Age
spirituality to ancient Gnosticism, a heresy that nearly took over the
church in the second century AD.

It is important to note that the renewed interest in Gnosticism
in the 1960s paralleled the invasion of Eastern religion. A library
of ancient Gnostic texts was discovered in Egypt in 1948 and made
available to the public in 1977 as *The Nag Hammadi Library in English*.[31] In the 1960s and '70s, liberal Christians and critical scholars
claimed that these newly found Gnostic texts were superior to the

biblical texts of the New Testament and that original Christianity was really a Gnostic movement. This undermining of Christian orthodoxy by liberal scholars, especially Carl Jung, who promoted Gnosticism as a method of healing,[32] was clearly part of the radical transformation of spirituality in the 1960s, and shook the faith of many Christian believers. Eastern religion and Gnosticism entered the West hand-in-hand.

Scholars have argued that ancient Gnosticism was a version of ancient Hinduism, and that early contact was made between these two schools.[33] We continue to see that relationship in our time. One leading Gnostic scholar, Elaine Pagels, with whom I studied at Harvard, eventually embraced Buddhism.[34] Similarly James Robinson, translator/editor of the Nag Hammadi Gnostic texts, declared that the Gnostic library had much in common with "eastern religions and with holy men of all times…and with the counter-culture movements coming from the 1960s."[35]

Before going further, I would like to assert here that the idea that original Christianity was Gnostic is preposterous. The ancient Gnostics taught that the created material world is evil and that you can only rely on your inner spirit. The Gnostics claimed to offer a path to the true self, based neither on the scriptural revelation of God as Creator and Redeemer, nor on God-honouring reason, nor on evidence from the flesh (biology), but on one's inner spirit. This search for the true self culminated when a person entered mystical, out-of-body experiences and trances. In the Gnostic system, the Creator of material things, the God of the Bible, is actually Satan, and the Old Testament Scripture is a worthless collection of diabolical lies and fools' tales. The true Gnostic god was called the "Father of the Totalities," the spirit in and behind all things. The true Jesus is a spirit being, sent from this pantheistic spiritual source. Like the

58

Indian Hindus, the Gnostics considered physical matter an illusion, what the Hindus call maya, whose evil goal is to take your mind off spiritual things.

In both its "Christian" and its Eastern pagan spiritual forms, Gnosticism is alive and well a generation or two after the 1960s. Its followers revere the famous second-century Gnostic, Marcion, who eliminated from the Christian canon the entire Old Testament (with its lawgiving, wrathful God), as well as significant sections of the New Testament. Marcion's goal was to distil a pure gospel of non-binary love—which has a particularly contemporary ring. This spirituality has sexual implications, as Robert Reilly notes:

> Gnosticism does not accept the evidence of reality. It is not a matter of what Gnostics do not know, but of what they refuse to acknowledge.... [T]he homosexual ideologue relocates the source of good from what is to his will. Only then can he successfully rationalize his moral misbehaviour.[36]

For ancient Gnostics, the sexual and spiritual goal was the realization of the imagined notion of androgyny,[37] which joins male and female in one person, and joins human and divine in one being. Homosexuality was considered a practical expression of androgyny, since both partners function as male and female. The obvious God-ordained male/female binary is dismissed as unenlightened foolishness.[38]

Harvard professor, Harvey Cox, a great believer in Gnostic inner knowledge, claims that modern scholarship has proven that the early church was dominated by Gnosticism. He cites James Robinson, who says that in early Christianity "there seems not yet to be a central body of orthodox doctrine distinguished from heretical [Gnostic] doctrine."[39] Cox concludes that "early Christianity was 'hugely kaleidoscopic,'"[40] not a universal, orthodox church.[41] He wonders what will happen when the "cat [the findings of modern scholarship] is completely out of the bag," and he has high hopes that this spiritual Gnosticism will be the basis of interfaith dialogue and communion between Christianity and other religions in the days ahead.[42] If we could finally realize that original Christianity was Gnostic, he maintains, then we would see that we no longer need creeds, canons or Scripture.[43] Instead we would have the inner spirit knowledge that inhabits all the religions.

In point of fact, "scholarship" has never succeeded in showing this. All evidence points in the opposite direction: early Christianity was deeply united.[44] 1 Corinthians 15:1–11 contains the earliest written gospel creed, which celebrates the authority of the Old Testament and the historicity of the resurrection of Jesus. The creedal structure here has never been disproven. The Apostle Paul is citing one of those creeds to which Cox is so allergic. Paul states that what he is writing was not his own invention: "For I *delivered* to you as of first importance *what I also received*" (1 Cor. 15:3). Paul uses a similar phrase in 1 Corinthians 11:23, where he cites another text from the eyewitness apostles and now passes on to the Corinthians: "For I *received from the Lord* what I also *delivered to you*." "Received" and "delivered" are the same Greek words he uses in chapter fifteen, which is the way the rabbis described the receiving and passing on of important teaching. The material in chapter 11 is the verbatim account of the words of Jesus instituting the Lord's Supper. "From the Lord" is doubtless Paul's way of saying these words were the very words of Jesus. So the Corinthians had two texts from the earliest times: one directly from Jesus, affirming his atoning death according to the Scriptures; and the other, the earliest creed of the original believers, affirming both his death and resurrection according to the Scriptures. There was not a hint of Gnosticism anywhere. The cat is well and truly out of the bag, and it is not yowling Gnostic catcalls, but rather a beautifully harmonious gospel hymn that is unmistakably orthodox. Paul preserves some of the earliest texts of the Christian movement, and they are clearly not Gnostic.

Joachim Jeremias, one of the most respected New Testament specialists of the twentieth century, in his book *The Eucharistic Words of Jesus*[45] notes that the quantity of non-Pauline vocabulary and syntax in 1 Corinthians 15:3b–5, and their Semitic character is so great that it is unlikely Paul was the author of this text. In other words, Paul was passing on something he had not created.

Today's Gnostic approach is a major theological deconstruction of Christian orthodoxy, occurring especially in liberal churches, a trend that warms the heart of Hindu guru, Deepak Chopra. This pagan mystic calls Cox's book, *The Future of Faith*, "a fresh vision for the resurrection of a new global Christianity."[46] What Chopra means is that Gnosticism is a form of his own Hindu religion and that the acceptance of "Christian" Gnosticism in the church produces interfaith globalism and spells the end of true Christianity. The Gnostic thesis is a historical scam, a profound intellectual falsehood, intending to serve the purposes of gospel-denying liberal theology.

Alas, this soft-Gnostic, Hindu-like spirituality has now entered even the evangelical church. Doubtless full of noble intentions, evangelicals now seek, in Carl Teichrib's words, "mystical, contemplative and Eastern approaches—refashioned for mainstream Christianity," that promise "spiritual formation to those earnestly desiring a deeper 'God experience.' The believer's intention may be noble, yet spiritual syncretism is the actuality."[47]

The Franciscan mystic Richard Rohr (popularizer of the Enneagram)[48] has had an enormous influence in evangelicalism. He speaks of the Divine Flow in which we all find ourselves, whether Christians, Hindus, Buddhists—people from every race and nationality. "We'll begin to experience God almost like a force field.... And we're all already inside this force field, whether we know it or not,"[49] he writes. Such apostasy appears in the oddest places. Fuller Seminary, founded by the great gospel preacher and radio evangelist Charles Fuller (1887–1968), had Richard Rohr teaching "non-dual spirituality" in the doctoral program. David Crumm, a liberal journalist with interfaith blog ReadtheSpirit, interviewed Rohr about his new book, *Immortal Diamond: The Search for Our True Self.* Here is how Crumm introduced the book:

> As is usually the case with Richard Rohr's books, the idea can be conveyed in a single sentence: At the core of each life is true, eternal goodness—and the key to a successful life is opening up that true self so that we can compassionately connect with God's world. After reading that sentence, dozens of questions spill from our lips: You mean, we're born good!?! We're not born evil? We're not trying to deny the deepest truths about ourselves? We don't need to fear what's truly and honestly in our heart? So, how do we find that true self? And, why didn't anyone tell me this before?[50]

FROM POSTMODERN TO POSTSECULAR

When postmodernism attacked secularism's claim to objectivity, it paved the way for a postsecular age of mysticism in a liberated Oneist world of relativism, in which good and evil are joined. The community now establishes politically correct truth through personal experience, a trend easily adapted by LGBT activists to insist on the right to sexual self-determination. Straights and non-straights must all agree that no absolute truth determines our sexuality. In fact, no absolute truth connects any of us in any area.

Postmodernism might still be thought of as a form of secularism, but some now call for a new term: postsecular—an era that has created a synthesis of science and myth[51] for a new way of thinking.[52] Postsecularism is lauded as having traced a middle path of wisdom between two now-defunct ways of living and thinking, namely theism and atheism. Mike King, a proponent of postsecularism, seeks to show that it "does not accept that reason must rule out religion." Like all self-respecting, intelligent multiculturalists, King opposes religious extremism, whether extreme theism (the old religion of the Bible which is dismissed as superstition) or extreme atheism (dismissed as self-assured dogmatic rationalism). King opts for a spiritual cocktail of ingredients, from the religious Left, to the new science, to mature New Age spirituality and deepening mysticism, which awaits "a new all-encompassing Oneist synthesis."[53] Between theism and atheism is pantheism. As we have seen, however, there is nothing "between" theism and atheism. The "Oneist synthesis" is, in fact, paganism.

Ross Douthat, columnist for the *New York Times* states: "I've become interested in books and arguments that believe...the term 'paganism' might be reasonably revived to describe the new American religion, currently struggling to be born." He believes secular humanism is taking on a religious form by denying any sense of civic neutrality and adopting convictions of unshakable religious dogma.[54]

Douthat is impressed with Steven Smith's[55] description of this pagan religious renewal, as is journalist Robert Knight, who summarizes Smith's argument that:

> much of what we understand as the march of secularism is something of an illusion, and that behind the scenes what's actually happening in the modern culture war is the return of a pagan religious conception,[56] which was half-buried (though never fully so) by the rise of Christianity. What is that conception? Simply this: that divinity is fundamentally inside the world rather than outside it, that God or the gods or Being

are ultimately part of nature rather than an external creator, and that meaning and morality and metaphysical experience are to be sought in a fuller communion with the immanent world rather than a leap toward the transcendent. This is quite different from, "In the beginning, God created the heavens and the earth" (Gen. 1:1) and "All things were made through Him" (John 1:3).[57]

In his relatively recent cultural and theological analysis, Smith is one of numerous scholars who grant that the 1960s Cultural Revolution has caused our present culture to resemble the ancient pagan Greco-Roman Empire. Both in its spirituality and in its sexuality, ancient paganism was deeply opposed to emerging Christianity and tried to stamp it out. If we are indeed facing a similar set of circumstances, Christians cannot accept the ideology of our present pagan culture as inspired by the Holy Spirit or by Jesus. Also, the church should expect serious religious opposition, even persecution. Discussion of the Christian position meets with animosity, and public vilification of Christians grows more and more frequent. Subconsciously, Christians often self-censor, knowing that they will not fare well if they speak out loud what they may wish to say. The conflict is becoming very religious.[58]

We are back to the confrontation between two views of existence. In Oneism the world is self-creating and self-explanatory, sharing the same substance, whether matter, spirit or a mixture, to be worshipped as divine or as of utmost import. As one author puts it, "All the gods of pagan religion and the first principles of pagan philosophers are gods and principles for the world and they could not be without the world."[59] Everything shares in the same this-worldly, ultimately meaningful substance. All distinctions are eliminated and everything has the same worth. This homocosmology is a worldview based on sameness, a Oneism of essence.

Twoism believes the world is the work of a personal, transcendent God, who creates *ex nihilo* and is not constrained by or dependent on the creation or on any pre-existing conditions. God's free act of creation displays his transcendence and sovereignty. No human analogy is adequate to "explain" the mystery of this unique Creator. There are two kinds of existence—the Creator who is uncreated, and everything else, which is created. We worship as divine the unique, distinct, personal, triune Creator, who wove distinction throughout creation as the essence of existence, revealing a heterocosmology, a worldview based on otherness and difference.[60]

Oneism and Twoism have always and in all parts of the world competed for the spiritual worship of human beings.[61] They are not mere variations or alternative spiritual options that share the same spiritual and religious foundations, such as we find, for example, in denominations that share a common commitment to the Word of God and the basic doctrines of salvation, yet vary on minor, particular issues. Oneist thinkers are in adamant opposition to a belief in a Creator God and treat with disdain the fundamentalism that "seeks certainty, fixed answers... a fearful response to the complexities of the world."[62] The Oneist option is painted as noble, a "transformative relation with the sacred, ...able to sustain levels of uncertainty."[63] In fact, both a Oneist and a Twoist worldview is held with "fundamentalist certainty." The conflict is between two mutually exclusive, antithetical belief systems. If one is true, the other must be false. That is why Paul calls them "the Truth" and "the Lie" (Rom. 1:25),[64] for in the moral universe of the Bible, knowledge is never amoral, and data are never neutral.

Current church conflicts over sexuality and spirituality must be seen against the backdrop of our culture's acceptance of a 'not-two' Hindu spiritual ethos. Sexual confusion goes hand-in-hand with a

God-denying, pagan, egalitarian theory of human identity. Unfortunately, in a desire to show compassion to hurting fellow human beings, some Christians inadvertently advance a godless culture by blurring the binary distinctions God the Creator knit into our world to remind us of himself. This binary structure emerges as the focal point of the struggle between two overarching political, cultural, and religious visions of existence, about which Scripture has much to say. This struggle is played out not only in the culture, but also in the Christian church. It is to a consideration of the effects to be seen in our Christian organizations and churches that we now turn.

CHAPTER 4

ASHES, ASHES, THEY ALL…

Derby Cathedral of the Anglican Church in England refused to allow a fellow evangelical Anglican pastor who is in favor of biblical sexual norms to preach in the cathedral at a Christmas Carol service for students, even though the students had extended the invitation. That seems peculiar enough, yet it gets stranger: the same church authorities gladly sponsor a semi-pornographic film series in the same cathedral.[1] How can this happen in the Christian church?

AN URGENT PROBLEM *FOR* THE CHURCH

Not long ago, the cultural normalization of same-sex practice seemed to concern only a few individuals in the secular domain and represented no threat to the church's freedom to practice and teach biblical sexuality. This situation is rapidly disappearing. In the United Kingdom, even though the church of the nation officially opposes same-sex "marriage," a senior government minister, from purely political motivations, recently pressured Anglican church leaders to let gay couples marry in the church. Equalities Minister Justine Greening urged faith leaders to keep up with twenty-first century attitudes. She stated:

> I think it's quite important that we recognize that for many churches, including the Church of England, [same-sex marriage] was something they were not yet willing to have in their own churches.... I think it is important that the church in a way keeps up with and is part of a modern country.[2]

An individual's right to maintain a traditional position on this subject was once normal; it is no longer. Most of us have read about Christian bakers, photographers, foster parents, and even a funeral home director who have been taken to court or lost their jobs or businesses for refusing to submit to the LGBT thought police. In an interview in *Rolling Stone*, the high-tech millionaire and LGBT activist Tim Gill called for punishment of Christians who refuse to take part in same-sex weddings. In the interview, the 63-year-old Colorado resident—who has funneled over four hundred million dollars into pro-LGBT social reform causes for over twenty years—claimed that it's time to "punish the wicked."[3] The sexuality issue has led some to consider Christ's church not merely as a relic of the past, but as a current and "wicked" threat. How will the church find a place in our non-binary culture to preach with faithfulness and clarity the gospel of divine love for sinners?

An Urgent Problem *in* the Church

These threats cause a problem not only *for* the church but *in* the church. I am convinced that the new definition of human sexuality will lead to the next great apostasy in the church of Jesus Christ—undermining not only marital and family structures but our understanding of God and the gospel. This indeed is the burden of this entire book. Already churches and denominations are splitting into warring factions, as progressive and traditionalist Christians are unable to agree over the nature of human sexuality as it touches the essential meaning of the gospel.

"Apostasy" is a stronger term than "heresy." Heresy means a deeply important disagreement on a particular doctrine. According to Webster, apostasy is "an act of refusing to continue to follow, obey, or recognize a religious faith" or the "abandonment of a previous loyalty." The Greek is *apo*—"away from," and *stasis*—"standing." So apostasy is "standing away from" or "refusing to recognize" something once considered fundamental. Attitudes toward sexuality are not harmless personal choices; "standing away" from the Bible's view of sexuality deals a mortal blow to the church's faithfulness to the Christian gospel.

The window of opportunity for arresting this movement is closing. Southern Baptist Theological Seminary president Albert Mohler states that Christians in the United States now face an inevitable moment of decision that cannot be avoided.[4] Journalist Terry Mattingly sees the same issue looming on the evangelical horizon: "There is no way to avoid the showdown that is coming."[5] So the unity of the Christian faith is at stake, unity based on clear thinking about the meaning of the gospel relative to the human situation. This split became evident when even Christians responded with strong opposition to the biblically orthodox Nashville Statement on Sexuality. In the debate concerning homosexuality, Christian consensus has unraveled.

The Pew survey, mentioned in chapter 2, showed that 47% of

young white evangelical Millennials support gay marriage, while the total evangelical support more than doubled over the last ten years.[6] If these figures are correct, more than a third of evangelicals have abandoned the traditional biblical understanding of sex and marriage, as have almost half of the next generation of evangelical believers. Al Mohler understands the pressing nature of the problem:

> [T]here is nowhere to hide. Every pastor, every Christian leader, every author—even every believer—will have to answer the question. The question cannot simply be about same-sex marriage. The question is about whether or not the believer is willing to declare and defend God's revealed plan for human sexuality and gender as clearly revealed in the Bible.[7]

As the liberal churches began accepting practicing gays as members—and even as ministers—many Christians walked out the doors. From 2015 to 2018, the Presbyterian Church (U.S.A.) lost over 200,000 members,[8] and the Episcopal Church over 100,000 members.[9] The persistent sexuality question now threatens to cause a great rift, not just in the mainline denominations, but in evangelical Christianity, the community of believers once defined by unwavering faith in Scripture. Though this study focuses on the historic evangelical church, breaches have also been made in the Roman Catholic Church and in mainline denominations worldwide. Below are simply a number of examples that illustrate a wide and deep movement in our day.

THE ROMAN CATHOLIC CHURCH

Under the leadership of Pope Francis, the Roman Catholic Church, once a great defender of the normalcy of male/female sexuality and marriage, is changing. Francis recently appointed Cardinal Christoph Schönborn as a theological spokesman for the church. Schönborn had caused a controversy shortly after the October 2015 Synod on the Family when he proposed to see positive elements in homosexual unions. The Austrian Cardinal said: "We can and we must respect the decision to form a union with a person of the same sex, [and] to seek means under civil law to protect their living together."[10] In 2006, his Vienna Cathedral blessed two unmarried couples on Valentine's Day, including homosexual partners. Fr. Faber, the rector of the same cathedral, expressed his regret that: "Today there is no possibility in the Church to bless a union of people with homosexual feelings." The priest explicitly welcomed "people with homosexual inclinations to receive a blessing for their longing for love."[11] One cannot deny the presence of genuine human affection in long-term homosexual relationships, but the church must surely see itself as the guardian of biblical definitions of sexuality and marriage for the good of the human community.

In 2014, Archbishop Scicluna of Malta presided at a Eucharistic celebration put on by the Drachma Community, a pro-homosexual group aimed at ending homophobia. The group stated:

> The Drachma Community hopes that this celebration can serve as a clear message against all forms of homophobia and transphobia in our society. This celebration also demonstrates that it is possible for LGBTI persons to fully integrate their sexuality with their spirituality.[12]

Georgetown University, headed by the Jesuit order of the Catholic Church, approved a gender and sexuality dormitory for students, intent on exploring the topics as part of a living, learning community, intended to "promote knowledge, critical conversation and a deeper understanding of LGBTQ histories, cultures, and social and political movements." Grace Smith, a Georgetown student who pushed for the gender and sexuality dorm and manages a school LGBT group, called the dorm approval "a really big deal at a Jesuit university."[13]

Pope Francis named Blaise Cupich (Archbishop of Chicago) to the College of Cardinals in 2016. The Archbishop's elevation came as a shock to many Catholics aware of his public dissent from Catholic teaching on sexual morality. During the 2015 Synod on the Family, which Cupich attended at Pope Francis's personal invitation, the then-Archbishop proposed a pathway based on what he called an "inviolable" conscience for allowing active homosexuals to receive Holy Communion. He later defended his view in an American Broadcasting Company interview, stating that if gay people in good conscience discern that they should receive Holy Communion, then "they have to follow their conscience."[14] Cupich does more than recognize genuine human affection. His acceptance normalizes non-binary homosexual practice as a valid part of the life of the church.

At the same synod, the subtle but insistent approval of homosexuality was moving toward acceptance. As French Jesuit Father Alain Thomasset said, "[H]omosexual relationship[s] lived in stability and fidelity can be a path of holiness."[15] With the liberalizing leadership of Pope Francis, the situation seems to be worsening almost on a daily basis.

MAINLINE PROTESTANT CHURCHES

While the situation in the Catholic Church is concerning, the mainline Protestant churches have nearly all capitulated to the LGBT agenda. The situation is in flux, but the following is an overview of what has been happening in many denominations worldwide.

- The Anglican Church numbers about 85 million members and is divided over allowing homosexuals to hold church office. At a meeting of the primates in 2015, 8 of the 38 provinces (United States, Canada, Scotland, Wales, New Zealand, South India, South Africa and Brazil) were open to changing doctrine on marriage to allow for same-sex unions. The African provinces, however, boldly affirmed heterosexual marriage as the only form for the church.[16]

- In 2015, after three decades of debate over its stance on homosexuality, the largest Presbyterian denomination (PCU-SA), voted to include same-sex "marriage" in its constitutional definition of marriage.[17]

- A leading Protestant denomination in Germany, Rheinische Evangelische Kirche, which has 2.6 million members, overwhelmingly voted to perform same-sex "marriages," beginning in 2016.[18]

- In 2016, Norway's Lutheran Church voted in favor of allowing same-sex "marriage." Elsewhere in Scandinavia, police are investigating a Christian politician in Finland, Päivi Räsänen, for an alleged "hate crime" because she shared a Bible verse on Facebook to criticize the Evangelical Lutheran Church of Finland, of which she is a member, for participating in the Helsinki LGBT Pride event. She merely cited Romans 1:24–27 that describes same-sex relationships as "shameful." With no support from the church, she wondered: "How can the church's doctrinal foundation, the Bible, be compatible with the lifting up of shame and sin as a subject of pride?"[19]

- In 2015, the United Methodist Church, at a meeting of its governing committee, the Connectional Table, voted in favor of supporting a localized option that would permit ministers to officiate same-sex weddings and conferences to ordain openly gay clergy. In 2019, the church, with the help of the African Methodist churches, voted to adopt biblical sexuality as the basis of the denomination. It is feared that the denomination will split.

- The Evangelical Lutheran Church in America (which is theologically liberal) allows individuals in committed homosexual relationships to serve as ministers.

THE EVANGELICAL COMMUNITY

While mainline churches have been compromising for years, the same process in evangelical churches was unexpected. Within the evangelical world this issue is dividing a once-unified theological community.

Once-evangelical figures in the Emergent Movement, such as Brian McLaren, Tony Jones, Jim Wallis, Rob Bell, and Tony Campolo, have all come out in favor of normalizing homosexuality in the church. Millennial Christians are often open to homosexuality as a normative, healthy lifestyle, and so tend to join churches associated with the Emergent movement or other groups that have already normalized homosexuality. The following examples show evangelical organizations that are quickly changing their thinking about LGBT issues.

- An open letter from Concordia University in Portland, Oregon – a school in the very conservative Lutheran Missouri Synod – announced in January 2018 that a Queer Straight Alliance is now a chartered campus club.[20]
- When World Vision (which controls a budget of $1 billion for overseas missions) sought to legitimize same-sex "marriage" in its staff hiring, the evangelical community was

shocked. Donations began to dry up, so World Vision revised its position. Trevin Wax, Bible and Reference Publisher
at LifeWay Christian Resources and managing editor of The
Gospel Project of the Southern Baptist denomination, is also
a writer for the Gospel Coalition. About the World Vision
situation, he states: "The World Vision decision was a tremor
that warns us of a coming earthquake in which churches and
leaders historically identified with evangelicalism will divide
along all-too-familiar fault lines."[21]

- Steve Chalke, pastor of the evangelical Oasis Church in
London, now supports LGBT marriage. Chalke says: "We're
registering at the moment to marry LGBTs…. This is not
because we're liberal, it's not because we're light on the Bible,
it's because we take the Bible very seriously." Christian Concern in the United Kingdom explains: "Chalke's move to
promote the LGBT agenda is another step in his departure
from orthodoxy, since he rejected substitutionary atonement
in 2004….Oasis Trust was expelled from the Evangelical
Alliance in 2014 for taking this position on same-sex 'marriage.'"[22]

- In 2008 Rev. Richard Cizik, Vice President for Governmen-
tal Affairs with the National Association of Evangelicals, was
asked to leave because he endorsed same-sex unions.

- Stephen W. Cobb, executive director of Waterbrook Mult-
nomah, defends publishing Matthew Vines's book, *God and
the Gay Christian: The Biblical Case in Support of Same-sex
Relationships*. Cobb calls the book "thoroughly evangelical."

- A flurry of books appeared in 2013–2014, representing the
new wave of United States evangelical reflection on LGBT
matters: Evangelical New Testament scholar, James Brown-

son, *Bible, Gender, and Sexuality*;[23] Vineyard pastor, Ken Wilson, *A Letter to My Congregation*;[24] young evangelical scholar, Matthew Vines, *God and the Gay Christian*;[25] director of Generous Space Ministries, Wendy VanderWal-Gritter, *Generous Spaciousness*;[26] Presbyterian Church (U.S.A.) pastor, Mark Achtemeier, *The Bible's Yes to Same-Sex Marriage*; ethicist, David Gushee, *Changing Our Mind*;[27] and professor of religious studies, Eugene F. Rogers Jr., *Sexuality and the Christian Body*.[28] David Crumm, publisher of two of these books, rejoices when evangelicals leave the faith. As he says about author Amy Julia Brecker:

> Like many of the other Christian writers we publish in our online magazine and in our own publishing house—writers like David Gushee and Ken Wilson—Amy Julia is a devout Christian whose faith is the key to her vision of a compassionate world. However—much like David, Ken and other Christian writers we have featured over the years—Amy Julia is now no longer interested in trying to defend the old "evangelical" label.

"I describe myself as a Christian, today," Brecker said in an interview. "I wrote a piece for The Washington Post that described why I am walking away from the term 'evangelical.'"[29]

- At Wheaton College, the "Harvard" of evangelical higher education, once-celibate lesbian Julie Rodgers, appointed as a chaplain at Wheaton, has since come to embrace active homosexuality and same-sex "marriage" and has resigned from her post.[30] She now believes:

> Same-sex couples are getting married, and many of these cou-
> ples are decisively Christian.... No amount of disagreement
> with these marriages will invalidate their Christ-like example
> of love and faithfulness.... [A]fter all, that is what a Christian
> marriage is all about.[31]

Rodgers left many pro-gay students behind at Wheaton,
though the administration is still holding to its biblical principles opposing the normalization of homosexuality.

- In April 2017, the entire seven-member Faculty Senate
  of Gordon College came out in support of LGBT issues,
  against the policy of the Board and Administration to uphold biblical principles.[32]

These examples could be multiplied. I will let two key churches
known for their place within historic Christianity represent the future of the adoption of homosexual practice in evangelical Christian
circles.

The first is First Baptist Church in Greenville, South Carolina,
which, since 2015, has been offering same-sex "marriage" ceremonies, membership, leadership positions, and ordination to openly gay
and transgender individuals.[33] This historic church was founded in
1831 by William Bullein Johnson, who later served as the first president of the Southern Baptist Convention upon its organization in
1845. The church was the original home of Furman University and
Southern Baptist Theological Seminary. Such a history of theological
faithfulness has not hindered this church from sliding into compromise. The pastoral couple who were ordained in the Greenville
church now serves at Calvary Baptist Church in Washington D.C., a
church that disassociated from the theologically conservative Southern Baptist Convention.

The second church is an evangelical church in the Reformed tradition. City Church, San Francisco, was founded under the inspiration of Tim Keller's Redeemer Presbyterian Church in New York City by Rev. Fred Harrell, once a bright light in the Presbyterian Church in America's church-planting program. City Church eventually joined the Reformed Church in America, in order to ordain women to the pastoral ministry, thereby already moving away from a biblical understanding of sexual differentiation of roles in the church. In 2015, City Church opened its membership and ministry rolls to credibly confessing LGBT persons, under the rubric: "the doors of this church are as wide as the arms of the Savior it proclaims."

IDENTITY CRISIS

A new-look evangelicalism merges gay rights with issues of sexism, feminism, and racism. According to Wheaton professor of psychology Michael Mangis, evangelicalism has been too long "entrenched in a white male evangelical groupthink," and must be redefined. Many evangelicals find themselves in step with Maggie Rowe, a pro-gay TV producer, who is planning a TV series based on her new memoir of being raised in an evangelical home—*Sin Bravely: A Memoir of Spiritual Disobedience*. Her testimony appears in ReadtheSpirit, an interfaith blog:

> Over the years, I did change from my earlier beliefs that everything in the Bible is literally true. Now, I see the Bible as containing figurative language, poetry and lots of pointers to the truth, but it's not a book to be read literally in the way I experienced it as a child. Today, I like to follow people like Rob Bell and Peter Rollins. I also like to read mystics—Christian and Buddhist and Hindu mystics. I'd say I'm a spiritual person with ties to a Christian faith.[34]

This multi-faceted theological challenge, while provoked by the LGBT agenda, goes beyond that issue, using the same rhetorical and emotive power to join a variety of current justice issues that are, perhaps, better considered separately. The church's crisis of belief is not limited to sexuality. Present apostasy from orthodoxy focuses on the redefinition of both God and the human person—which is the central question in apologetics today, namely, the question of personal identity.

One can sense the frustrated tone in the question Trevin Wax asks in his *Gospel Coalition* blog: "What can evangelicals do to show that our belief in the sanctity of true marriage is just as uncompromising and unwavering as our love for gay and lesbian people created in the image of God? ...I don't know all the answers to that question. Nor am I sure of the best way forward."[35]

No doubt many evangelical churches and pastors are asking Wax's question, "What can evangelicals do?" They share a sense of deep concern about a problem that is not going away. How should the church formulate her answer to this burning issue? The next evangelical generations need to hear a clear statement of the truth about God and sexuality so they will not be influenced by the pagan revolution noted in chapters 2 and 3. Instead, they need to heed God's way of speaking the gospel, in grace and truth: "Let your speech always be gracious, seasoned with salt, so that you will know how to answer each person" (Col. 4:6), but without conforming to the world (Rom. 12:2).

Under the influence of modern culture, both spiritually and sexually, many in the evangelical community are seeking to be inclusive and to follow the example of the "welcoming Jesus," in order to normalize the open presence of homosexuals in the membership and ministry of the church. How does the slide from evangelical orthodoxy to liberalism and eventually paganism occur? This is the subject of the next chapter.

CHAPTER 5

LOVE, SWEET LOVE

I was born and raised in Liverpool, England, so it would seem natural for me to like Beatles music—which I do—however, my favorite 1960s composer is Burt Bacharach, who transformed the popular music scene of the 1960s and 1970s with unforgettable melodies in songs like "Raindrops Keep Falling on my Head," and "Walk on By." Perhaps his most influential piece was his 1965 hit, "What the World Needs Now Is Love, Sweet Love." This haunting song has been recorded or performed live by over one hundred leading artists, proving the success of the tune and the popularity of the words.

THE ROOT OF EVANGELICAL APOSTASY

Everyone knows that the world needs love. It is understandable that those who wish to justify homosexual practice in the church appeal to the overriding demand of love, as they understand it. After all,

Christianity is the most powerful message of love in the world. How could love ever be wrong? Heart-wrenching stories make any opposition to the agenda of love seem heartless and "unchristian." Many Christians ask: "How can the love of gay couples, joined in marriage, as the embodiment of commitment and fidelity, be wrong?" The image of Jesus, arms outstretched in love, seems to provide the last and definitive word.

Two essential convictions mark many affirming churches who seek to normalize homosexual practice: 1) that ambiguous Scriptures, read from just the right angle, do not oppose the full inclusion of gay people in church life, because the biblical writers would not have known about homosexual orientation; and 2) that in the absence of Scriptural clarity, there is sufficient Christian love and wisdom in the body of Christ (and in the culture) to justify full acceptance of homosexual believers. Later I will discuss the key texts in Scripture that deal specifically with the issue of sexuality. Here I want to examine the arguments that affirming Christians employ to justify the normalization of homosexuality. They use four main arguments: 1. Inner Wisdom, 2. Jesus, 3. The Spirit, and 4. Love.

1. INNER WISDOM

The mistake some Christians are making today is a form of Gnosticism, mentioned in chapter 2. This second- to fourth-century heresy claimed that salvation could only be gained through mystical/spiritual experience (gnosis, which means knowledge). It was a special, secret "knowledge" that helped the believer realize that humanity is divine. Gnostics taught that the created material world is evil and that you can only count on your inner spirit. They offered a search for the true self, based neither on scriptural revelation of God as Creator and Redeemer; nor on God-honouring reason; nor on evidence from the flesh (biology), but on one's inner spirit. This search for the true self culminated when a person entered mystical, out-of-body experiences and trances to discover true inner wisdom.

Diana Butler Bass takes this Gnostic tack. Once an evangelical, this historian of Christianity has become a leading voice of its progressive version. In her book, Christianity After Religion[1] she wrote (in quite Gnostic language) that God is now "defined in less dualistic terms," in favor of "finding one's self in God and find[ing] God in one's self."[2] Notice the non-binary approach. For Bass, this involves praying to God as "our Mother," the purely pagan idea that the goddess represents the womb of the universe from which we all emerge as divine. She sees God "less in terms of an absolutist, sin-hating, death-dealing 'almighty Father in Heaven' and more in terms of… the nourishing spirit of mother earth."[3] Meet the god within!

As we saw earlier, the ancient Gnostics were the first liberals, seeking to blend the Christian faith with the pagan culture of their day. Because they gave no place to the importance of God the Creator, they disdained the flesh, including all its physical manifestations and creational structures, as the work of an unworthy god. Of course, to reach such opinions, they also had to reject the authority of Scripture. Contemporary liberal churches have embraced homosexuality in their membership and ordination decisions, rejecting the Old Testament Scripture and the God of creation. Evangelical churches, though less radical, also appeal to personal, subjective spirituality and a weakened view of Scripture as they seek to embrace homosexuality. Without using the term Gnosis, the evangelical version subjectively appeals to Jesus, the Spirit, and love to bolster an acceptance of homosexual behaviour as a worthy Christian practice, based on true wisdom as the "spiritual wisdom within."

2. JESUS

Modern Gnosticism emphasizes Contemplative Spirituality and a subjective Jesus, who leads the church into interfaith communion. (Interfaith believes that all religions are true.) Seemingly timeless Gnosticism also explains the current lack of interest in theology, doctrine, and exegesis. As an example of the trend, though not as radical as liberal churches, a new denomination with historical ties to the Emergent[4] and Vineyard movements is developing. It goes by the name Blue Ocean Faith[5] and feeds on subjective and contemplative approaches to Christian truth.

Blue Ocean Faith pastor David Schmelzer reveals his own thinking when he finds "delightfully provocative" Harvey Cox's book *The Future of Faith*, that calls for a return to Gnostic spirituality.[6] Schmelzer has been fooled. Cox is a radical pagan, disguised in semi-Christian clothing! You can see, however, why Cox is a hero for Schmelzer, an urban church-planter seeking to develop a body of believers without drawing any boundaries. A man with a pastor's heart, Schmelzer lives by one principle: *Solus Jesus* (Jesus alone). He rejects "traditional notions of God,"[7] and the classic Reformational norm of *sola scriptura*, since the Bible, while a great gift, is "just a book."[8] Clearly now a long way from Protestant evangelicalism, Schmelzer prefers "the living Jesus" to written Scripture. In following Jesus, he says, there is no bad news (such as exclusionary boundaries).[9] In pressing non-binary thinking in this direction, he claims no one is "in" or "out." There is no "correct religion," only "following Jesus,"[10] the way you think best. No longer at ease with the term "evangelical," he prefers calling fellow believers "all people," with no labels.[11] "The secret of the kingdom of God [consists of] responding to the living, interactive Jesus,"[12] "with intuitive skill."[13] This "Jesus only" principle, based on individual "intuition," sounds so pious,

88

yet in Schmelzer's entire 140-page book, Jesus is never once defined, and thus has little if any relation to historic Christianity. "Jesus" is whoever "all people" imagine him to be at any given moment. Not all who appeal to this "Jesus" are as honest as Schmelzer, who openly observes: "Figuring things out about life with Jesus didn't seem to be as helpful as it sometimes claimed to be."[14] Thinking is not useful, for even in moral issues we often "do not know" where Jesus is leading us.[15]

Such optimism about human beings (with no mention either of original sin or of the radical cultural changes since the Sixties) suggests a belief that comes from the "spiritual transformation movement," which (though not specifically mentioned by Schmelzer) is part of the Emergent Movement and of Blue Ocean Faith theology in particular.[16] According to this mystical approach, there is an inner "true self" that needs to be awakened through mystical techniques in order to experience union in the divine Presence deep within the soul. When this union occurs, the person can realize a state of "non-dual consciousness," in which there is no distinction between God and the individual soul. It follows that in Schmelzer's entire book there is not one mention of the atoning work of Jesus on the cross, his moral teaching, his judgments and curses, his divine person, or his specific place in history. All that's left is a timeless "living Jesus" who justifies one's own good vibes. The only semblance of a definition of Jesus that Schmelzer offers his readers is by way of the Roman Catholic St. Francis of Assisi,[17] who famously prayed: "Praise be to you, my Lord, through our Sister, Mother Earth, who sustains and governs us, and who produces various fruit with coloured flowers and herbs."[18] Worship of the earth is specifically denounced in the Bible (cf. Deut. 4:19; Jer. 8:2; Rom. 1:25), but is celebrated everywhere in religious paganism. From this mystical foundation,

Schmelzer makes a confident evaluation of the question of homosexuality. With solid conviction, he states that "the LGBT person who is gifted and called to serve as pastor is free to do so, ...and who[ever] wants to marry a person of the same gender is free to do so."[19]

The interpretive principle guiding the Blue Ocean Faith approach in the debate on homosexuality is personal spiritual intuition, an inner sense of what Jesus would do. Of course, what one individual's "Jesus" would do might well conflict with another's, which is not a very solid foundation for church polity or unity. If you are seeking Jesus in Schmelzer's Blue Ocean, you are likely to drown in waves of individual subjectivity.

Another example of the subjective Jesus argument, pushed to the extreme, is seen in the work of massively popular Christian blogger Glennon Doyle Melton, who made her name writing about families and motherhood. In 2016, she wrote that Jesus had led her to divorce her husband and marry international lesbian female soccer star, Abby Wambach. In 2013, Melton wrote: "Figuring out my stance on homosexuality felt like a life and death decision.... I know my Jesus, I love Him, and I think if he needed me to believe that homosexuality was a sin, he would have mentioned it."[20] Perhaps she should have looked closer at the words of Jesus. Jesus does mention it in his rejection of "sexual immorality" (*porneia*), a term inclusive of all sexual sins, in Matthew 15:19. See also Matthew 5:32 and 19:9. The inspired New Testament authors follow the teaching of Jesus—see Romans 13:13; I Corinthians 5:1, 11; 6:13; 2 Corinthians 12:21; Galatians 5:19; 1 Thessalonians 4:3, as a start.

3. THE SPIRIT

"Ken reports experiences with God's Spirit that will seem alien to those of us whose faith is not quite as supernatural as is his own tradition. This is...a gift from the Spirit-attuned part of the evangelical world to the rest of us."[21] Such is David Gushee's estimation of Ken Wilson's view of the Spirit. Gushee (an ethicist who defends gay integration into the church) was a natural to write the introduction to Ken Wilson's book, *A Letter to My Congregation*, which takes the same position.

Like Schmelzer, Wilson is a pastor associated with Blue Ocean Faith and influenced by the Vineyard.[22] Wilson's pastoral heart, which marks his work, is now deeply affected not by the classic evangelical piety he once embraced, but by Roman Catholic Ignatian spirituality, in which his church is deeply involved.[23] As an evangelical Vineyard pastor intrigued by the renewalist (i.e. mystical) wing of faith, Wilson says, "I am perhaps less suspicious of the role of experience in the moral discernment process."[24] Wilson describes as his spiritual director Rev. Don Postema, a campus chaplain at the University of Michigan in Ann Arbor, and life-long practitioner of interfaith fellowship.[25]

Ignatian (or Jesuit) Spirituality involves a developed system of rules and exercises based on the experience and teaching of Ignatius of Loyola, the founder of the Society of Jesus in 1539. It is ironic that, having recently celebrated the 500th anniversary of the Protestant Reformation, many evangelicals are committing to a spirituality central to the Roman Catholic Jesuit order, which led the Catholic struggle against Protestantism in the Counter-Reformation.[26] During the Reformation, believers returned from medieval mystical spirituality to the Word as final authority, and the Protestant church turned away from monasticism and mysticism as people began to place their faith in Scripture and in Jesus' finished work on their behalf. We now find Christian pastors like Ken Wilson accepting homosexuality, rejecting the five solas—including *sola scriptura*[27]—and turning back to Ignatian Spirituality to create structures for Spiritual Direction, or Spiritual Formation, practices popular in some evangelical churches.[28] The terms sound pious and are sometimes used by Christians to describe perfectly orthodox approaches to Christian growth. However, most programs with these labels encourage mystical transformation and seek insight through subjective contemplation, not through biblical teaching and faithfulness.[29]

In the sixteenth century, in his deep mystical and visionary encounters with Jesus and the Virgin Mary, Ignatius Loyola experienced either "consolation" (leading him to God's will) or "desolation" (leading him in another direction). He learned to discern between good and evil spirits. Ken Wilson admires Ignatian Spirituality and refers to it in his own experiences. He recounts a period of "extended consolation," during which he had a vision of the Son of Man, sitting next to him on a log in a cave.[30] In Ignatian fashion, this vision was a true consolation: he was pleasing God and walking "faithfully with Jesus" by publicly defending the right of gays to be full members of the body of Christ. To oppose this, he believed, would be "a sign of desolation." It would allow "a phantom [the unimportant gay issue], projected from below over American evangelicalism," to take the church's eyes off much more important issues like denouncing "greed, war-making, and gossip."[31] Emerging from such a mystically-based background, Wilson's book focuses entirely on the question of homosexuality in the church, and has been widely influential in many evangelical churches, including City Church in San Francisco.[32]

Wilson believes in "the reasonable possibility" that the biblical texts are not addressing the morality of present day same-sex couples who love each other. He does grant that "the traditional view may be correct but not indisputably so."[33] So he concludes that there are "no right answers," as far as Scripture is concerned.[34] He states: "I might be wrong on this matter, but I am determined to not let the fear of that keep me from following Jesus as I understand him to be leading me."[35] His experience of "consolation" confirmed his decision.

Wilson does seek to wrestle with Scripture, but he believes the ambiguity he claims to find there creates an unlivable church experience, since no one can agree. Because of this, he believes we must base our decision on other ways of knowing—beyond Scripture—such as his direct encounter with Jesus. He agrees with the following contemporary arguments for receiving gays into full fellowship in the church—arguments that have nothing to do with Scripture:

- Young people who accept gays are abandoning the church.[36]
- In a period when he was part of a Roman Catholic charismatic renewal community, Wilson "met more openly gay people who didn't seem to be conflicted about their spirituality."[37]
- "Excluding gays was inconsistent with my duty as a pastor."[38]
- Hating homosexual sin "did not feel like a Jesus approach," because, for Jesus, "love is the fulfillment of the prophets."[39]

Wilson's solution is "a third way through the gay controversy, one that is neither 'love-the-sinner, hate-the-sin' nor 'open and affirming.'" It abandons all church discipline of gay couples as long as they are faithful to each other.[40] The Scriptural ambiguity Wilson claims to discover implies that our unity should not depend on the Bible.[41] As a pastor, Wilson seeks a "non-exclusionary approach, accepting rather than affirming," whatever that means. He believes our relationship in the church should not be "contingent on extending moral approval to each other." We should "let God be the judge."[42]

Such church life would require "restraint" on all sides, but it would require "conservatives" to accept the ministry of gay pastors and allow their children to sit under the teaching of gay Sunday school teachers. Could this work? Wilson says yes, because it would be an "advantage to expose children to diversity of thought and practice while they are living at home."[43]

Wilson's solution fails to take seriously: 1. the clear teaching of Old and New Testament Scripture, 2. the two thousand years of Christian history and of the church, and 3. the impossibility of genuine church unity on the basis of this third way. Finally, his solution derives from one man's mystical experiences, and so it can hardly serve as a basis for general church unity. On the contrary, it will surely cause church division. What Wilson claims to hear from the Spirit he eventually identifies as "the voice of God."[44] Incredibly, the Holy Spirit of God Almighty is now leading him to accept what the godless ideology of sexual liberation has been demanding for a generation, namely the non-binary denial of the male/female distinction. He says as much. In a crucial concession to this agenda, Wilson states: "We're all—male and female—part of the bride of Christ. Maybe we are being asked to relax around gender distinctions a little."[45] Yes, we are being asked to relax, but only because of the influences of a godless, pagan culture, a fact of which Wilson seems oblivious. Also, Wilson's relaxation on sexuality automatically entails relaxation on biblical orthodoxy, as he admits in his book, *Solus Jesus*. Wilson's approach is a specific example demonstrating the thesis of this book, namely that compromise on the Bible's teaching that regards homosexuality as unnatural inevitably leads to theological liberalism and, eventually, to paganism.

4. Love

We hear everywhere the siren call to make decisions on the basis of (undefined) "love," especially in the discussion of homosexuality. Here are but a few examples:

- The Scottish Episcopal Church allows same-sex "marriages" in its churches, citing the principle: "love means love."[46]
- The website "Above All, Love: Unfundamentalist Christians"[47] considers the Nashville Statement, a Scripture-honouring document on sexuality, to be full of hate.
- On the Oprah Winfrey show, Kristen Bell read a quote from the book she and Rob Bell wrote on marriage: "Marriage, gay and straight, is a gift to the world because the world needs more, not less love, fidelity, commitment, devotion and sacrifice."
- Nicholas Wolterstorff, a leading Reformed philosopher and professor of Philosophical Theology at Yale University, also calls for love in normalizing homosexuality. He says,

> When those with homosexual orientation act on their desires in a loving, committed relationship, [they] are not, as far as I can see, violating the love command.... If homosexual orientation is not morally blameable or a disorder, and if members of the church are to accept people as they are, then why is it wrong for people with [homosexual] orientation [to act] on their desires in a loving and covenantal relationship?[48]

- Jen Hatmaker, a highly influential speaker in many Christian ladies' circles, in a Facebook post, wrote: "It is high time Christians opened wide their arms to the LGBT community.... Your life is worthy and beautiful. There is nothing 'wrong with you.' Jesus still loves us beyond all reason and lives to make us all new, restored, whole. Yay for Jesus!"[49]

- In a similar vein, Christian blogger Glennon Doyle Melton, whom we met above, appealing to "Jesus," exhorts her faithful fan base of seven million followers: "My beloveds—please never give up on love. Life could surprise the [expletive] out of you. Trust me—you might just wake up one morning and find yourself smack dab in the middle of heaven. I love my wife. LOVE WINS."[50]

- Finally, the same justification is evoked by a Reformed church we referred to in chapter 4. The elders of City Church, San Francisco ask: "If Jesus were the pastor of City Church, what would he say to the people who are asking if they can belong? As we consider the life of Christ, his example of love, his call to embrace the outsider and cast down, and his patience with those earnestly seeking him, what is a Christ-like response?"[51]

To use the argument of love, one must first define what Scripture means by love. David Gushee is one of the most influential of those who justify gay inclusion in evangelical churches on the basis of "love." Brian McLaren hails him as "the Billy Graham or Pope Francis of Evangelical ethics."[52] In his book on loving homosexuals, however, Gushee neither defines love nor asks what it might mean to love God. He is another example reinforcing a conclusion that the acceptance of the homosexual agenda leads both individuals and churches to reject biblical orthodoxy and adopt liberalism.

THE PLACE OF SCRIPTURE

New Testament scholar Denny Burk says of David Gushee: "The key issue for Gushee is not what the Bible says but what experiences have led him to have more sympathy for gay people."[53] This characteristic is hardly limited to Gushee, but is common among those who argue for full acceptance of practicing homosexuals in the church. Just as the culture now bases laws about sexual rights on feelings, so the church is creating its theology of sexuality not on God's truth, but on feelings of love. This appeal exclusively to experience is a tactic often used now in churches. A Christian Reformed church in Grand Rapids, Michigan, the "holy land" of Dutch Reformed tradition in America, held a meeting to convince the congregation to accept homosexuality as normative for Christians. A member of the panel stated:

> Do not use Scripture to convince your fellow Christian Reformed Church members of the beauty of full inclusion. Instead, rely on personal stories.... Everyone has a story.... We can argue back and forth all day about Scripture, but we're never going to win that way. Nobody can argue with your story.

The article goes on:

> Another member of the panel shared the focal point of this "personal story" strategy. He said it is all about convincing people, through stories about real people who have embraced the gay/lesbian/bisexual/transgender lifestyle, that such people bear healthier fruit than those who are non-inclusive. The panel at the meeting referred to "the old teachings of the church" as "toxic."[54]

David Gushee even warns churches whose convictions he shared only a few years ago that they will be left behind and totally marginalized by the "secular" culture if they, with the traditionalists, attempt to maintain a false notion of orthodoxy. Perhaps Gushee has forgotten to heed the warning of Scripture: "Do you not know that friendship with the world is enmity with God? Therefore, whoever wishes to be a friend of the world makes himself an enemy of God" (James 4:4).

As Christ's church, we face a crisis of belief as apostasy creeps in, focused on redefining both God and human identity. The redefinition of human sexuality and spirituality is the greatest issue of theology today, an issue that pastors and churches cannot afford to avoid, in spite of very real fears of losing members, eliciting strident slander from the community, or feeling inadequate to articulate biblical teaching on gender without sounding political or moralistic. The twenty-first century church needs a clear scriptural and cosmological foundation from which to preach and cogently defend biblical sexuality. Its mandate is also to preach the love of Jesus, who wants the best for his children. It was Jesus who, with the Father and the Holy Spirit, worked in creation to give us physical life. He it was who died on the cross to give us new life in him. How can "new look" evangelicalism, which integrates homosexuals, reject traditional orthodoxy as ossified, bigoted, and out of touch?

A simplistic, sentimental, or well-meaning appeal to inner knowledge, to "Jesus," to the Spirit, or to love fails to provide a solid theological basis for the church's teaching on sexuality (which we shall develop in chapters 8 and following) and thus threatens the body of Christ with deep division about what it means to love.

Trevin Wax's question about the way forward, raised in chapter 4, is not limited to a debate within the church. Our problem has planetary implications. Younger Christians are feeling enormous social pressure to conform to the culture's redefinition of justice and freedom. What is happening, even in evangelical churches, is not happening in a vacuum but reflects an ideological movement of global proportions. The "best way forward" must face this need squarely.

We do not have the luxury of shrugging off opposition to the historic understanding of biblical sexuality. The issue has pierced the heart of the Christian faith. By naïvely Christianizing pagan views of sexuality and spirituality, Christians lay a match at the doors of their churches and will watch in horror as the conflagration guts the edifice, leaving behind only the ashes of a Christian belief system. In the name of love, will we lose everything but a singed family photograph?

Ken Wilson, David Gushee and Rob Bell, lamenting the departure of Millennials from church, have compromised with the pagan, non-binary culture in an attempt to rescue the church from oblivion. Bell is willing to compromise on homosexuality:

> I think culture is already there and the church will continue to be even more irrelevant when it quotes letters from 2,000 years ago as their best defense, when you have in front of you flesh-and-blood people who are your brothers and sisters, and aunts and uncles, and co-workers and neighbours [who are homosexual], and they love each other and just want to go through life.[55]

Bell's clarion call is not to gospel fidelity but to an emotion-fueled desire to be loved by the culture. It is heart-wrenching to see these and other progressive evangelicals seeking spiritual guidance from a culture hell-bent on denying the Creator and proposing to their spiritually hungry followers a solution of self-identity. As David Wells notes, "Evangelicalism has lowered the barricades. It is open to the world."[56] "Open to the world" in this case does not mean moving *out* in evangelistic fervor. It is opening the doors to invite pagan evangelists *into* the church of Christ. Our authoritative teacher, the Apostle

Paul, lays down a principle for our situation:

> I wrote to you in my letter not to associate with sexually immoral
> people—not at all meaning the sexually immoral of this world, or the
> greedy and swindlers, or idolaters, since then you would need to go out
> of the world. But now I am writing to you not to associate with any-
> one who bears the name of brother if he is guilty of sexual immorality
> or greed, or is an idolater, reviler, drunkard, or swindler—not even to
> eat with such a one. (1 Cor. 5:9–11)

Paul doesn't want us to hide out from the world, but God's standards
must be maintained in the church. Christians must not conform
their message to that of the world but take the message of the gospel
of salvation to lonely, broken sinners, which includes all of us. Only
a compelling and courageous account of what it means to love both
God and neighbour will represent accurately and effectively the
gospel of Jesus Christ to our culture, which has eliminated God the
Creator in favor of setting our own agenda.

Because the approaches discussed in this chapter all reject the orthodox view of the inspiration of Scripture, they also reject scriptural
statements about the person and being of God. Such a compromise
with the ideology of a Oneist culture will, in the name of the love
of Jesus, cause believers to fail in their love for God and in their love
for their neighbour, as they end up in liberalism, and then paganism. From that dark place, the church can no longer declare the true
gospel to the world.

CHAPTER 6

HELLO, INTERFAITH LIBERALISM

Fear of offending homosexuals and ignorance of the larger cultural issues produces much naïveté in evangelicalism. A staff member at Redeemer Church, New York City, states: "How does homosexuality effect [sic] you and other Christians? I guarantee it doesn't directly or even indirectly effect [sic] Christians as much as greed, gluttony, theft, rape, racism, or even foul language."[1] This person needs to read the works of ex-gay Joe Dallas, once an active member of the gay Metropolitan Christian Church, who knows the problem from the inside and is not so sanguine. He states: "The pro-gay interpretation of Scripture...is arguably the most divisive, emotionally heated issue the modern [evangelical] church faces."[2]

As we have seen, contemporary Western culture made a radical turn into both pagan spirituality and pagan sexuality. Unaware of this turn, many progressive and/or Millennial Christians naïvely take the values of the present culture as the norm for biblical teaching. In addition, they take the encouragement the culture gives for showing respect and love and rejecting "judgmentalism" (again, none of these terms are defined) as proof that they must be right.

So we ask the question: What will happen to our Christian message concerning purity, holiness and the radical nature of the gospel if "gay Christianity" becomes a normal foundational element of Christian belief and practice? It is not too difficult to foresee. Many leaders in the "gay Christian" movement are testing the waters of theological liberalism. Theology professor John Barber still remembers a conversation with a lesbian student some years ago at Yale Divinity School who said: "Pay attention to this issue...We're going to change the churches. Give us 30 years, and it will happen."[3] Some 30 years later, that revolution is taking shape. The inevitable connection between theology and anthropology has taken place. Oneist theology leads to Oneist sexuality. David Gushee is a prime example of this movement. He dismisses any concern for biblical faithfulness as evangelical narrow-mindedness and meanness, but his dismissal only shows how simplistic his theology is. Everything is at stake here.

In spite of the culture's positive affirmations, accepting homosexual and transgender practice as a valid expression of biblical truth is the next great theological apostasy to face the church. Radical changes in Western culture since the Sixties have largely driven theism from the public square. Evangelicals are making exactly the wrong move in their desire to hang on to something of their faith. To gain wisdom in this time of confusion, one must see the profound disjunction between biblical values and those of contemporary progressivism.

The mainline churches have shown us how devastating their

theological choices have been, taking once-Christian churches and the individuals who stay in them into radical apostasy. On July 8, 2012, Katharine Jefferts Schori, the presiding or leading bishop of the Episcopal Church, preached her brand of post-Christian religion. An attendee gives this stunning report:

> She mocked most of the crucial doctrines of the Christian faith, including the God of creation, the Incarnation, and the Trinity. She accomplishes this through her demeaning use of rhetoric. She taunts the Lord by the use of the name "Big Man" and then points her finger at everyone listening and tells them that they have "missed the boat." [She] then proclaims that she has the answer for this. We all need the "act of crossing boundaries" to become God after which our hands become a "sacrament of mission." [4]

As part of this new-look theology she declares that same-sex union ceremonies are perfectly welcomed in her Nevada diocese. If this is an outreach tactic meant to welcome the unchurched, it should be re-evaluated. Statistics made available by the Episcopal Church General Convention Office in September, 2017, showed a denomination continuing a sustained decline, shedding 34,179 members, with a net loss of 37 parishes.[5]

Responses to the Nashville Statement on Sexuality

The mainline churches are gone, but where are evangelical churches headed? We noted earlier the antagonistic reactions to the 2017 Nashville Statement on Sexuality. I gladly signed this Scripture-honouring statement, written and endorsed by leading evangelical theologians.[6] The Nashville Statement raises two crucial questions: 1. What is God-honouring sexuality? The content of the statement answers that, and 2. Who is truly Christian? That is at least partially answered by the many responses claiming to be Christian but reject-ing the teaching of the Bible. Here are a few examples:

A *Sojourners* magazine article had the title: "Thousands of Christians Respond to Nashville Statement with Emphatic 'No.'" Sojourners' own president, Jim Wallis, rejected the statement as damaging to people and to the evangelical witness.[7] One wonders what Wallis means by "evangelical" any more, granted his appearance at the non-Christian Parliament of the World's Religions. Lutheran Pastor and writer Nadia Bolz-Weber offered a point-by-point ref-utation of the statement that was compleltely devoid of Scriptural support.[8] A "Christian" group known as the Liturgists drafted a statement called "God Is Love," signed by authors like Rachel Held Evans and Nish Weiseth (among others), affirming: "We can no longer project first-century notions of sex and sexuality on people today." They further state:

> We believe that people of all sexual orientations and gender identities are fearfully and wonderfully made, holy before God, beloved and beautiful as they are. We believe all people have full autonomy over their bodies, sexual orientations, and gender identities, and the diver-sity of identities reflects the creative power of a loving God. We believe that God is love, and that 'anyone who loves is born of God and knows God' (1 John 4:7).[9]

Alas, "full autonomy" will take people way beyond the confines of Scripture and the historic Christian faith. The group Christians United in Support of LGBTQ+ Inclusion in the church, immediate-ly proposed its own statement that begins:

> As followers of Jesus Christ, we are compelled to bear witness to the love, grace, and truth of God in every generation…So it is that we, like each generation before us, are called to reflect, repent, and reform our

teachings and practices to be ever more closely aligned with the heart and will of God revealed to us in Jesus Christ.[10]

This group not only claims to be Christian, but claims to be the most Christian expression of what God is now doing. It goes so far as to state that evangelical orthodoxy is "resist[ing] the Spirit's leading in various ways and cling[ing] to the dogmas and traditions that God is calling us to rethink and reform." evangelical orthodoxy is redefined as heresy.

Pastor John Pavlovitz, in the name of evangelicalism, offered a damning description of the Statement, claiming it was born out of fear. Understanding the present cultural opposition to biblical faith, he states: "Evangelical Christians are at the precipice of extinction—and we know it. We are a profoundly endangered species coming to grips with the urgency of the moment, of our impending disappearance, of the whole thing going sideways here in the Bible Belt—and we're in a bit of a panic." He goes on: "We are leaking people from our churches, watching multitudes walk away in disgust, and losing market share in the religious landscape, as well as the vice-like stranglehold we've had on American politics for the past 241 years—and we are rightly terrified."[11] To survive, he makes the culture the defining word of truth, and can only propose a rejection of the biblical teaching on sexuality, which he believes is the statement of a "bullying of marginalized people." In its place, he embraces a progressive socio-political gospel.

THE CULTURE KNOWS BEST

This acceptance of our contemporary culture's progressive social gospel by certain evangelicals finally undermines Scripture. Young evangelicals, rightly eager to invite outcasts into the body of Christ, feel that they must redefine evangelicalism, too long "entrenched in a white male evangelical groupthink."[12] Award-winning journalist and radio producer Deborah Jian Lee left the evangelical world, due to its entrenchment in conservative politics. In her book *Rescuing Jesus: How People of Colour, Women, and Queer Christians Are Reclaiming Evangelicalism*, she rejoices that the evangelical culture is changing. She seeks to give women, racial minorities, and the LGBTQ community a voice within evangelicalism.[13] As Kathleen Dupré puts it, those on the "leading edge of progressive evangelicalism—LGBTQ and straight; white, black, Asian, Hispanic, and indigenous—are working to wrest political power away from conservatives."[14] But with no serious definition of the nature of biblical Christianity, these "evangelicals" accept same-sex "marriage" and are inclined to define pro-life issues as merely helping society's disenfranchised. Those associated with the Gay Christian Network (GCN), such as Rachel Held Evans and Baptist theologian Tony Campolo, plan to "rescue Jesus," and save the church by means of "another gospel."

Allyson Robinson, also associated with the Gay Christian Network, is the first openly transgender minister to be ordained in the Baptist tradition. "She" served as "transitional" pastor at Calvary Baptist Church in Washington D.C. Robinson believes that

> our society has watched the Church grapple with these questions of alternate sexuality, and many are disappointed that it has taken the church longer comparatively than the rest of society to come around. … [T]he cultural war has come to a close on this front, and those of us on the affirming side have won.[15]

For Robinson, the future has left traditional Christianity far behind. "Her" redefinition of the Christian faith comes directly from the progressive ideas in the culture, ideas like those of Frank Bruni, a gay journalist at the *New York Times* and a severe and constant critic of orthodoxy. Bruni sees in traditional Christianity a group of ossified bigots, lost in a past that will never return.[16] Many now see the church as "an antiquated backwater, out of step with the times and the latest findings of psychology," believing the culture sets the moral norms for the church.[17]

A leader in this revision of Christianity is former evangelical, Brian McLaren, who endorses same-sex "marriage" and claims that God must no longer be understood as the separate "omniscient, omnipresent, and omnipotent" Creator and cosmic Ruler.[18] God must be redefined as the spirit of love flowing within everything.[19] With not one mention of the Trinity, McLaren presents an entirely impersonal god. "We must become atheists in relation to the Supreme Being of violent and dominating power."[20] Christianity must "lose its monotheistic notions to embrace a grander, inclusive God who demonstrates solidarity with all." We need "a bigger, non-dualistic God,"[21] a non-binary God who is "in the story, not outside of time and space like a prime mover or divine watchmaker."[22] It saddens me to have to say of a once-evangelical pastor, still claiming to be a Christian theologian, that McLaren's god is a Oneist, pagan god—a part of creation rather than the Bible's Twoist Trinitarian God, who is separate from creation.

Here, without shame, the non-binary understanding of God is proposed as the inevitable expression of Christianity in the third millennium. Many are trying to force the biblical message into the amorphous pagan agenda of freedom for all. Paul's exhortation to the Roman church, which was beset by the same kinds of sexual practice, is surely still true: "Do not be conformed to this world, but be transformed by the renewal of your mind, that by testing you may discern what is the will of God, what is good and acceptable and perfect" (Rom. 12:2). We should not be surprised to see the same confrontation about which the Apostle Paul spoke to the church in the first century—the confrontation of two kinds of radically opposed minds:

- The undiscerning, debased mind that elevates the creature (or all of nature) into god by worshipping and serving the creation. The undiscerning mind is bound in darkness and builds a worldview on the Lie.
- The transformed, discerning mind, that understand God to be separate from creation and so worships and serves him alone. Free from the blindness of sin, the discerning mind builds a worldview on the Truth.

The "discerning" mind of Romans 12:2 and the "undiscerning" mind of Romans 1:28 are expressed in words that share the same root. Here we find not only a clear antithesis between two ways of using the mind to process ideas, but a moral element as well. For Paul, one way of using the mind is true (discerning who God is); the other is false (undiscerning, failing to recognize who God is). The created world ultimately faces us with a moral choice. Are we *for* or *against* our personal Creator?

These two worldviews, the Truth and the Lie, are as much in conflict now as they have always been. Today, in the name of love, the Lie (disguised in evangelical clothing) seeks to redefine both sexuality and spirituality in ways that deny God's good and loving creation. It is against this background of cultural decline that Christians must consider the questions that currently trouble our churches, specifically those about sexuality. We cannot afford to ignore the debate but must meet arguments without capitulation, seeking to honour God's nature and his creation order.

LIBERALISM

Like the intellectual, J. Michael Clark, who left Christianity because he saw no future in it for homosexuals, people like David Gushee and Colby Martin have started down that same slope. Martin is one of the signers of the Christians United document, opposing the Nashville Statement. In his book, *UNclobber*,[23] he tells how he left "conservative Evangelical orthodoxy" over the issue of homosexuality. Eventually, he founded a welcoming community that was "uniquely Christian" but "not exclusively so," a community that gives space to people "regardless of ethnicity, orientation, age, creed or socioeconomic status." What does it mean for Martin to be Christian in today's world? On the website of his church in San Diego, an attendee commented:

> Sojourn Grace Collective is still a church as they do have regular Sunday services that examine Bible scripture with a non-denominational angle. The sermons usually don't interpret the Bible literally and are geared toward lessons applicable to everyday life, i.e. how can I be a better person, achieve my full potential, and make the world a better place? Some might call that liberal Christianity, but it makes a lot more sense to me than fire and brimstone theology.[24]

In the final pages of his book, Martin[25] acknowledges the people who have most influenced him in his "Christian" thinking:

- Glennon Doyle Melton, (whom we met above), the Christian author and speaker who divorced her husband to marry a woman;
- Rob Bell, who has publicly abandoned Scripture and appar-

ently no longer attends church;[26]

- Doug Pagitt, pastor of Solomon's Porch in Minneapolis, who sees Christianity as an evolving system and has no doctrinal statement;
- Brian McLaren, who champions interfaith spirituality.

These people would doubtless no longer call themselves "evangelical," since they no longer believe that the Bible is the standard for Christian faith. The essence of liberalism throughout church history has been the belief that God's spirit speaks through the spirit of the age rather than through Scripture. Anyone who says that Scripture is worthless in the light of human desires for love becomes a classic liberal.

A Brief History of Liberalism

The first version of Christian liberalism took place early in the church's history in the form of Gnosticism, a system by which compromising Christians rejected the Bible and sought to blend the pagan spirituality of the mystery religions with their Christian faith. Interestingly, there are no accounts of Gnostic Christians martyred by the Romans. They were too much like the Romans. Hippolytus, the second century anti-Gnostic church father, documented that the Gnostics of his day sought "the wisdom of the pagans,"[27] in particular by attending Isis-worshipping ceremonies, in order to understand "the universal mystery."[28] This is akin to interfaith worship services attended by liberals today. However, it was clear in those early days that Gnosticism had nothing to do with the faith of the Bible, especially since it favored personal experience and denied any value to God the Creator or to the Christian scriptures.

Much later, in the nineteenth century, the movement of "Christian Modernism" sought to erase the miraculous from the Bible in order to blend the Christian gospel with materialist secular humanism. Secular liberal values—the Fatherhood of God and the brotherhood of man—became the all-inclusive social gospel of the sophisticated liberal churches. For some, biblical spirituality was transformed into this-worldly philosophical existentialism, which required that the Bible be "demythologized," scrubbed of its preposterous supernatural "myths"! Again the Bible was dismissed as the norm of the church.

Currently, pluralistic Neomarxism's destruction of the binary is creating a global interfaith movement and an all-is-one, pagan spirituality, as the culture absorbs Eastern spirituality and sets the agenda for the church. "Gay Christianity," which does not see any problem in this trend of modern culture, is beginning to associate with this massive attack on the biblical binary, especially in its turn toward androgyny. The warning of Paul is timely: "Do not be conformed to this world, but be transformed by the renewal of your mind" (Rom. 12:2). In today's thinking, ethical issues are determined by the intelligence and judgment of well-meaning people of good will. This is nothing less than human autonomy, which is the foundation of secular humanism.

The Canadian philosopher George Grant well understood how liberalism is destroying the Anglican Church of Canada. It is conforming to the principles of social justice as defined by secular liberalism and has rejected its own Christian beliefs:

> Justice is understood to be something strictly human, having nothing to do with obedience to any divine command or conformity to any pattern "laid up in heaven." Moral principles, like all other social conventions, are something "made on earth." Human freedom requires that the principles of justice be the product of human agreement or

113

consent, that is …they must therefore be rooted in an understanding of the interests of human beings as individuals rather than in any sense of duty or obligation to anything above humanity.[29]

J. Gresham Machen, the great orthodox theologian at the beginning of the twentieth century, saw "Christian" liberalism as an early form of paganism in Christian dress. He adeptly put his finger on the essence of this apostasy at a time when it was not so obvious that the mainline Christian churches were denying biblical orthodoxy:

> The truth is that liberalism has lost sight of the very center and core of the Christian teaching. In the Christian view of God as set forth in the Bible, there are many elements. But one attribute of God is absolutely fundamental in the Bible; one attribute is absolutely necessary in order to render intelligible all the rest. That attribute is the awful transcendence of God.[30]

That "awful transcendence" is supremely expressed in God as the distinct Creator. In the last few decades, mainline churches who downplay biblical authority have adopted a defence of homosexuality, thus rejecting how God created mankind. In Liberalism, "personal experience becomes a filter to determine the meaning of the Bible."[31] Cardinal John Henry Newman once wrote that "liberalism is the halfway house to atheism."[32] I would argue that it is a halfway house to paganism.

Michael Brown, in *Can You Be Gay and Christian?*[33] warns that the sexual and theological excesses of the Metropolitan Christian Church, the one specifically "gay" denomination, are the end point that begins with evangelical compromise. Brown shows that a cavalier dealing with Scripture to realize personal aims and desires, especially unhealthy sexual desires, finally produces a theology and practice that undermine the faith of genuine orthodoxy. He cites the case of a Metropolitan Christian Church-licenced minister, Patrick Cheng, professor at the Episcopal Divinity School, who entitles a chapter in his book: "Model One: The Erotic Christ"[34] and presents Jesus as both "straight, lesbian, bisexual, tri-sexual,"[35] whose love life varies from masturbation to incest—"since we are really all one Being."[36] So spiritual life becomes a male "falling in love with a [naked] man." Brown notes that many "gay Christians" are celebrating these theologians,[37] not bothering to find any theological structures to oppose them.

THE KEY: SCRIPTURE

It might seem that the debate or conversation is merely about intramural issues of interpretation, but the question of homosexuality is now focusing us on what the Bible is and how much authority it has over the church. Any church or individual who concludes that the Bible is an error-filled, out-of-date, socially-conditioned document written by authors giving us their subjective ideas, which are irrelevant for today's issues—that church or individual will find it natural to affirm homosexual inclusion. Once the Bible is stripped of its normative authority, its contents can be seen through the autonomous presuppositions of the modern culture.

Machen and others throughout the history of the church understood that the only way to resist Liberalism is to place the Scriptures as primary authority in one's life, which has been the practice of the church from the earliest times. This is not mindless, easy believism. The doctrine of Scripture has a noble place in the life of the church and accurately describes the nature of the world. The essential nature of Scripture is tied to the person of God himself, our Creator, who is distinct from the creation. The creation cannot use itself as its final reference point; humans cannot be the starting point of truth. Creation on its own cannot understand itself or God. Paul brings a solemn word of testimony as an inspired teacher appointed by God to describe the ignorant and rebellious state of humanity:

> Now this I say and testify in the Lord, that you must no longer walk as the Gentiles do, in the futility of their minds. They are darkened in their understanding, alienated from the life of God because of the ignorance that is in them, due to their hardness of heart. (Eph. 4:17–18)

Without a word from the God who is outside of us, we are lost, and so is the culture to which we so often turn for direction and approval.

If, in the beginning, there was the Word (John 1:1) rather than senseless matter that mysteriously organizes itself in unimaginably logical complexity, it should not surprise us that God spoke into the universe language, meaning, beauty, morality, joy, love, and a host of other things that matter could never have created. Yet the physical creation is only one revelation of God to us. We would not know enough about him unless he revealed himself more specifically.

How vain would be our Christian faith if there was no sure Word from God the Creator about the nature of human existence. How frustrating would be a situation in which God, having created us as intelligent, thinking beings, would give us no dependable way of understanding him and the mystery of who we are. Our thinking would be in vain. The whole idea of human existence depends on God's revelation of himself and of his purposes in creating us. As opposed to all the various forms of Eastern spirituality and the mystical religions of the West, Christianity begins with the affirmation that God is a speaking God, known not through subjective inner feelings, but by objective forms of communication.

GOD SPEAKS

God speaks in different but complementary ways:

1. *God speaks by making human beings in his own image* and thus showing us divinely given human logic. If we say that something is true, we affirm an intelligent universe. Even postmodernists announce with great assurance that there is no overarching truth—for they have to believe, at the very least, that their overarching denial of truth is in fact true.

2. *God also speaks through his works of creation* in their beauty and complexity, as Paul says: "For what can be known about God is plain to them, because God has shown it to them. For his invisible attributes, namely, his eternal power and divine nature, have been clearly perceived, ever since the creation of the world, in the things that have been made" (Rom. 1:19–20). The character of the God of creation is seen in the things he has made. When we see "made" things, we immediately assume there is a Maker. When we look at the world around us, we do catch a glimpse, as Paul says, of the immensity and power of God. We see intricacy, attention to detail, and frightening power. We experience an uneasy sense of the vastness of time and space. We watch animals that make us laugh and stare at beauty that brings us to tears. But we must not forget the apex of God's creation—human beings, who are the only creatures made in God's image. It is in humanity that we see the most about God. We see personhood, creativity, intelligence, language, and—most of all—love! All this we see in God's creation. Yet we need more.

3. *God speaks through his special words of Scripture.* In an intelligent universe that human beings did not create, it makes sense to hear that God "entrusted" his people with special speech, "the oracles

of God" (Rom. 3:2), the gift of the Scriptures, inspired by his Spirit. Though his people are unfaithful, God's faithfulness is "vindicated by means of (his) words" (Rom. 3:3–4). These particular words are "inspired" (God-breathed) and can be counted on to give us true knowledge. As a Scripture-producing prophet, the Apostle Paul tells us: "All Scripture is God-breathed and is profitable for doctrine, for reproof, for correction, for training in righteousness, that the man of God may be complete, equipped for every good work" (2 Tim. 3:17). This is a special work of the Spirit: "Men spoke from God as they were carried along by the Holy Spirit" (2 Pet. 1:21). Scripture is essential for good works. Numerous texts within the Scriptures testify to this special work of God.[38]

Scripture is both authoritative and sufficient, though not exhaustive. It does not speak directly to every subject, but recounts and applies God's acts of redemption in history. Nevertheless, the Bible claims authority over human tradition,[39] miracles,[40] prophets,[41] angels[42] and men.[43] Moreover, the law of God, rightly understood, is a continuing factor in the life of the church.[44] Christians may not build an understanding of the world without a deep dependence on this graciously provided Word of God.

If emotionalism and subjective feelings are the ultimate criteria of truth, the church is doomed to descend into liberalism, and then into outright paganism. "Gay Christianity" is the emotional toe in the door of the sanctuary, marking the arrival of egalitarian, politically-correct cultural Neomarxist progressivism—the ultimate political expression of individual autonomy and of the essence of pagan Oneism.

True liberals, when they see the conversion of evangelicals to pro-gay convictions, smell victory. Three particular "evangelical" authors I mentioned earlier—Dave Schmelzer, Ken Wilson, and David

Gushee—are all in favor of full inclusion of active homosexuals in the church, and are all published by the same committed interfaith/ liberal publisher, ReadtheSpirit. Every week, on a popular blog of the same name, David Crumm, the publisher, celebrates the success of interfaith spirituality and honours these authors, together with Matthew Vines, as important contributors to the church's future thinking.

And here is "Christian" interfaith from the horse's mouth, that is, from J. Herbert Nelson II, the Stated Clerk of the Presbyterian Church (U.S.A.): "Despite cries proclaiming the death of the Presbyterian Church (U.S.A.), we remain a viable interfaith and ecumenical partner in many local communities while proclaiming a prophetic witness throughout the world."[45] The content of this prophecy is that all religions are one. In the opening worship service of the 2016 General Assembly, an Islamic leader offered a prayer in which he referred to Mohammed as a prophet alongside Jesus and decried "bigots" and "Islamophobes."[46]

DAVID GUSHEE'S SAGA

David Gushee once held an orthodox position on human sexuality, co-writing a textbook entitled *Kingdom Ethics: Following Jesus in a Contemporary Context*,[47] published by InterVarsity Press, in which he wrote: "Homosexual conduct is one form of sexual expression that falls outside the will of God."[48] In that textbook, he opposed the full inclusion of LGBT Christians in the churches, as well as same-sex "marriage." So how was it, that in 2016, he received an award from the interfaith Religion Communicators Council?[49] Why would the liberal Society of Christian Ethics and the liberal American Academy of Religion, along with the Society of Biblical Literature, name Gushee as their president for 2017? In its 100 years of existence, this academy (which hosts 10,000 scholars of all religious confessions and convictions at its annual meeting) has never named one respected evangelical scholar to be president. Indeed, in recent years this post-Christian "scientific" academy has never elected a theologian, even a liberal one. But along comes Gushee, with no particular academic prestige or scholarly body of work, and, seemingly overnight, he is their titular president.

What might account for this? Gushee received these honours *after* publishing *Changing Our Mind*, in which he recounts that his mind was changed on LGBT issues by following "the way of Jesus"[50] and by "transformative encounters with gay, lesbian, bisexual and transgender Christians," one of them being his "own beloved [lesbian] sister."[51] He wrote that his younger self had made "an unthinking assumption" that to be gay was automatically to be liberal. Now his mind has changed.[52] The change is massive and instructive. Ironically, the younger Gushee had failed to see that he had probably already become a liberal, though his favorite term is "progressive." In any case, old or young, the change happened. In May 2017, Gushee announced his definitive and happy departure from evangelicalism, led by "Jesus." In his column for *Religion News Service*, Gushee said:

> I now believe that incommensurable differences in understanding the very meaning of the Gospel of Jesus Christ, the interpretation of the Bible, and the sources and methods of moral discernment, separate many of us from our former brethren—and that it is best to name these differences clearly and without acrimony, on the way out the door. I also believe that attempting to keep the dialogue going is mainly fruitless. The differences are unbridgeable.[53]

Gushee's journey has been long. Twelve years passed between his orthodox ethics textbook and his later book, *Changing Our Mind*. His current theological reasoning follows an unusual principle; he "leans forward towards Jesus rather than leaning backwards to the primeval creation narratives,"[54] such as Genesis 1:27–28 and Genesis 2:24. He argues that because these texts have "proven remarkably problematic in Christian history,… we cannot rely on them for sexual ethics."[55] He states: "We cannot get back to Genesis 1 and 2, to a primal sinless world,"[56] so the primary texts of biblical anthropology (Gen. 1:27–28) and the foundation of marriage (Gen. 2:24) no longer apply.[57]

Gushee places his experience beyond critique: "It became clear to me—in a deeply spiritual place that I will allow no one to challenge—that God was sending LGBT people to me."[58] "Experiencing the suffering oneself—or a loved one's or a parishioner's—is the major path into theological reconsideration."[59]

Erick Erikson, the well-known conservative commentator, states that Gushee is "actually leaving Christianity itself, despite trying to claim otherwise, with a book titled *Still Christian*. In fact, I think Gushee will eventually be as honest about leaving the faith as he is about leaving evangelicalism."[60] Will all the evangelicals who faithfully follow their master walk out the door as well? Gushee wrote recently that he is among millions of others "who have made their exits, or had their exits made for them, and now wander in a kind of exile."[61]

How is it that Gushee, who claims to hold so strongly to following Jesus, can directly oppose his Savior, who verbally cites Genesis 2:24 as an essential part of his teaching on divorce (Matt. 19:4) and his understanding of the human lot? Gushee is not "leaning forward to Jesus," for if he rejects Genesis 2:24, he must reject Jesus' teaching of that passage in relation to marriage: "Have you not read that he who created them from the beginning made them male and female"

(Matt. 19:4)? Jesus did not consider this text to be "remarkably problematic." He saw it as foundational. In contradicting the Pharisees' view of marriage, Jesus reaffirms the validity of Genesis 2:24 for all time, saying: "Have you not read that he who created them from the beginning made them male and female (Matt. 19:4)? "Because of your hardness of heart Moses allowed you to divorce your wives," he goes on to tell them, "but from the beginning it was not so" (Matt. 19:7–9).

In this debate with his opponents, Jesus solemnly evokes "the beginning," driving them back to the beginning of creation as the norm on which he bases his inspired teaching. In such a short span our Savior uses the phrase "in the beginning" twice, clearly marking how important it is to him. He is not "leaning forward" in an attempt to get away from the original creation pattern. As the personification of Wisdom in the process of creation, and as the eternal Son, he says: "The LORD possessed me "at the beginning" of his work, the first of his acts of old (Prov. 8:22). The proof that what God says is true over against the lies of the false gods is that he is the one "Who declared it from the beginning, that we might know, and beforehand, that we might say, 'He is right'" (Isa. 41:26). John begins his gospel by stating that God the Son, as the Word, was there "at the beginning" (John 1:1), he "was in the beginning with God" (John 1:1–2). This is one of his titles. As Paul says, "he is the beginning" (Col. 1:18), so when Jesus speaks about the beginning he speaks as a divine witness of the beginning. He was there. "The words of the Amen, the faithful and true witness, the beginning of God's creation" (Rev. 3:14). This is why the triumphant Lord declares: "I am the Alpha and the Omega, the beginning and the end" (Rev. 21:6, see also 22:13).

Coming from the heights of glory of the "in the beginning" Savior down into the deception of "gay Christianity" brings us up with a jolt. Can we still call ourselves Christian if we eliminate the Bible's foundational texts, reject the clear and explicit teaching of Jesus— Creator of the universe—replacing them with our self-justifying and self-creating theories and practices about sexuality? This is a dangerous and unparalleled route for evangelicals to follow.

Professor Denny Burk, who spearheaded the writing of the Nashville Statement, is right: "It is time for folks on both sides of this debate to come to terms with just how much of a watershed this issue [homosexuality] is. The evangelical movement is facing a moment of crisis over this issue. We are about to find out who is for real and who isn't."[62] This is evident in the language of Gushee. The acceptance of homosexual practice by evangelicals eventually creates "incommensurable," and "unbridgeable differences."[63] A Twitter feed reacting negatively to the recent Nashville Statement draws the obvious conclusion: "If you love LGBT+ folk, leave the evangelical church."[64] A line in the sand is being drawn publicly on this issue that will distinguish evangelicalism from the rest of the culture.

Abandoning evangelicalism will happen to others who have followed Gushee. Matthew Vines, another pro-gay advocate, expresses deep admiration for Gushee's work as of "pivotal importance,"[65] and says that Gushee shows "where we're headed."[66] At the same time he affirms: "I believe all of Scripture is inspired by God and authoritative for my life."[67] How long will this attachment last?

Another example of the theological slide due to the need to justify homosexuality is the story of Mark Yaconelli, son of Mike Yaconelli. The father is the founder of Youth Specialties, a ministry in which his son Mark participated, taking young people into the theologically dangerous arena of Contemplative Spirituality. Mark has pursued his father's youth work in a ministry called The Youth

Ministry & Spirituality Project. The website is now for sale, which may be one endpoint of a sad story. Mark has come to believe that

> God did not write the Bible…The Bible itself must be judged according to Jesus' Rule of Love. When we do that, we find that the teachings of the Bible that discriminate against homosexuals are plain wrong. The Bible was never meant to be a book about sexuality and it shouldn't be treated that way.[68]

As always happens, the rejection of the historic Christian interpretation of Scripture leads to "Christian" liberalism. This is followed in short order by an openness to all religions and to their "methods of moral discernment," as Gushee says, so that interfaith becomes part of the dominant agenda for liberalism, and the term "Christian" begins to disappear or at least lose any kind of significant meaning.

Interfaith liberalism has indeed walked out of the door of evangelical faith. "Christa," a bronze sculpture of a "female Jesus" by artist Edwina Sandys, appears alongside the work of 21 other contemporary artists in the high and holy place of "Christian" liberalism, the Cathedral of St. John the Divine in New York City. The *Juicy Ecumenism* website justifies its inclusion among all the pieces of artwork since they are all "exploring the language, symbolism, art, and ritual associated with the historic concept of the Christ image and the divine as manifested in every person—across all genders, races, ethnicities, sexual orientations, and abilities."[69] With this kind of hermeneutic, the man Jesus can be turned into a woman, "Christa." Indeed, liberalism ultimately finds its place in the religion of interfaith, since there is no authoritative Scripture defining spirituality… or anything else.

INTERFAITH

Feeling-based exegesis only gives rise to various forms of mysticism, which become the fast route to interfaith heresy. Diana Butler Bass, mentioned in the previous chapter, who once taught at the orthodox Christian Westmont College and attended a Reformed evangelical church, now no longer considers herself an evangelical.[70] In a sermon at the National Cathedral, Washington D.C., another high place of Christian liberalism, Bass, reflecting on the themes in her recent book: *Grounded: Finding God in the World—A Spiritual Revolution*, speaks of finding God in nature and other people. She believes we must understand God horizontally not vertically, denying God's transcendence. Top-down religion is over, she claims. "My faith is broad and eclectic including Jews, Moslems, Buddhist and Hindus—I'm spiritual but not religious."[71] She is also pro-gay, for interfaith and intersex[72] seem to go together, as we shall see.

Brian McLaren is another notable pro-homosexual, ex-evangelical, interfaith thinker and author. In 1993, strictly as an observer, I attended the Parliament of the World's Religions, where 8000 delegates from 125 religions assembled in the immense Palmer House Hotel in Chicago. It was an unforgettable experience. On the stage were Hindu gurus in saffron robes, Buddhist teachers in brown mantles, liberal bishops in solemn academic regalia, and a pagan witch from the Fellowship of Isis, with an enormous exotic headdress. There was not one sign of orthodox Christian faith. Not one speaker at any occasion, in the plenaries or seminars, was an orthodox Christian. Indeed, the historic Christian message was not only silenced—it was attacked throughout the week as the great enemy of true religion. As I gazed at this vast assembly, called together to epitomize the unity of all religions, I believed I was seeing the future as the confrontation between orthodoxy and interfaith heresy, with

125

interfaith heresy set to dominate world culture for years to come.

To my surprise, by 2015, all that had changed. Interfaith liberalism had succeeded in seducing *evangelical thinkers* to be part of its gospel-denying movement. I never saw that coming! One plenary speaker at the 2015 *Parliament of the World's Religions* in Salt Lake City was none other than Brian McLaren, accompanied by an evangelical we already met, Jim Wallis of *Sojourners*. McLaren's message had become a poem to interfaith spirituality: "Brothers and sisters, the Earth is singing to us, the Earth is crying to us, the Earth is groaning to us. That people of faith need to tell a new healing story, bigger and better and more gracious, rooted in the diverse riches of our various traditions. This [is the] new story."[73]

When you've taken the slide all the way down, you basically lose any resemblance to Christian faith. J. Michael Clark, mentioned above, is now a "gay theologian." He describes himself as "a scripturephobe" who "studiously avoids the Bible whenever [he] can." Says he, "[I]t is not the scripture that holds authority; it is the standpoint of oppression that…provides me with a hermeneutic of suspicion."[74] Cultural and personal experiences are the only sources of revelation. "Gay Christianity" ends up in the radical heresy of mainline, interfaith, free-floating liberalism, and beyond, as we shall see. Wittingly or unwittingly, it denies the basic Christian revelation of who God is, and ends up relying on subjective experience, losing touch with the essence of the person of God. Those who follow this road travel into various forms of Gnosticism or paganism, and end up in a desperate physical and spiritual state. A false love of neighbour without consideration of the foundation and truth of the love of God leaves the neighbour in a worse state than he or she was at the beginning.

The theological naïveté of "gay Christianity" is expressed in the sad statement of Julie Rodgers, whom we met above. Rodgers recently left her chaplaincy post at Wheaton College to engage fully in homosexual behaviour:

> The fire I've come under (publicly and privately) as I've sought to live in the traditional ethic causes me to question whether this is about genuinely held beliefs or straight up homophobia... The...dream of GC [gay Christianity] is one I truly believe in, full homosexual acceptance...If it turns out that I'm wrong, I trust God will be faithful to catch me.... For now, though, I hope those of you who disagree will continue to welcome my friendship and serve alongside me. It's not too late to call it quits on all the fighting. We could choose instead to focus on all we share in common and seek to mend what's been broken in this fragile world.[75]

Clearly this is a woman who has struggled deeply with temptation, for whom we can feel great concern and Christian sympathy. But we appeal to her to hear the words of a German scholar of a generation ago, the respected Wolfhart Pannenberg, who, though sometimes teetering on the edges of intellectual liberalism himself, was fearful of the break-up of the church, and had the conviction to prophetically declare:

> Here lies the boundary of a Christian church that knows itself to be bound by the authority of Scripture. Those who urge the church to change the norm of its teaching on this matter must know that they are promoting schism. If a church were to let itself be pushed to the point where it ceased to treat homosexual activity as a departure from the biblical norm, and recognized homosexual unions as a personal partnership of love equivalent to marriage, such a church would stand no longer on biblical ground but against the unequivocal witness of Scripture. A church that took this step would cease to be the one, holy, catholic, and apostolic church.[76]

Does Julie Rodgers see the theological implications of her words and actions in this larger perspective? Does she stop to think that what she promotes as her own sexual self-expression will have such immense theological implications: the being and glory of God and the maintenance of the liberating power of the gospel? The biblical vision is much more than what she dismisses as the moral disapproval of narrow-minded killjoys.

The diminution of liberal churches in the United States is tied to their view of sexuality. Ironically, this is true of the great center of the Protestant/Presbyterian Reformation, the country of Scotland. The Roman Catholic Archbishop Tartaglia reported that Catholics now constitute the most active religious group in Scotland, because the Protestant churches are steadily shrinking, having adopted the normalization of homosexuality within their churches. Ironically, the Catholic Church becomes the primary representative of Christianity in the historic land of the Reformation.[77]

Unfortunately, the evolution from subjective Bible interpretation to liberalism and then to interfaith finally blossoms into full-orbed pagan thinking, which we shall examine in depth in the next chapter. In interfaith we are already describing a form of paganism. Manifestly, spiritual communion between "evangelicals" and the other religions is a form of paganism that recognizes the gods of other religions.

The next chapter is a warning to believers who are hesitating between the two views. The right choice may mean suffering, but the wrong choice will take you out the door of Christian orthodoxy and into the dark world of paganism.

CHAPTER 7

HELLO, PAGANISM

Christianity's decline in the West is not producing austere secularism but rather a wild flowering of shamanic healers, spirit crystals, transcendental maharishis, and a plethora of pansexual practices. The once-Christian West is becoming both spiritually and sexually pagan, helped by churches eagerly adopting the culture's norms. Unless God calls them back from the brink, Christians who associate with certain theological and sexual movements will end up in liberalism and finally in pagan apostasy. There is a deep spiritual power associated with homosexuality, an aspect rarely mentioned in discussions of the subject. Homosexuality is presented as part of a blossoming Western defence of civil and human rights and as an essential and beneficial building block of a progressive moral agenda. As the West converts to forms of spiritual paganism, it also freely adopts sexual expressions that characterized the pagan world but were largely abolished by the spread of biblical faith.

I hope it will be helpful for my readers to understand the spiritual destination of those who have rejected a strong view of the Bible and who now promote an "affirming" view of homosexuality. Individual homosexuals may have no idea of the ideological meaning of the gay agenda. But the truth is that liberal Christians who make the culture their authority will end up worshipping culture's god, Nature. The Apostle Paul said that we worship and serve either God the Creator or some form of the creation (Rom. 1:25).

Today it is in vogue to understand omnigender (all genders) to be an expression of intrinsic human sexuality, and omnireligion (all religions) as an expression of intrinsic human spirituality; the two go hand in hand. Which "omni" comes first is not significant, for they are in a circular relationship. When people begin to accept many forms of sexuality, they stop thinking in a binary, either/or fashion in the area of religion as well. "Unnatural" sexual expression has emerged "naturally" in the many forms of pagan religion throughout time and space. In other words, pagan religious thinking has produced pagan sexual action—and vice versa.

Christian de la Huerta, gay author of *Coming Out Spiritually*,[1] once presented his work as spokesman for "queer spirituality" at a global summit for the United Religions Initiative. In his address at this important interfaith meeting, he stated: "before patriarchal [theistic] times, when women and the divine feminine were honoured… we [homosexuals] were the shamans, the healers, the visionaries, the mediators, …the people who walk between the worlds."[2] The crowd of interfaith visionaries gave him a standing ovation, clearly approving his pagan message and its interfaith spirituality, in which homosexuality plays a central role. A person who still identifies as an evangelical while advocating interfaith liberalism has, in fact, become a pagan, since all the gods and all the spiritual truths of religious practice are honoured in such interfaith gatherings, whereas the God of the Bible is consistently denied. De la Huerta mentioned his meeting with an Argentinian tribal representative who said about Christianity: "Ask them to stop evangelizing. Tell them we do not wish to be evangelized. For if you do away with our traditions, who will tell you about the Earth or remind you of Nature?"[3] Pagan animism, which has for centuries celebrated homosexuality, understands the great divide between its own presuppositions and those of theistic thinking.

PAGAN—REALLY?

Perhaps you baulk at the description of modern culture as "pagan," wondering if that is a term reserved for times when witches, Wiccans, Satanists, and occultists were much in evidence. Of course, in a general sense, anyone who lives without recognizing, honouring and thanking God, anyone who is dominated entirely by this-worldly concerns, can accurately be described as pagan. That person worships natural things. Under that description, the great majority of those living in the secular West are pagan. But today we are seeing an increasing number of exotic pagan spiritual practices, right here in the sophisticated, intellectual West. As we saw in chapter 3, secularism is on the decline as we enter the postsecular age.[4]

The pagan nature of our times is well illustrated by a leading contemporary spiritualist, Jean Houston. This brilliant woman was a spiritual advisor to the first lady Hillary Clinton during the 1990s, helping her make spiritual contact with (deceased) first lady Eleanor Roosevelt, doubtless as a kind of occult medium.[5] From the halls of ultimate political power, Houston observed in 1995: "we are living in a state both of breakdown and breakthrough...a whole system transition …requir[ing] a new alignment that only myth can bring…. Never has mythic knowing been more needed than today."[6] Her book, *The Passion of Isis and Osiris: A Gateway to Transcendent Love*, was a call to discover the powers of Isis, goddess of the underworld. Houston assures us that "we are living in mythic times [a time when] we communicate with those mythic beings remembered as Isis and Osiris."[7]

Elsewhere, I document the increase of ancient animistic paganism among leading intellectuals in the sophisticated West.[8] Here, I wish to show that to normalize alternate sexualities not only affects personal and civil rights but provides a natural bridge to pagan spirituality.

THE RADICAL JOURNEY OF RELIGIOUS LEADERS

Progressive Christians may not realize where they are likely to end up if they follow the crowd out of evangelicalism. The following leaders are but a few examples of those still calling themselves Christians who have gone into apostasy.

Rev. Eugene Monick

For many years, an outspoken Episcopalian priest in Minnesota and New York City, Monick declared with assurance that "the effort to dictate who a man should love is perverted theology. It is the psychological counterpart of monotheism, dominated by patriarchal triumphalism, demanding adherence to the patriarch's one true god."[9] Monick correctly realizes the culminating union of interfaith and intersexuality. According to him, the unique patriarchal God of the Bible is far too limited and such a view of God creates a far too limited concept of sexuality. He argues that we need as many gods and as many sexual choices as possible. This is unabashed paganism dressed up as progressive Christianity.

Frank Griswold

In 2003, as Presiding Bishop of the Episcopal Church (U.S.A.), Frank Griswold preached the ordination service for the first homosexual bishop in the denomination. Here again, paganized Christianity was in evidence. Griswold's sermon was based not on a passage of Scripture but on a citation from the poet Rumi, a medieval Sufi master. The poem teaches that in the final analysis, there is neither right nor wrong. In other words, the event was sanctified by pagan Oneist spirituality, not by Scripture, in order to justify homosexuality. This Christian bishop cited a mystic Muslim who was, to boot, a pedophile.

Marilyn Sewell

Unitarian Universalist minister and writer, Marilyn Sewell claims to be a spiritual woman—spiritual because, for her, the joining of male and female in homosexuality functions as a deep form of spirituality. In contemporary culture, she sees an "emerging shift... towards balance—a balance of the masculine and feminine modes of consciousness, of *anima* and *animus*, of yin and yang, both in the culture at large and within our personal lives as well."[10] The shift is not just about sex. She calls this a "spiritual revolution" that radically changes how we see ourselves in relation to others," a sort of new birth, understanding "that there is no stranger, no "other,"[11] which clearly means no otherness to God himself.

J. Michael Clark

The trajectory of this gay American scholar and professor at Emory University serves as a solemn warning about where the move out of evangelicalism will end. Clark, raised as a Christian, states cogently: "being a gay man or lesbian entails far more than sexual behaviour alone…. [It entails] a whole mode of being-in-the-world."[12] Clark could not find in the Scriptures a model for his chosen lifestyle, and he therefore self-consciously adopted the lifestyle and spirituality of the *berdache*, the American Indian homosexual shaman of pagan animism.

THE SPIRITUAL IDEOLOGY OF HOMOSEXUALITY

M. Stanton Evans—a nationally syndicated columnist for *The Los Angeles Times* and later a professor of journalism—in his book, *The Theme Is Freedom*,[13] recognizes the connection between paganism and the acceptance of homosexuality among those calling themselves conservatives: "The campaign to change societal views of homosexuality adopts a 'pagan ethic.'" He cites acceptance of homosexuality in ancient civilizations such as Babylon and notes: "All of this was unequivocally condemned by the religion of the Bible."[14]

Another informed historian of religion, John N. Oswalt, distinguished professor of Old Testament at Asbury Theological Seminary in his book, *The Bible Among the Myths*, makes an important statement about ancient paganism: "There are only two worldviews; the biblical one and the other [pagan] one."[15] In a section entitled "Denial of Boundaries," he states that in the ancient world boundaries between realms (humans and gods, gods and nature) had to be eliminated. All the boundary-crossing immoral behaviours (cult prostitution, incest, homosexuality) of the ancient world are not "primitive behaviours…or unfortunate aberrations…They are theological statements, necessary expressions of the worldview [of Oneism] of which they are part."[16]

These scholars confirm that a pagan understanding of God as a spiritual life-force within nature produces a deconstruction of normative creational sexuality. The Bible's theistic teaching reveals God not as the Spirit within nature but as nature's distinct Creator. Scripture also, therefore, emphasizes the created distinctions of heterosexuality, which the church maintains as a witness to the pagan world. Many evangelicals fail to understand how crucial this is.

Bereft of a robust view of Scripture and a solid understanding of this world's pagan cosmology, naïve "gay Christians" can hardly avoid falling into this pagan way of thinking. In line with contemporary pagan spirituality, Ken Wilson's statement comes to mind again: "We're all—male and female—part of the bride of Christ."[17] He is right, in one sense, but remember that he recommended 'relaxing' gender distinctions.[18] Wilson's thinking is a naïve, evangelical version of ancient pagan, ideological androgyny, which is now running riot in parts of the church (in addition, of course, to our schools, libraries, TV programs and so on).

There is a deep spiritual ideology behind the practice of homosexuality (whether individual homosexuals know it or not), which goes back into the mists of time as the preferred sexual embodiment of paganism. I return to the example of J. Michael Clark, who gave up searching for a spiritual model in the Scriptures. He well understood at the beginning of the modern gay movement that embracing homosexuality was not an option that one could add to one's Christian faith. It was not a valid possibility for Christian unity, as Julie Rodgers proposed, asking evangelicals "to call it quits on all the fighting….[and] to focus on all we share in common and seek to mend what's been broken in this fragile world." What is broken is the biblical worldview.

Julie Rodgers's hope for unity dissolves in the heat of the immense worldview importance of normalizing homosexuality. There is little, if anything, in common, which is why Clark chose to reject entirely the God of the Bible.[19] He understood that the spirituality animating homosexuality moves outside of biblical faith. "Something in our gay/lesbian being as an all-encompassing existential standpoint...appears to heighten our spiritual capacities."[20] Clark claims these "religious impulses are being killed by [traditional] Judeo-Christianity."[21] For him, the problem lies not with mean-spirited or hateful Christians who fail to love enough. Rather, he deeply understands that, for gays, the problem lies with the overarching biblical worldview and theological paradigm.

SACRED BALANCERS

Seeing the impossible divide, Clark, with remarkable honesty, turned to the sexual model of the American Indian *berdache*, the androgynous shaman of animistic paganism. For Clark, the *berdache* (born male, but choosing to live as female), constitutes a desirable gay spiritual model. He understood the spiritual meaning of this, since the *berdache* achieves "the reunion of the cosmic, sexual and moral polarities," or the "joining of the opposites." *Berdaches* were known as "sacred balancers", unifying the polarities to "nurture wholeness."[22] This powerful spirituality involves the denial of distinctions: between male and female and (the chief of all distinctions) between God and the creation. In the *Star Wars* series, millions of Westerners were introduced to Obi Wan Kenobi, a hero figure and the sacred balancer of the Force. Clark's androgyny lands him squarely in the balancer's pagan camp, facilitating the conscious acceptance of all one's contradictions and perversions. With such liberating power, one can reign divinely supreme over issues of right and wrong.

SHAMANS

Another source for this spiritual view of homosexuality is Walter L. Williams's study *The Spirit and the Flesh: Sexual Diversity in American Indian Culture*.[23] He shows that prior to the Christian influence that accompanied the invasion of the Spanish *conquistadores*, homosexual shamans dominated the animistic, earth-worshipping spirituality of the Mayans and Aztecs. Homosexuality is a common theme in the history of paganism, which proves Michael Clark right: there is no commonality between the biblical and pagan views of homosexuality. Elsewhere, I have developed the key place of homosexuality in the pagan *cultus*, citing numerous sources.[24] This history is crucial for understanding the theological implications of homosexuality for the thinking of today's church.

At the heart of religiously inspired, homosexual, pagan Oneism is a mystical experience, as Clark testifies—a state in which distinctions disappear and opposites are joined. The clearest textual testimony in ancient times comes from nineteenth-century BC Mesopotamia. Androgynous priests were associated with the worship of the goddess Ishtar.[25] Their condition was due to their "devotion to Ishtar who herself had 'transformed their masculinity into femininity.'"[26] They functioned as occult shamans, who released the sick from the power of demons just as, according to the cult myth, they had saved Ishtar from the devil's lair. "[A]s human beings," says a contemporary scholar, "…they seem to have engendered demonic abhorrence in others. …[T]he fearful respect they provoked is to be sought in their otherness, their position between myth and reality, and their divinedemonic ability to transgress boundaries."[27]

RITUALS OF ANDROGYNY

The renowned history of religions scholar, Mircea Eliade, calls this "ritualized androgynization."[28] Professor Eliade holds that many myths, symbols, divine figures, and religious practices encountered in varying sociocultural contexts are likely to be reminiscent of one another, despite the latitude of their culture-specific difference. They are human documents that "express typical human situations" and "form an integral part of the history of the spirit."[29]

We see the myth of a bisexual or androgynous god and androgynous or homosexual priests in ancient Mesopotamian and Indo-European nature religions, as well as in the myths of Australian Aborigines, African tribes, South American Indians and Pacific islanders. Even though they are separated by many centuries and many miles, Eliade shows an evident historical and "theological" connection between the Mesopotamian homosexual shamans called *assinnus*, which the Canaanites called *qedeshim*, the Scythians *ennares*, and the Syrians *galli*. In the North American tribes there were *berdaches*, amongst the Navajo known as *nadle*, among the Zuñi, *awonawilona* (literally "he-she").[30] Eliade believes that "ultimately, it is the wish to recover this lost unity in existence that has caused man to think of the opposites as complementary aspects of a single reality,"[31] hence the importance of the religious symbolism that androgyny expresses.

Such a widespread practice over time and space, now brought to light by modern scholarship, surely explains how the Old Testament knew of the spread of this custom in all the pagan nations surrounding the nation of Israel, and therefore warns Israel to avoid the practices, as well as the pagan beliefs these practices expressed. The warning, "You shall not do as they do in the land of Egypt, where you lived, and you shall not do as they do in the land of Canaan" (Lev. 18:3; see Lev. 20:23) is not only national, ceremonial and moral, but deeply theological. God's people are to avoid engaging in homosexual activity which, by eliminating distinctions, embodies the worship of the many gods of paganism. Their sexual purity thus maintains the witness of the only true God—the theistic, distinct Creator revealed to Israel.

Eliade explains the spiritual meaning of androgyny as "a symbolic restoration…of the undifferentiated unity that preceded the creation,"[32] in direct opposition to the Old Testament account of creation, which is marked by distinctions. The androgynous being sums up the very goal of the mystical, Oneist quest, whether ancient or modern: "In mystical love and at death one completely integrates the spirit world: all contraries are collapsed. The distinctions between the sexes are erased: the two merge into an androgynous whole."[33] In short, "at the center one knows oneself, is known, and knows the nature of reality."[34] According to Eliade, androgyny functions as "an archaic and universal formula for the expression of wholeness, the co-existence of the contraries, or *coincidentia oppositorum* (joining of the opposites)…symboliz[ing] perfection…[and] ultimate being."[35] The homosexual priest-shamans—true hermaphrodites who dress and behave like women—"combine the two cosmological planes—earth and sky—and also …in their own person the feminine element (earth) and the masculine element (sky). We here have ritual androgyny, a well-known archaic formula for the…*coincidentia oppositorum*."[36]

On the moral plane, the pagan monist—in an exercise of personal, autonomous power—assumes guiltlessness and takes personal control over all his actions, thus joining the opposites of good and evil, and relativizing the entire moral domain. Just as the distinctions inherent in heterosexuality point to the fundamental theistic notion of the Creator/creature distinction, so androgyny in its various forms, eradicates distinction and elevates the ideal of the spiritual blending of all things, including the idolatrous confusion of human and divine, as well as of good and evil.

CONTEMPLATIVE SPIRITUALITY

The theological implications of this opposition to sexual binary categories are enormous. Evangelical naïveté plays into the hands of non-binary spirituality, now popular in certain church circles, under the guise of "Contemplative Spirituality."[37] In its Hindu form, such spirituality is taking over much of the Western mind and soul. Philip Goldberg, mentioned in chapter 2, calls this a spiritual "revival," based on the acceptance of *advaita*, the Hindu term meaning "not-two." The spiritual synthesis, to which progressives believe we are advancing, will be non-dual, non-binary. Goldberg declares that *advaita* and "non-dual...oneness, unity around non-separation" are "the generic term[s] increasingly used to describe the present and coming spirituality in America—meaning that God and the world are not two."[38]

Such apostasy from God and from the biblical notions of gender is pagan to the core and has produced, in the Christian West, a torrential flood of the same spirituality and sexuality that has always characterized occult paganism. Understanding where such radical theology has always taken a society in its sexual practice will help us to see the necessarily close association between theology and sexuality, as well as the manner in which the one affects the other. It is not civil rights. It is the abandonment of theism in the last two generations of Western history, and the embrace of the spirituality of Eastern paganism. These same years have produced the most radical social engineering in America's history—the deconstruction of normative biblical heterosexuality and the revival and pagan idealization of homosexual androgyny.

In chapter 2, I dedicated some time to describing the contemporary culture as the direct result of the 1960s Cultural Revolution. One of the architects of this culture whom I mentioned was the Jungian psychologist[39] and Gnostic spiritualist,[40] June Singer. She was directly and consciously involved in influencing this modern culture, founded on homosexuality[41] and its spiritual meaning. We have inherited that culture. In 1977, at the end of the Sixties revolution, Singer made a programmatic statement in her book, *Androgyny: Toward a New Theory of Sexuality*. Others are now proving her predictions: "What lies in store as we move towards the longed-for conjunction of the opposites? [C]an the human psyche realize its own creative potential through building its own cosmology and supplying it with its own gods?"[42]

Singer called for a coherent, all-encompassing, attractive, and religiously pagan account of the nature of existence. Actually, the new paradigm she predicted fits perfectly with paganism's past. She saw that the spiritual Age of Aquarius was also the Age of Androgyny. A new humanism required a new view of sexuality, which she found in androgyny. She also understood its implications, and declared: "We have at hand…all the ingredients we will need to perform our own new alchemical opus…to fuse the opposites within us. This is what individuation [the Jungian state of human maturity] is all about." She goes on to say: "The archetype of androgyny appears in us as an innate sense of…and witness to…the primordial cosmic unity, [which was] nearly totally expunged from the Judeo-Christian tradition…and a patriarchal God-image."[43] Singer, a true Jungian, is conscious of promoting the deeply important sexual element in the coming "new humanism": "The androgyne participates consciously in the evolutionary process, redesigning the individual…society and…the planet."[44] A fundamental element in this "new sexuality" is its affirmation of Monism or Oneism, which is a radical rejection of the biblical God and cosmology of the Western Christian past.[45]

COSMOLOGY OF SYNTHESIS

I noted in my book *The Other Worldview*[46] that the era now unfolding is neither post-Christian nor postmodern, but postsecular. I cited English philosopher, Mike King, for whom the new day in spirituality involves "a renewed openness to questions of the spirit while retaining the secular habits of critical thought."[47] The tandem increase of homosexuality and pagan spirituality is the startling phenomenon of the twenty-first century world. It is not a footnote of Western history. Secular humanism is in decline[48] and, against all expectations, spirituality is breaking records as the major preoccupation of the average citizen. Religious secularism, more accurately called renewed spiritual paganism (in which the Dalai Lama feels at home)[49] includes "a spiritual cocktail of various ingredients, from 'the religious [political] Left,' to the new quantum science, to mature 'New Age' spirituality and to deepening 'mysticism.'"[50] This is a new kind of spirituality; beyond religion, beyond binary thinking, which—it is claimed by progressive thinkers—will bring a new synthesis between the intellect and the spirit to produce a great convergence of spirituality and science—and sexuality. Pagan philosopher Richard Tarnas brilliantly unpacks the content of this new synthesis: "Platonic and Pre-Socratic philosophy, Hermeticism, mythology, the mystery religions…Buddhist and Hindu mystical traditions…Gnosticism and the major esoteric traditions…Neolithic European and Native American spiritual traditions—[are] all gathering now on the intellectual stage as if for some kind of climactic synthesis" by which "every society and individual symbolically interprets and engages

144

the ultimate nature of being." [51] We await the final coming of a total worship of divinized creation.

Interfaith believers from many religions and many churches eagerly await this ultimate synthesis. Wayne Teasdale, a Catholic interfaith mystic, predicted the longed-for utopia: "We are at the dawn of a new consciousness, a radically fresh approach to our life as the human family in a fragile world.... Perhaps the best name for this new segment of historical experience is the Interspiritual Age."[52] Another term might well be the Intersexual Age.

ORTHODOXY UNDER SIEGE

With the recent transformation of Western culture, we are facing the ultimate question: What is Christian orthodoxy? In the name of love for mistreated sexual outcasts, many now claim the title "Christian," but what is a Christian and what does a Christian confess? The church is not accustomed to associating issues of doctrinal correctness with seemingly peripheral issues like human sexuality. But questions of doctrinal orthodoxy now face us because of the deep integration of a new/ancient, sexual/spiritual, all-embracing pagan cosmology.

Theologian Al Mohler rightly observes:

> We are living in the midst of a massive revolution in morality, and sexual morality is at the center of this revolution. But the question of same-sex relationships and sexuality is at the very center of the debate over sexual morality, and our answer to this question will...determine or reveal what we understand about everything the Bible reveals and everything the church teaches—even the gospel itself.[53]

A naïve evangelical approach, seeking wisdom from modern culture without any serious analysis, leads both individuals and the church into betrayal of biblical orthodoxy. The case of Bart Campolo—son of the famous evangelist, Tony Campolo (who accepts "gay Christianity")[54]—sadly illustrates the process. Bart's journey to secular humanism took him through every stage of heresy, as he says, "from conservative to liberal to entirely secular."[55] He states: "Progressive Christians tend to reject the historic biblical understanding of marriage and sexuality, and generally deny or redefine doctrines such as the atonement and biblical authority. …in 10 years, 30 percent to 40 percent of so-called progressive Christians will also become atheists."[56]

The legal uproar in the United States (and in other countries) caused by the LGBT agenda (and accompanying issues, such as abortion) is the greatest threat to free expression of the Christian faith in centuries. A naïve evangelical commitment to the normalization of the practice of homosexuality will only further the intense opposition to the free public expression of biblical truth, an opposition the culture is already exerting through social shaming and penal sanctions. In the United States, this may well come in the form of legislation like that of "the Equality Act," a bill that was passed by the United States House of Representatives in May 2019, with the help of eight Republican congressmen. According to James Dobson, founder of Focus on the Family, this Act will "spell disaster for Americans…[for it] is nothing but a thinly veiled attempt to finish off religious liberty in America once and for all… and places Christians who believe in traditional marriage at grave legal and civil jeopardy."[57] If it is passed by the Congress and signed by the President, the Equality Act will amend the Civil Rights Act of 1964 and the Fair Housing Act of 1968 by adding to the categories already protected by anti-discrimination laws, "sexual orientation and gender identity" (SOGI). This new social category of LGBT rights would

146

join categories such as race and religion, under the assumption that one's subjectively defined sexual identity is a right as fundamental and as unchangeable as racial identity.

In a short article, I noted the legal implications. "Such a law would ban sex discrimination in public accommodations, which are redefined to include retailers, banks, transportation, jury service, children's education, Christian colleges and universities, federal programs, and credit and health care services…[without being able to] use the federal Religious Freedom Restoration Act (RFRA) to maintain religious and theological convictions."[58]

WHAT CAN WE DO?

How seriously we must take Paul's exhortation: "Walk as children of light, and try to discern what is pleasing to the Lord. Take no part in the unfruitful works of darkness, but instead expose them" (Eph. 5:8–11). The warning of this book does not simply involve being sensitive to the personal feelings of our gay friends. Christians must realize that major cultural and theological implications are involved.

First, we must seek to protect our neighbours and family members from a way of life that will increasingly resemble the dissolute life of ancient pagan Rome, where both the worship of the gods and sexual licence were freely practiced.

Second, we must seek to maintain, by all legal means possible, freedom of speech to declare publicly God's truth and announce the glorious good news of God's gracious forgiveness for all those who seek it. Speaking and hearing the gospel is of ultimate importance.

Third, we must understand the present and coming conflict over truth. We need to know not only what the Bible says about sexuality, but why the Bible ties the honour of God's person to our sexuality. Every Christian should know how to explain these truths in a clear and winsome fashion, without hatred or moralism.

And finally, if we want to love our neighbour well, we must love God first.

CHAPTER 8

LOVE GOD FIRST

The song *Love Is a Many-Splendoured Thing* has been popular since its appearance in the 1995 movie of the same name. It pierces to the heart of the deepest human emotion: love, which the song says is "nature's way of giving a reason to be living." Christians are not the only ones to consider love as "a reason to be living," yet evolution's "survival of the fittest" cannot explain why this "many-splendoured" reality should exist at all. What exactly is the essence of love and where did it come from? In this and the following chapters, we will seek to define what love of God and love of neighbour mean in relation to sexuality. To love God, we must consider the binary distinction between God and the world. Remember the theme of our previous chapters: God is the only uncreated being. All else that exists, he created. Difference and distinction are fundamentally good and right. To love God means honouring him as distinct and prior—the God who has placed his Trinitarian image on us by making us male and female. We are then called to witness to God and to love him by preserving that image in our sexuality.

The binary of sexuality is reflected in the binary of spirituality, which preserves God's otherness and his gracious condescension. Preserving and honouring God by life and word is the most loving gift any human being can offer another.

A KEY TO THE MEANING OF LOVE

Christian believers hold the key to the meaning of love. We turn not to nature, as stunning as it is, for the definition, but to God. In 1 Corinthians 13:13 we read: "So now faith, hope, and love abide, these three; but the greatest of these is love." One day, in the presence of our Savior, when we no longer need faith or hope, love will still last! Our answer to the question "What is love?" has the deepest of implications for the meaning of life. When asked by the religious leaders of his day what the greatest commandment is, Jesus responds without hesitation:

> "Hear, O Israel: The Lord our God, the Lord is one. And you shall love the Lord your God with all your heart and with all your soul and with all your mind and with all your strength." The second is this: "You shall love your neighbour as yourself." There is no commandment greater than these. (Mark 12:28–31)

Here is the essence of Old Testament faith: loving God with everything in us, and then loving our neighbour. "On these two commandments," says Jesus, "depend all the Law and the Prophets," that is, the entire message of the Old Testament (Matt. 22:40). This statement, known as the *Shema*, from the first Hebrew word of the text, "Shema Israel—Hear, Israel," is the essential affirmation of the

Old Testament monotheistic worship of God as revealed in Scripture. In speaking of two kinds of love, Jesus is referring implicitly to the Ten Commandments, which have two basic sections: the first four tell us how to honour and love God exclusively (Ex. 20:1–11) and the latter six tell us how to honour and love our fellow human beings (Ex. 20:12–17).

The affirmation: "the Lord our God is one," with which Jesus begins his answer, is the fundamental statement of Twoism. Calling God "one" here is not to deny the Trinity; it means that God as the Creator is unique. The prophet Isaiah declares that God is "he who sits above the circle of the earth, and its inhabitants are like grasshoppers; who stretches out the heavens like a curtain, and spreads them like a tent to dwell in" (Isa. 40:22). In Isaiah, the Holy One asks us, "To whom then will you compare me that I should be like him? Lift up your eyes on high and see: who created these?" (Isa. 40:25). The answer follows: "He who brings out their host by number, calling them all by name, by the greatness of his might, and because he is strong in power not one is missing.... The LORD is the everlasting God, the Creator of the ends of the earth" (Isa. 40:25–28).

There is no one like God. The Shema is the oldest daily prayer in Judaism, recited morning and night since ancient times as the central element of Jewish piety. It is the Old Testament confession of the uniqueness of the God of Israel. Jesus makes this affirmation central to the New Testament faith. In both Old and New Testaments, love for God our Creator precedes love for others. The Twoist biblical faith shows us how to love by teaching us to love God first. Asking and answering the question "What is love?" is essential for a Christian understanding of existence.

What happens if we fail to love God first? Brian McLaren

believes that "Only through loving neighbours do we prepare our hearts to love God."[1] But reversing the love order, as McLaren does, means that God is no longer the omniscient, omnipresent, and omnipotent Creator and cosmic Ruler. McLaren says Christianity must "lose its monotheistic notions to embrace a grander, inclusive God who demonstrates solidarity with all."[2] McLaren's description fits a non-monotheistic view of God, precious to Hindus and pagans of all stripes,[3] but is totally foreign to what Jesus taught.

Jesus knew that the true source of love is neither nature nor other human beings, but the Creator himself. Reversing the order is the chief diabolical temptation. When Satan promised Jesus rule over the kingdoms of the world and their glory at the price of worshipping him, a created being, Jesus replied: "Be gone, Satan! For it is written, 'You shall worship the Lord your God and him only shall you serve.'"[4] The Apostle Paul echoes this in Romans 1:25. True worshippers "worship and serve...the creator who is blessed forever."

To follow Jesus, we must not ask first about how to love our neighbour, but what it means to love God. Love is not a vague sentimental feeling that we can use to justify any action we choose. Our love must be defined and empowered by God himself. Everything else in our life depends upon it.

It is tempting to start with the love of neighbour, but to do so brings woeful consequences. Christians realize that God has set his unconditional love on us *in Christ*. Naturally, we want to follow Jesus and the Holy Spirit by loving others unconditionally as well. This is an excellent and godly instinct, but it is different than the push to accept "gay Christianity," which posits that "love" is supreme and covers everything. Such an approach is fraught with danger. Placing the love of humanity before the love of God inevitably ends in the worship of creation and full adoption in the church of religious paganism. The love of God, as Jesus expressed it, requires Christians to ground their understanding of love in the person of God the Creator and Redeemer. Anne Kennedy, a perspicacious blogger, understands that behind the use of the same word 'love' are two major, conflicting views of existence:

> We...are living side by side with two incompatible world views and definitions of love. One view says that the only objective truth that can be known are the feelings and inclinations of the self.... And the other view says that the only objective thing that Ultimately matters are the feelings and inclinations of God Who Can Be Known, in the scriptures, whose love extends so far that he entered his own creation to save his creatures from eternal destruction.... These two pictures of the world cannot be reconciled.[5]

Kennedy underlines our point: our question about love gives rise to a cosmic conflict over the very meaning of life. Under seven headings in this chapter, we will explore the Bible's teaching about why and how we love God first. This foundation will prepare us for our reflections about how to love our suffering neighbours, especially those involved in sexual confusion.

1. We love God first because He is first.

This statement might sound abstract, but it expresses some really good Christian news. It is where everything starts. Appearing to Moses at the giving of the Law, God identifies himself as "The Lord, the Lord, a God merciful and gracious, slow to anger, and abounding in steadfast love and faithfulness" (Ex. 34:6). The term חֶסֶד (*hesed*) used here, translated as "steadfast love," is found in hundreds of references to Jehovah God. Moses cannot look to the faithless Israelites as a source of love. Nor can he look into his own heart. The source of love is God, who is full of faithfulness. We must love God first because God precedes us as our loving Creator. He is the source of everything, including love. Long before there was any neighbour to love, God was expressing perfect love, because the Scriptures say "God [in his essence] *is* love" (1 John 4:8). He is the very definition of love. Jesus, who was "with the Father," was a part of that eternal, personal love, as was the Holy Spirit, who pours the love of God into our hearts (Rom. 5:5). The source and foundation of all love is that pre-existing, Trinitarian love of the Father, Son, and Holy Spirit.

Before the cross and the coming of Jesus, before God's dealings with his people Israel, God revealed himself as a loving, personal Creator. God did not need to create. The reason he created was lovingly to share the goodness of existence with creatures. As the Roman Catholic philosopher Robert Sokolowski creatively observes, cosmic goodness—from which derive morals—flows from the nature of God as transcendent Creator: "Because God is so independent of the world, we can say that he created the world out of sheer generosity, not out of any sort of need.... In doing so he has shown the charity that is at the heart of things."[6] According to the Apostle Paul, everything human, everything historical, starts with the prior reality of God as Creator.

There are only two kinds of reality: first, the reality of God the Creator, and secondly, created reality. All existence is under the rule and protection of God the Creator, whom we love by worshipping and serving. Worship and love of the Creator is the truth—about everything. To deny this is to accept the lie. The first verse in the Bible is a programmatic statement of existence: "In the beginning God created the heavens and the earth" (Gen. 1:1). The Christian faith begins right there, and we must understand, accept, and embrace that truth.

Those who worship creation as ultimate will move through life negotiating their path as best they can. The standard of truth for Christians, however, must start with the love for, and worship of, our Creator God. He made everything according to his great wisdom and we must seek to worship and serve him in accord with that originating wisdom.

2. We love God first because He is holy.

The holiness of God is more good news. To call God "holy" is to say that he is different in his being. Relative to everything else, he is totally "Other." The all-wise, un-created Creator has made this vast universe and knows every one of the millions of galaxies, as well as every DNA strand in every human being. Yet our infinite and all-powerful Creator condescends to enter into a love relationship with us! Before matter was created, there is God, a personal being who, in himself, is love and loves the creation he made. This is the ultimate statement of the binary—the Creator/creature distinction, Twoism.[7] Though by his Spirit he can dwell within a human person, the God of Scripture, in his essence, is outside of creation, existing in holiness before he creates the cosmos.

The sixteenth-century theologian, John Calvin, understood that we owe our existence to this loving Creator. Calvin put into practice what Jesus demanded—love of God first. This youthful genius, who was only twenty-six years old when he wrote his famous *Institutes*, explains that our knowledge of ourselves depends on our knowledge of God. We are born first for God, not for ourselves, and we cannot attain true knowledge of ourselves until we have understood who God is.

God reveals himself to Moses with the name *Jahweh*, a name that affirms his *difference* from us (Ex. 3:14). *Jahweh* means: I AM

WHO I AM. God is self-existent, depending on no one, and thus self-defining. This is reassuring. Today, many claim the right and the power to self-define, especially in terms of their sexuality, and their experimentation will not end well. God is the only being who self-defines. He is also the being who defines all other existence. As our Creator, he has already defined us as creatures who reflect his nature—made "in his image." In the words of Calvin, "the Creator was pleased to behold [in human beings], as in a mirror, his own glory."[8] This is the source of human dignity, glory, holiness, and safety.

3. We love God first because He is Trinity.

The Trinity is one of the most ignored and most important truths of biblical revelation, though it is a mystery we cannot completely understand. The ancient Athanasian Creed states that "whoever will be saved must hold the faith of the universal church, that we worship one God in Trinity."[9] The liberal bishop, John Shelby Spong, says there is "not much value in the doctrine of the Trinity,"[10] and both Judaism and Islam reject the Trinity as a major heresy. Even evangelicals do not always see its importance. But in spite of its mystery, there is profound significance in the Trinitarian nature of God.

The word "one" in the Shema from Deuteronomy 6:4 is the Hebrew אֶחָד ('ehād). The same word is used in Genesis 2:24, where Adam and Eve become "one" flesh. The term means unity or fullness, not singularity, which is expressed using יָחִיד (yachid), a word never applied to God in the Hebrew Bible. 'Ehād seems at least to imply a Trinitarian essence in God, a truth that becomes clearer later in Scripture.

To "love the Lord your God," as Scripture requires, means we love him as Trinity. God did not become loving by creating the world. As eternal Trinity, he is a loving Father of the loving Son and the loving Spirit in all eternity before he is the Creator of the universe.[11] If God were just one in the sense of *yachid*, an eternal divine singularity like Allah, his "love" would be impersonal and narcissistic. Can an impersonal force even love at all? To love, this kind of abstract singularity would need something or someone outside of itself in order to have a relationship, at which point love of the creation would become central to this being's eternal essence. Indeed, an essential attribute of such a god—his "person-ness"—would depend on created things and he would then lose his transcendence and become one with everything else.

The notion of true love, so extravagantly and naïvely employed by many to justify the practice of homosexuality and of same-sex "marriage," is the love that we cannot invent, the love that is essential to the transcendent being of the Trinity. If Trinitarian love is the origin of all human love, then human love must reflect the original love that God defines in his revelation of himself to us.

4. We Love God First by Respecting the Holy Character of His Creation.

God, who is prior and distinct from his creatures, expresses who he is in the things he makes. The God whose Trinitarian being includes both separateness and complementarity, diversity and unity, creates things that are both distinct and yet in beautifully designed relationship with other created things. This, remember, is the meaning of holiness: things in their rightful, ordained places.

In Genesis 1, God separates day and night, seas and dry land, male and female, setting them in their proper places. He creates different kinds and gives them specific, individual names and calls everything "very good."[12] To create is to separate—to set apart for a particular purpose, and to set apart is to make holy. Thus, created things—in their separateness and in their functional unity—reflect in some creaturely way the holiness or separateness of God. Twoism, another word for holiness, is not incidental. It is the way the cosmos is made. Twoism—the principle of difference or the binary—is the key to the cosmos.

5. We love God first by preserving the heterosexual image He gave us.

Holiness or Twoism, is reflected biologically in heterosexuality. "Hetero" in Greek means "other." In Scripture, God states programmatically: "Let us make man in our image, after our likeness" (Gen. 1:26). How do we reflect God's holy image on this earth and thus show love to God? As image-bearers of God's identity, we show our love for God by seeking to reflect his character in our humanity. The summit of the glory of God's handiwork is captured when the psalmist exclaims: "What is man that you are mindful of him?" (Ps. 8:4). He is astounded that God should care for us. Human beings are special to God.

Our creation in God's image is the reason for our unique human dignity. We reflect in human form elements of God's personhood, such as intelligence, moral sense, and creativity. We see the stunning inventiveness in human history—in medicine, architecture, space travel, music, poetry, and a myriad of other talents. In our expression of these characteristics, we love God by preserving his clear image within us. But there is more to be said about God's image.

"So God created man in his own image, in the image of God he created him; male and female he created them" (Gen. 1:27). In this time of raging conflict on the emotive subject of gender, Twoism brings clarity. We cannot create our own identity. The image of God, male and female, and the principle of otherness is our true identity.

160

The image of the Trinitarian God who is both one and many is given both to male and female, and explains their differences and their "one flesh" unity. The text of Genesis is very clear. In Genesis 1:26, image is associated with God as in some sense a plurality: Then God said, "Let us make man in our image, after our likeness." "Us" and "our" in the mouth of God imply a Trinitarian God. Genesis 1:2 already refers to the Spirit as participating in the creative work: "And the Spirit of God was hovering over the face of the waters." Genesis 1:27 specifically names "male and female" human beings as reflecting God's image. This implies that both the male and the female are given God's image separately, but they also reflect together the creative being of God by "procreating as he created."[13] This is specifically stated in the very next verse: "And God blessed them. And God said to them, 'Be fruitful and multiply and fill the earth and subdue it.'" Their essential goal is to produce offspring and thus to ensure the emergence of the human race.

Professor James B. DeYoung captures this thought perfectly:

> God could have made a thousand males for Adam, yet he would not have fully achieved his own image and its internal diversity. Without that full-orbed picture, his own being would have gone unknown and unknowable. Only a woman, not another man, could complete the divine design for humankind.[14]

Michael Reeves observes that "the Father, Son, and Spirit have always been in delicious harmony, and thus they create a world where harmonies—distinct beings, *personas* or notes working in unity—are good, mirroring the very being of the triune God."[15] This is why God pronounced the separations in creation "very good" (Gen. 1:18).

Loving God by preserving his clear image within us is a profound expression of the Bible's cosmology. God created a cosmos structured on distinction within unity, reflecting his own being. This is why the Bible presents a heterocosmology, not a homocosmology—a created universe based on "otherness," not "sameness." The Bible's view of sexuality is not one of small-minded, unloving moralism, discrimination, violence, or bullying, as some critics claim. God's revelation in the Scriptures goes to the heart of the nature of existence. A theistic understanding of the universe reveals that our difference and unity in sexuality is meant to reflect the difference and unity of God himself in his Trinitarian being. This is why homosexuality is "unnatural," as Paul says in Romans 1:26. Because of the Fall, it is "out of order" with the physical cosmos. Homosexuality is both a misuse of the natural world as God made it and—by consequence—a rejection of God, the moral judge and the intelligent, ordering Creator of all things. Homosexuality serves another kind of divine being—the god within, the gods of nature, the false god of paganism.

The Trinitarian being of God has further implications for human identity. Just as the persons of the Trinity are separate in identity and function, so must men and women keep their sexual identities separate and not attempt to merge them in some androgynous or "third-being" fashion.[16] If the ultimate dignity of men and women is a reflection of the person of God, then homosexuality inevitably reflects another expression of divinity—a Creator-denying, all-is-one, non-binary pantheistic god. Clearly, "Christian gay marriage," often proposed by pastors in order to regularize the gay couples they counsel, cannot find a place in genuine biblical practice, for their practice denies the very person and being of the only true God.

6. We love God first by loving Jesus, the final gracious image of God.

Jesus is the definitive revelation of the image of God in human form: "There is one God, the Father, from whom are all things and for whom we exist, and one Lord, Jesus Christ, through whom are all things and through whom we exist" (1 Cor. 8:6). Jesus says: "He who has seen me has seen the Father" (John 14:9). In this one human being we see the deep essence of the transcendent, loving Creator God, who is also our Redeemer. In the incarnation, Jesus makes God accessible. He reveals the eternal, unfathomable, mysterious God in understandable human terms. In his birth, life, obedience to God's Law, atoning death, resurrection, and ascension, Jesus is the heart of the gospel; the good news that God the Creator and Lawgiver is also the Savior. Thus Jesus is the supreme expression of God's love for fallen humanity. "God shows his love for us in that while we were still sinners, Christ died for us" (Rom. 5:8). If we want to love God, we must "love our Lord Jesus Christ with love incorruptible" (Eph. 6:24). "The love of Christ controls us" (2 Cor. 5:14). The Son, as the image of the Father, is an amazing revelation of God as Trinity. Jesus is the example of perfect obedience in his love for the Father and the Father's law, and in the Father's love for the world.

7. We love God first by honouring heterosexuality and heterosexual marriage.

Just as Jesus honoured heterosexuality and heterosexual marriage, we also must honour it. This created structure teaches us deep things not only about the nature of God in his Trinitarian being as Creator, but also about his compassionate heart that reaches down to us in love as our Redeemer.

The institution of marriage in Genesis 2:24 states: "Therefore a man shall leave his father and his mother and hold fast to his wife, and they shall become one flesh." The "therefore" refers back to verse 23, where the new human being is "called woman" and is "taken out of man." So we see the creation of two gender-distinct persons. Yet we already know from Genesis 1:27 that both are made in God's image: "So God created man in his own image, in the image of God he created him; male and female he created them." Being different (male and female), yet "one," reflects God's Trinitarian image.[17] God creates this first, fundamental human structure not only to fill the earth but also to reflect his own character.

The Apostle Paul makes the clear connection between the structure of Trinity and heterosexual marriage. In 1 Corinthians 11:3 he states that just as the husband is the loving head of his wife in a God-honouring marriage, so in the dynamic of the distinct personal relations within the mystery of the Trinity "the head of Christ is God." The comparison is explicit. A God-honouring male/female marriage is a powerful reflection of the very being of God. God the Father is the loving head of Christ, the Son, just as a husband is the loving head of his wife.

Heterosexual marriage also reveals God as Redeemer. In Matthew 19, Jesus cites Genesis 2:24 to embrace the institution of normative human marriage. This is his court of appeal in answering the trick question posed by the Pharisees about sexuality and divorce. Paul also appeals to this text, once in 1 Corinthians 6:16 and once in Ephesians 5:31–32, where he says that marriage is a profound mystery because it prophesies Christ's love for the church. Right at the start of God's creation, he reveals the mystery about himself as Redeemer. The "mystery" Paul mentions is not immediately obvious in Genesis 2:24, but it is there—hidden, waiting to be revealed at the end of time.[18] Paul says his call as an apostle is "to bring to light for everyone what is the plan of the mystery hidden for ages in God who created all things" (Eph. 3:9). Paul was "entrusted with the mysteries of God" (1 Cor. 4:1), "who created all things." Paul's writings reveal immense truths about what the Creator was doing and who the Creator really is. What Paul was given by Christ, namely "my gospel and the preaching of Jesus Christ," he even calls "the revelation of the mystery that was kept secret for long ages" (Rom. 16:25).

The Great Mystery

The great mystery of the cosmos is the redemption God provides for his creation. Here we see the outreach of God the Creator's love, by coming himself to be our Redeemer in the flesh. Luther said it well: "the cross alone is our theology,"[19] for it is Emmanuel, God himself, hanging on the cross for us. This disarming truth teaches that at the very beginning of the world, God the Creator, distinct from his creation, reveals himself in the institution of marriage as lover of the "other," the creation. Genesis 2:24 is the *proto proto evangelium*, the first announcement of the gospel, even before the so-called *proto evangelium* of Genesis 3:15. The Old Testament text that institutes marriage is a prophecy of the fulfillment of redemptive history—the gospel mystery of God's love for the church, as the Son sacrifices his life for her (Eph. 5:32).

This is how it can be said of God already in the Old Testament: "just as a husband loves his wife, and as a bridegroom rejoices in his bride, so shall your God rejoice in you" (Isa. 62:5). Robert Gagnon rightly notes that "every narrative, law, proverb, exhortation, poetry and metaphor in the pages of Scripture that has anything to do with sexual relations presupposes a male-female prerequisite for sexual relations and marriage."[20]

In 2013, Doug Mainwaring—a well-known American journalist

who once promoted same-sex "marriage"—finally understood. He publicly stated:

> I am now a Christian, and even though I am same-sex attracted—or, more likely, because I am same-sex attracted—I marvel at the extraordinary significance of marriage in God's eternal plan. Marriage is under siege because it stands at the heart of the Good News of the gospel.... At its heart, this is a spiritual battle.[21]

As an ex-gay man, Mainwaring sees the issue of sexuality and of same-sex "marriage" with extraordinary clarity and has understood what true love is.

The author of this heterosexual, Twoist universe is God the Creator.[22] The world is not a blank page on which people write their own self-definitions. God's knowledge of himself and his revealed plan for creation are the objective blueprint and structure of reality. Cornelius Van Til notes that God's perspective is not merely one among others. On the contrary, it determines and finalizes *all* significance. Reality is what God made it and declared it to be. The Bible is God's authoritative interpretation of creation. Only he comprehends all the facts and their interaction with all other facts.[23] Christians must affirm this perspective on creation with confidence. In Romans 1, Paul has explained that we know enough about God by seeing his creation to be without excuse for our failure to thank and glorify him (Rom. 1:19–20). But his divine revelation—in nature and in Scripture—goes farther, showing us both God's authority and his fatherly, selfless love.

God's love for his people is love of creatures other than himself. Of course, love is not limited to marriage. But the intimacy of heterosexual marriage is the love used in Scripture to show us the distinction/union aspect of divine Trinitarian love. That particular "one flesh" union is set apart in the Scriptures. A man engaging in sex with another man cannot express the "otherness" of married union, nor can this unnatural couple have true "one flesh" union. As noted, Paul, in 1 Corinthians 6:16, cites Genesis 2:24, showing that human sexual union cannot be expressed in just any kind of twosome, especially in forbidden sexual unions. "Shall I then take the members of Christ and make them members of a prostitute? Never!" The significance of holy sexual union is underlined: "For, as it is written, 'The two will become one flesh.'" God is jealous of the sanctity of sexual union because it reflects the union of the divine Trinity. This is why we talk of "holy matrimony."

Ultimately, sexuality is intimately linked to spirituality. In the creation of human sexuality, God reveals himself as different from us yet intimately related to us. In revealing himself, he defines us. Our great cosmic task as humans is faithfully to carry his image throughout our lives and to bear witness to it in the world, in particular, through our sexuality. This is part of how we love God. Being "straight" does not put you right with God, but it does reflect in your created sexuality something right about God.

The principle of the binary and the mystery revealed in marriage is a vital cosmological concept for all human beings. Without it, there is no future human civilization, no love, and no gospel. This is how the cosmos works. This is the foundation on which we build to love our neighbour. Jesus, the faithful celibate male, comes to reveal the ultimate redemptive meaning of marriage as it will be fulfilled in the cosmic reconciliation between the Heavenly Groom and his bride, the church at the "marriage supper of the lamb" (Rev. 19:7).

A culture that has eliminated God the loving Creator has cut itself off from true love. If God is the all-wise Creator who made us both for his glory and our good, then his definition of love is the only ultimate hope for fallen, sinful creatures. This unique message, given to the church, is what we offer to a lost world. We love our neighbour by passionately preaching the great cosmic love story of the Creator, providing his perfection for us and dying on the cross to bear the punishment of our sins. There is no greater love than this. We speak the clarity and power of the gospel in this fallen world, without which people have no hope of genuine, everlasting love. We must also passionately bring this good news by living out and holding out this love with sensitivity and courage to gender-confused people who are searching for real love. Those who are "in Christ" by the Spirit can display in our marriages the mysterious image of God and offer to others what they have already received: love, forgiveness, acceptance, a worthy goal for living, a freedom from the power of death, and the promise of eternal life. We have the majestic gospel of an incredible God, who is the only source of human dignity and whose power can transform lives.

May the Lord grant his church courage and loving gospel clarity as she engages in faithful, courageous teaching and living. Her humble practice of God-honouring heterosexuality is a powerful expression of the mystery of the Bible's amazing message of divine, redeeming love. Our human attempts to show love are woefully insufficient. Only God's love will last, as Martin Luther wrote 500 years ago:

> Let goods and kindred go,
> This mortal life also;
> The body they may kill:
> God's truth abideth still.
> His Kingdom is forever.

CHAPTER 9

LOVE GOD? LOVE HIS LAW

The once-evangelical ethicist, David Gushee, believes that Bible-believing Christians are guilty of having caused great distress to the homosexual community by "telling people that something they cannot change about themselves is fundamentally disordered and wicked."[1] He blames the Christian community for causing turmoil, and for making suffering people "want to kill themselves."[2] Jesus certainly would not do that, he argues. Gushee cites a statistic that "LGBT kids from religiously condemning homes are 14 times more likely to be homeless and 8 times more likely to make an attempt on their lives than those in affirming ones."[3] But Christian author Jake Meador notes the unfair character of Gushee's analysis who, in spite of his training as an ethicist, places everything in emotional, accusatory terms, rather than in the context of worldview. Says Meador:

> To read Gushee is to be told that we aren't seeing a fight between two

fundamentally different visions of reality with competing claims about the nature of human beings, sexuality, and family life. We're simply seeing a fight between the inevitable forces of progress objectively understood, and those backwards people who would oppose it. The trouble here is that this completely misrepresents what is actually happening. What we are witnessing is the triumph of one understanding of reality over another.[4]

Gushee has abandoned the teaching of Scripture and the good news of the gospel for the sake of clearing his conscience. The issue is worldview, not personal animosity or closed-mindedness. The stakes are toweringly high. While far from refusing to love homosexuals, orthodox Christians understand that homosexuality faces us with an essential conflict of worldviews, a conflict that was at the heart of the 1960s sexual revolution. Without God's mercy and compassion, the continuation of that revolution will functionally eliminate Christian values from the culture, depriving it of any understanding of Christian love.

THE DILEMMA

To follow the teaching of Jesus about love we must obey the two great commandments that he laid out: to love God with all our heart, soul, mind, and strength, and to love our neighbour as ourselves, in that order. In the last chapter we examined what it means to love God. Such love demands that we place God the Creator in first place and human beings, made in his image, in second place. But there are further unavoidable implications. To love God is to love his law. This is an overwhelming principle of biblical truth.

I do not bring this up for purely theoretical reasons. It applies directly to the subject of this book and to how Christians love those engaged in homosexual behaviour, in the midst of sexual turmoil.

Some same-sex attracted people have been abused as children, felt loneliness and rejection (especially from the church) or frustration because they cannot seem to rid themselves of deeply ingrained sexual desires. Clearly these people need rich, dependable, nonjudgmental love!

The dilemma this situation creates is evident in the observation of Bekah Mason, a thoughtful same-sex attracted professing Christian woman, who describes with great clarity two options:

> Progressive Christians have to complete some relatively impressive theological gymnastics to work around the Bible's consistent prohibition of same-sex activity and relationships, and hyper-conservative Christians have yet to explain how disowning children or rejecting fellow parishioners with same-sex attractions can possibly fall under Jesus' instruction to love our neighbours as ourselves.[5]

In other words, how do you believe and put into practice the Bible's moral values and show love to homosexuals?

COMPROMISE

Nicholas Wolterstorff also faced this dilemma. As a specialist in questions of justice, he considered all the relevant biblical texts and concluded that homosexual practice and the acceptance of it in the church is in no way a violation of the biblical command to love one's neighbour as oneself.[6] On the contrary, is not part of the biblical command to love marginal people, particularly homosexuals, and to embrace their desire for same-sex marriage? Wolterstorff is able to call homosexuality "a creational variance not a creational disorder."[7] But what Wolterstorff fails to ask is whether law-keeping is an essential part only of Jesus' first summary commandment to love God, or also of the second summary commandment to love one's neighbour.

I read the testimony of a self-affirming Christian abortion doctor, who—interviewed in *Time* magazine—justified his life-long practice of performing abortions as arising from a heart-felt "compassion" for poor, single women who, he said, were "asking me to help them safely end their unplanned and unwanted pregnancies."[8] This attempted expression of love for suffering women ends up in the unloving, horrendous murder of defenceless unborn human beings.

In seeking to be loving, can our well-meaning sentiments, like those of professor Wolterstorff, make matters worse? Clearly, life in this fallen world is sometimes cruel, and complications from sin are seemingly unsolvable, but that surely throws us back to Scripture for revealed help and timeless divine wisdom, especially on the question of what is pleasing to God. Doubtless, the power and beauty of the Law of God revealed from heaven—written by God's finger—will inevitably come into conflict with a rebellious sinful culture. However, before we consign ourselves to a compromise, let us examine the nature and content of the Law whether it contains both the requirements for a loving approach to homosexuals as well as the necessary standards for life-promoting holiness in the body of Christ.

LOVE AND LAW WITHOUT COMPROMISE

We cannot ignore the Bible's ubiquitous command to love our neighbours. It is an essential element of early Christian piety, as shown in the writings of Paul and James. Believers took very seriously Jesus' teaching about this second great commandment. The Old Testament commands take form in the New Testament through the church, the body of Christ. Christians are to "do good to everyone, especially to those who are of the household of faith" (Gal. 6:10), for whom they show a deep, unselfish love.

For Paul, loving one's neighbour fulfils the entire Law. All the specific commands ("You shall not commit adultery, you shall not murder, you shall not steal, you shall not covet," etc.) are summed up in this word: "You shall love your neighbour as yourself." In other words, loving your neighbour means not committing adultery with them, not murdering them, not stealing from them, not coveting what they have—obeying the Law. In applying this text, Paul goes on to make selfless love the very goal of the Law: "Love does no wrong to a neighbour; therefore love is the fulfilling of the Law" (Rom. 13:8–10). You could surely also argue that the law is the fulfillment of love. This teaching is repeated in Galatians 5:14: "For the whole law is fulfilled in one word: 'You shall love your neighbour as yourself.'" The Epistle of James makes the same point: "If you really fulfill the royal Law according to the Scripture, 'You shall love your neighbour as yourself,' you are doing well.... For whoever keeps the whole law but fails in one point has become accountable for all of it" (Jas. 2:8–10). Here "law" and "love" are deeply related. The Psalmist declares: "I find my delight in your commandments, which I love" (Ps. 119:47).

We have come full circle. Treating one's neighbour as oneself is the outward effect of our obeying and thus loving the Law of God. Loving God and his Law is the essence of love for the neighbour. This close association of love and law explains the existence in Scripture of what could be called "law-keeping piety." In other words, to love God is to love his Law, of which the neighbour is the beneficiary.

LAW-KEEPING PIETY

In ancient Israel, there was national pride that Israel's God was an incredibly just lawgiver. Moses exhorts the people:

Keep them [the statutes and rules] and do them, for that will be your wisdom and your understanding in the sight of the peoples, who, when they hear all these statutes, will say, "Surely this great nation is a wise and understanding people." For what great nation is there that has a god so near to it as the LORD our God is to us, whenever we call upon him? And what great nation is there, that has statutes and rules so righteous as all this law that I set before you today? (Deut. 4:6–8)

Two hundred years before the giving of the Law on Sinai, the Babylonian king Hammurabi issued a series of legal decisions, most of them of administrative interest. But the Code of Hammurabi can hardly be compared to the Decalogue of Exodus. Clearly, this ancient code represents a lower view of human life than the Law given to Moses. It favors the privileged, the free and wealthy, rather than the protection of the oppressed. The Code of Hammurabi, an early attempt at codifying justice, includes much injustice, rare mercy, and no personal relationship with the divine lawgiver. On the contrary, in the Law of Moses, loving and honouring God and taking care of man's relationship to God is the ultimate focus of specific moral laws. Consider one illustrative example of the respective value placed on human life by the Code and the Mosaic Law:

If an ox be a goring ox, and it shown that he is a gorer, and he do not bind his horns, or fasten the ox up, and the ox gore a free-born man and kill him, the owner shall pay one-half a mina in money. (Code of Hammurabi, 251)[9]

But if the ox has been accustomed to gore in the past, and its owner has been warned but has not kept it in, and it kills a man or a woman, the ox shall be stoned, and its owner also shall be put to death. (Ex. 21:29)

Every law system protects with its most severe penalties the things that it most values. In Mosaic Law, negligence resulting in the death of another image-bearer of God was deserving of death, to demonstrate to the community the high value placed on human life. The identical situation in Hammurabi's Code lets the offender off with a nominal fine.

We see in Scripture a highly *personalized* law-keeping piety, a deeply emotive, intimate faith within the believer, who understands that to love the God who loves the sinner, we must love God in all his aspects, not only for his kindness and grace but for his holiness and righteousness—for the sake of others. Psalm 10:12–18 joins law and love in a harmonious whole. The passage describes God's fatherly compassion, the God who "knows our [weak] frame" and our tendency to sin, yet has removed our transgressions from us, "as far as the east is from the west." The psalm adds that this "steadfast love of the LORD is from everlasting to everlasting on those who fear him…to those who keep his covenant and remember to do his commandments" (Ps. 103:17–18). Divine grace and human law-keeping form an indissoluble bond.

This expression of piety or heartfelt love for God's law and thus for God himself is found both in the Old and New Testaments. In the Old, it appears especially in the Psalms. This is how the entire Psalter begins: "Blessed is the man who walks not in the counsel of the wicked, nor stands in the way of sinners, nor sits in the seat of scoffers; but his delight is in the law of the LORD, and on his law he meditates day and night" (Ps. 1:1–2). In the Psalter, lereHere ove and law-keeping are intertwined and constantly repeated

This law-keeping piety is expressed with deep passion in Psalm 119, the longest chapter in the Bible, written as a Hebrew acrostic poem in praise of the law. In verse 1, we read: "Blessed are those whose way is blameless, who walk in the Law of the LORD!" God's lifelong blessings are promised to law-keepers. The believer responds throughout the psalm: "Oh that my ways may be steadfast in keeping your statutes!" (Ps. 119:5). "For I find my delight in your commandments, which I love. I will lift up my hands toward your commandments, which I love, and I will meditate on your statutes" (Ps. 119:47–48). This is the way faithful believers praise God: "I will praise you with an upright heart, when I learn your righteous rules" (Ps. 119:7). This is the way believers live: by keeping the Law, "a young man keeps his way pure" (Ps. 119:9). To avoid sin against God, the believer stores up God's word in his heart (Ps. 119:11). So God's child declares: "In the way of your testimonies I delight as much as in all riches. I will meditate on your precepts and fix my eyes on your ways. I will delight in your statutes; I will not forget your word" (Ps. 119:14–16). "If your Law had not been my delight, I would have perished in my affliction. I will never forget your precepts, for by them you have given me life" (Ps. 119:93). "Oh how I love your Law! It is my meditation all the day" (Ps. 119:97). "I love your testimonies" (Ps. 119:119, 159, 163, 165, 167). "Therefore I love your commandments above gold, above fine gold" (Ps 119:127).

The theme of God's people keeping God's Law as an expression of their love for him, reflected throughout the Old Testament, is also prophesied for the community of the New Covenant: "For this is the covenant that I will make with the house of Israel after those days, declares the LORD: I will put my Law within them, and I will write it on their hearts. And I will be their God, and they shall be my people" (Jer. 31:33). In fact, the New Covenant will be a law-abiding community founded on the law-keeping of Jesus.

JESUS AND THE LAW

Law-keeping is taught by Jesus, who says unequivocally:

Do not think that I have come to abolish the Law or the Prophets; I have not come to abolish them but to fulfill them. For truly, I say to you, until heaven and earth pass away, not an iota, not a dot, will pass from the Law until all is accomplished. Therefore, whoever relaxes one of the least of these commandments and teaches others to do the same will be called least in the kingdom of heaven, but whoever does them and teaches them will be called great in the kingdom of heaven. (Matt. 5:17–19)

To the rich young ruler Jesus says programmatically: "If you would enter life, keep the commandments" (Matt. 19:17). For Jesus there is neither life nor love without law. He even intensifies the law in his teaching that follows the statement in Matthew 5:17–19. In verse 20, he states: "For I tell you, unless your righteousness exceeds that of the scribes and Pharisees, you will never enter the kingdom of heaven." Then come the well-known "But I say unto you" passages, such as, "You have heard that it was said to those of old, 'You shall not murder; and whoever murders will be liable to judgment;' but I say to you that everyone who is angry with his brother will be liable to judgment,'" or, "You have heard that it was said, 'You shall not commit adultery;' but I say to you that everyone who looks at a woman with lustful intent has already committed adultery with her in his heart" (Matt. 5:27–28). Jesus further states that everything he does is a fulfilment of the Law and the Prophets (Luke 24:44–45).

So Jesus adopts as his own the Law of Moses, intensifies it, and then ties the love of his person to this very law.

Whoever has my commandments and keeps them, he it is who loves me. And he who loves me will be loved by my Father, and I will love him and manifest myself to him…. If anyone loves me, he will keep my word, and my Father will love him, and we will come to him and make our home with him. Whoever does not love me does not keep

my words. And the word that you hear is not mine but the Father's
who sent me (John 14:21–24). ... If you keep my commandments,
you will abide in my love, just as I have kept my Father's commandments and abide in his love. (John 15:10)

PAUL AND THE LAW

Paul, one of the founding apostles of the church, clearly adopts the
law-piety of the Old Testament. Specifically, he personalizes the
law by presenting Jesus as the law's very embodiment. In the Old
Testament, the Lord says to Israel, at the reaffirmation of the Sinai
Covenant, that the law is an unspeakable gift, which he has brought
to them. They have no need to search the universe to discover what
is right and good:

> For this commandment that I command you today is not too hard for
> you, neither is it far off. It is not in heaven, that you should say, "Who
> will ascend to heaven for us and bring it to us, that we may hear it and
> do it?" Neither is it beyond the sea, that you should say, "Who will go
> over the sea for us and bring it to us, that we may hear it and do it?"
> But the word is very near you. It is in your mouth and in your heart,
> so that you can do it. (Deut. 30:11–14)

Paul cites this same text from Deuteronomy but places Christ in
the place of the law as the final incarnation of God's moral personal
expression of himself with the implication that as we love Christ, we
love the Law he embodies:

> But the righteousness based on faith says, "Do not say in your heart,
> 'Who will ascend into heaven?' (that is, to bring Christ down) or
> 'Who will descend into the abyss?' (that is, to bring Christ up from
> the dead)." But what does it say? "The word is near you, in your
> mouth and in your heart" (that is, the word of faith that we proclaim);
> because, if you confess with your mouth that Jesus is Lord and believe

in your heart that God raised him from the dead, you will be saved (Rom. 10:6–9).

This intensification of the Old Testament law, which we noted was part of the teaching of Jesus (Matt. 5:27–28), is carried on in the church when Paul speaks of "the law of Christ." He says: "Bear one another's burdens, and so fulfill the law of Christ" (Gal. 6:2). The coming of Christ is not the annulment of the Law of Moses but an intensification and personification of it.

DOES PAUL DOWNPLAY THE LAW?

However, at first it might appear that in Paul there is a negative approach to the law, as if the Old Testament piety of law-keeping had more or less disappeared.

- He speaks of "abolishing the law of commandments expressed in ordinances" (Eph. 2:15).
- He states: "by works of the law no human being will be justified in his sight, since through the law comes knowledge of sin" (Rom. 3:20).
- He speaks of "the curse of the law" (Gal. 3:13).
- He affirms the priority of grace: "you are not under law but under grace" (Rom. 6:14). Indeed, faith seems to have taken the place of law-keeping: "For we hold that one is justified by faith apart from works of the law" (Rom. 3:28).
- He utters the famous phrase: "The just shall live by faith" (Gal. 3:11).

But to read these passages as anti-law is superficial. It is true that the New Covenant recognizes *changes* in the law, as the book of Hebrews states clearly: "When there is a change in the priesthood, there is necessarily a change in the law as well" (Heb. 7:12). It was necessary to abolish "the law of commandments expressed in ordinances," that is, the ceremonial law, because the coming of Christ and the entrance of the Gentiles into the church creates a new situation. Here "commandments expressed in ordinances" refers to the theocratic and ceremonial aspects of the law, which, like circumcision, are fulfilled by the work of Christ, and no longer apply in the New Covenant. At that moment, Christ "create[s] in himself one new man in place of the two, so making peace" (Eph. 2:15). The work of Christ "redeemed us from the curse of the law, by becoming a curse for us by hanging on the tree" (Gal. 3:11–13).

However, in the New Testament, law-keeping is not abolished. First, Jesus specifically stated that the law is not abolished. In addition, he said he came to fulfill the law, as we saw in Matthew 5. Faith and grace become clear through the work of Christ, whose life of perfect law-keeping and whose atoning death to take the curse of our sins together remove the need for law-keeping as the *means* of our righteousness and salvation. Our salvation depends upon *Christ's* perfect law-keeping. A new understanding of "the righteousness of God has been manifested apart from the law, although the Law and the Prophets bear witness to it" (Rom. 3:21). We are now "justified by faith apart from works of the law" (Rom. 3:28). The law is not removed, but what emerges in the New Testament is a clear understanding that we are considered righteous because of the law-keeping of our Savior, which motivates us to please him by *responding in obedience* to his law of love. Thus, law-keeping truly finds its place of piety in the life of the believer. This is why Paul says: "Do we then overthrow the law by this faith? By no means! On the contrary, we uphold the law" (Rom. 3.31).[10]

182

The law is clearly not a means by which we justify ourselves before God. This would deny the very gospel that saves us. But law-keeping is the standard by which we live and show love to God, the author of the law. This is the connection that Psalm 119:64 made clear: "The earth, O LORD, is full of your steadfast love; teach me your statutes." The definition of brotherly love in the New Testament is to apply the Old Testament law to fellow believers, as enriched and expanded by Christ. So Paul says: "Owe no one anything, except to love each other, for the one who loves another has fulfilled the law" (Rom. 13:8).

SPEAKING THE LAW IN LOVE

In the early church, recalling the law to a Christian brother is an act of love, both as an expression of love-inspired selfless behaviour, but also – and this is more difficult – in "speaking the truth in love" (Eph. 4:15) and "stirring one another to good works" (Heb. 10:24), which fulfills in the life of the church what Jesus commanded: "If your brother sins against you, go and tell him his fault, between you and him alone. If he listens to you, you have gained your brother" (Matt. 18:15–17). Paul exhorts believers to identify sins in a brother. "Brothers, if anyone is caught in any transgression, you who are spiritual should restore him in a spirit of gentleness. Keep watch on yourself, lest you too be tempted" (Gal. 6:1). The Apostle James tells us that if a believer brings a fellow believer back from sinning, he will "cover a multitude of sins" (Jam. 5:19–20).

Obviously, defining transgression and sin is critical here, and the New Testament is clear about the sin of homosexuality, along with all the other sexual sins, included in the general term πορνεῖαι, "sexual immorality" (*porneiai*, a plural noun). Jesus defines "defiling" sins in the following phrase: "For out of the heart come evil thoughts, murder, adultery, sexual immorality, theft, false witness, slander. These are what defile a person" (Matt. 15:19). The early church clearly takes up this teaching of its master. Says Paul to the Roman church: "Let us walk properly as in the daytime, not in orgies and drunkenness, not in sexual immorality κοίταις (*koitais* includes various forms of sexual promiscuity, including homosexuality), and sensuality, not in quarreling and jealousy. But put on the Lord Jesus Christ, and make no provision for the flesh, to gratify its desires" (Rom. 13:13–14). This is why wanton homosexuality is named as one of the behaviours that bars one from inheriting the kingdom of God. In clear terms Paul declares: "Or do you not know that the unrighteous will not inherit the kingdom of God? Do not be deceived: neither the sexually immoral, nor idolaters, nor adulterers, nor men who practice homosexuality, nor thieves, nor the greedy, nor drunkards, nor revilers, nor swindlers will inherit the kingdom of God (1 Cor. 6:9–10).

To remain true to Scripture, believers must hold the love of God's law as an essential aspect of the love of one's neighbour.

CHAPTER 10

LOVE GOD? LOVE HIS HOLINESS

For a Christian, the love of God and the love of his law imply
living in a way that is set apart from the godless culture. This is why
the practice of homosexuality is not just an independent personal choice. Believers are reminded in 2 Corinthians 6:16 that since
God is our God, and since we are his people, there can be no agree-
ment between the temple of God and idols. "What partnership has
righteousness with lawlessness? Or what fellowship has light with
darkness?" (2 Cor. 6:14). Citing the Old Testament, Paul reminds
the church of God's promise to Israel, which is renewed in the New
Covenant: "I will make my dwelling among them and walk among
them" (Lev. 26:12; Isa. 52:11–12; Ezek. 37:27). The principle is to
"be separate from them, says the Lord, and touch no unclean thing"
(2 Cor. 6:16–17), so the church, as the holy body of Christ, must

"be separate from lawlessness, darkness, Belial, unbelief, and idols" (2 Cor. 6:14–16), and believers must "cleanse [them]selves from every defilement of body and spirit, bringing holiness to completion in the fear of God" (2 Cor 7:1). God's people of the New Covenant were called to be spiritually and morally separate from the pagan nations of the first century. As God's people, the church inherits the call God gave to Israel in Leviticus: "You shall not do as they do in the land of Egypt, where you lived, and you shall not do as they do in the land of Canaan, to which I am bringing you. You shall not walk in their statutes" (Lev. 18:3). As we saw in chapter 7, this warning includes avoiding homosexual behaviour. The point of the original Holiness Code (Leviticus 17–26) is to ensure that Israel would function as a holy witness to the corrupted nations around it. The call is to "walk in my statutes and observe my commandments and do them" (Lev. 26:3). The church, receiving that same call, becomes "the temple of the living God," God's special people. The Holiness Code of Leviticus is not limited to ancient Israel but is also meant for the life of the new Israel.

Moses assured the Israelites, "The Lord has declared this day that you are a people for [God's] treasured possession, as he has promised you, called for a special task—you are to keep all his command-ments" (Deut. 26:18). The church inherits this favored place, as the Apostle Peter reminds believers. They are a body of Levitical priests: "you are a chosen race, a royal priesthood, a holy nation, a people for his own possession, that you may proclaim the excellencies of him who called you out of darkness into his marvelous light" (1 Pet. 2:9). This is a verbatim citation of Exodus 19:5–6, as Israel is about to receive the Law of God.

Paul reemphasizes this fact with even more clarity in his epistle to the Thessalonians:

For this is the will of God, your sanctification: that you abstain from sexual immorality; that each one of you know how to control his own body in holiness and honour, not in the passion of lust like the Gentiles who do not know God; that no one transgress and wrong his brother in this matter, because the Lord is an avenger in all these things, as we told you beforehand and solemnly warned you. For God has not called us for impurity, but in holiness. Therefore, whoever disregards this, disregards not man but God, who gives his Holy Spirit to you. (1 Thess. 4:3–8)

If God's people love God, they must individually reflect to the world and as a body the character of God. In addition, they are not to "wrong" their brothers by their immoral behaviour, which leads others into temptation. Paul writes to the church in Ephesus: "I am writing these things to you so that if I delay, you may know how one ought to behave in the household of God, which is the church of the living God, the pillar and buttress of the truth" (1 Tim. 3:14–15). This privileged status and role lies behind the practice of church discipline, especially in the context of a church made up in large part of people who had been raised in Gentile paganism, who really did need to know "how to behave." This is why Paul is so insistent that we must not associate with those who call themselves Christian brothers and sisters, who are sexually immoral or who are greedy, thieves, idolaters, drunkards, or "revilers." Paul goes so far as to tell the Corinthian Christians not even to eat with such people (1 Cor. 5:9–11). Sexual immorality must not be tolerated in the church, which is to be a foretaste of the age to come—the temple of the Spirit and the body of Christ.

In 1 Corinthians 6, Paul picks up sexual immorality again:

Flee from sexual immorality. Every other sin a person commits is outside the body, but the sexually immoral person sins against his own body. Or do you not know that your body is a temple of the Holy Spirit within you, whom you have from God? You are not your own, for you were bought with a price. So glorify God in your body. (1 Cor. 6:19–7:1)

The body is made to reflect the Lord, and any activity outside of God's design dishonours the body.

There remains a place for discipline in today's church. If the church receives the same divine call as Israel to holiness, she uses New Covenant disciplinary procedures for law-breaking and correction in the community. Discipline was applied in the early church because of the importance of maintaining purity in the body of Christ. Discipline cleanses the church body from corrupting influences. "Do you not know that a little leaven leavens the whole lump? Cleanse out the old leaven that you may be a new lump, as you really are unleavened. For Christ, our Passover lamb, has been sacrificed" (1 Cor. 5:2–3). Loving the law and living by it is not limited to personal holiness for its own sake. Holiness is not only for a believer's personal good, but for the good of the whole church and for the good of its role as witness in the world. When someone in a church family lives in open and unrepentant sin, it not only makes that temptation harder to resist for fellow believers, but sends a false message about truth to the world.

The application of the law as discipline and as the moral standard applied to the community is thus a way of showing love to all, as the pastoral letter of Hebrews teaches when it presents God as a loving, disciplining Father: "For the Lord disciplines the one he loves, and chastises every son whom he receives. It is for discipline that you have to endure. God is treating you as sons. For what son is there whom his father does not discipline?" (Heb. 12:6–7). Notice that discipline is specifically associated with love and is a solemn warning for the morally weak person who may be tempted to fall into sin.

The law as loving discipline employed by the church is effectively rejected by Nicholas Wolterstorff's argument regarding Leviticus 18:20. He claims that the prohibitions in the Mosaic Holiness Code, including the prohibition on same-sex intercourse, only applied to ancient Israel for her ritual cleanliness, to distinguish her from the pagan nations. But Wolterstorff surely fails to see that ritual cleanliness contains a message, symbolizing moral cleanliness. Therefore, Leviticus does not only deal with "ritual cleanliness" (fulfilled in Christ—what Paul calls ceremonial "ordinances" in Ephesians 2:15), but also with life-promoting moral behaviour that always reflects the being of God and needs to be announced to the whole world. As noted earlier, Leviticus 18, which deals with the issues of sexual holiness, begins and ends with the command: "You shall therefore keep my statutes and my rules; if a person does them, he shall live by them: I am the LORD" (Lev. 18:5). It ends: "But you shall keep my statutes and my rules and do none of these abominations" [of the nations] (Lev. 18:26). These commands are not ritual and ceremonial laws but laws for ethical purity. When Wolterstorff concludes that these laws are no longer applicable for Christians today, it is because he fails to take into account how the early Christian church and Jesus himself used this very Holiness Code for the maintenance of holy living in the Christian community.

DISCIPLINE IN THE NEW TESTAMENT

The last Old Testament prophet, John the Baptist, who announced the coming of Jesus, baptized him to show symbolically that Jesus was called to bear the sins of the world. John, of course, lived under

Levitical law (Lev. 18:8; 20:11). Indeed, his ministry came to an abrupt end when Herod beheaded him for courageously defending the holiness of Levitical sexual laws. He denounced the illegal, incestuous marriage between Herod Antipas and the ex-wife of Herod's half-brother Philip, a woman who was also the daughter of another half-brother.

After John's execution, Jesus evokes the Old Testament law against adultery (Lev. 20:10) to show that the contemporary practice of divorce was illegitimate. Basing the legal authority of his argument on the eternal validity of the law, he says: "It is easier for heaven and earth to pass away than for one dot of the law to become void" (Luke 16:17). He then takes the principle of adultery expressed in Leviticus 20:10, from the Holiness Code, "If a man commits adultery with the wife of his neighbour, both the adulterer and the adulteress shall surely be put to death," and applies it to the illegitimate practice of divorce in his day, saying: "Everyone who divorces his wife and marries another commits adultery, and he who marries a woman divorced from her husband commits adultery" (Luke 16:18). Jesus is saying that those who think they are innocent are in fact guilty of adultery, as stated in the law of Leviticus. Adultery, as expressed in Leviticus, is still for Jesus an immoral act, not a mere expression of ritual cleanliness of no practical necessity.

Leaders of the early church met as a formal body in the Jerusalem Council, which took place a few years after Jesus' resurrection (Acts 15:19–20). They found the Holiness Code to be a useful reference for considering what to require of Gentile believers. The council required them to abstain from participating in things associated with the pagan cults of their past, such as the "things polluted by idols, and from sexual immorality, and from what has been strangled, and from blood," which are all prohibited in the Holiness Code (Lev.

17:14; 19:4, 18).

Loving God by showing love for the law and therefore loving the brother is demonstrated by Paul when he uses the Old Testament law as the final standard of holiness in the church. Like Jesus, who says, "Have you not read?"—basing his teaching on Old Testament law (Matt. 19:4)—Paul goes beyond "human authority" and appeals to divine law. He does this even for trivial things like paying workers. He quotes Deuteronomy 25:4: "e quotesHDo I say these things on human authority? Does not the law say the same? For it is written in the Law of Moses, 'You shall not muzzle an ox when it treads out the grain.' Is it for oxen that God is concerned?" (1 Cor. 9:8–9). He repeats this Scripture, and the principle therein contained, in 1 Timothy 5:18 for the church in Ephesus. This is clearly typical practice for apostolic teaching and church life.

For the Ephesian church, where the young Timothy was now the pastor, Paul continues to invoke the present role of the Old Testament law, and not just for the pastor's pay! Paul speaks about "using the law lawfully," indicating that the church should continually turn to the law to understand God's will. Beginning by underlining the timeless nature of the law in general, Paul implicitly evokes Old Testament law, including laws against homosexuality:

> Now we know that the law is good, if one uses it lawfully, understanding this, that the law is not laid down for the just but for the lawless and disobedient, for the ungodly and sinners, for the unholy and profane, for those who strike their fathers and mothers, for murderers, the sexually immoral, men who practice homosexuality, enslavers, liars, perjurers, and whatever else is contrary to sound doctrine, in accordance with the gospel of the glory of the blessed God with which I have been entrusted. (1 Tim. 1:8–11)

A number of these sinful actions are specifically underlined in the Levitical law, such as sexual immorality (Lev. 18:6–20) and homosexuality (Lev. 18:22 and 20:13), as well as the mistreating of parents (Lev. 19:3 and 20:9). Several times in his letters, Paul mentions specific cases of church discipline. Timothy, the young pastor, is encouraged to bear patiently with sinners—as Paul himself has done—but not to hesitate in taking action if a stubborn sinner refuses to repent. Timothy is to "wage a good warfare," which involves holding firmly to his conscience and his solid anchor of faith in Jesus Christ. That gospel, which is "trustworthy and deserving of full acceptance," must always be the foundation of faith and action. Some in the church, however, had "made shipwreck of their faith," by rejecting that foundation. What was to be done about their blasphemy? Paul, in his apostolic authority, handed Hymenaeus and Alexander over "to Satan that they may learn not to blaspheme" (1 Tim. 1:20). Notice that Paul does not hesitate to call these men to account publicly and by name. He urges Timothy to have no hesitation in warning those in his church, should they begin to wander from Christ, the anchor of their faith. "As for those who persist in sin," Paul says, "rebuke them in the presence of all, so that the rest may stand in fear" (1 Tim. 5:20).

DISCIPLINE AND LAW IN TODAY'S CHURCHES

How many churches in our time have the courage to call out those who are working against the gospel? We may feel we should not dare such a judgment, but Paul has put this issue squarely into a gloriously fearful context. We are to give "honour and glory forever and ever" to "the King of the ages, immortal, invisible, the only God" (1 Tim. 1:17). He is the one to whom we will give account—not the cultural judges that see such discipline as hateful.

Paul writes instructions to Timothy so that Gentile believers will "know how one ought to behave in the household of God" (1 Tim. 3:15). In other words, the law was constantly invoked in the Gentile churches to maintain moral standards in the Christian communities that had emerged out of the "lawless" Greco-Roman world.

Paul's most obvious employment of Old Testament law as a justification for church discipline—specifically a law enunciated in the Holiness Code of Leviticus—is found in 1 Corinthians 5:1ff, concerning the sin of incest. Paul states with shock that "it is actually reported that there is sexual immorality among you, and of a kind that is not tolerated even among pagans, for a man has his father's wife." Paul is concerned about the church's witness to the pagan world, and his disciplinary action is clearly motivated by the law of Leviticus, which states: "you shall not uncover the nakedness of your father's wife; it is your father's nakedness" (Lev. 18:8). This command is repeated in Leviticus 20:11 with a specific punishment: "If a man lies with his father's wife, he has uncovered his father's nakedness; both of them shall surely be put to death; their blood is upon them."[1]

Because of the spiritual reality of the church, which is no longer a physical theocracy, Paul, like Jesus (John 8:5–11), does not demand the punishment of physical stoning, but requires its spiritual equivalent, namely some form of excommunication or exclusion from the spiritual life of the community. In the exact words of Paul, "you are to deliver this man to Satan for the destruction of the flesh, so that his spirit may be saved in the day of the Lord" (1 Cor. 5:5). Being "put to death" in the Old Covenant has its woeful parallel in the New, though with the hope of ultimate salvation. The destruction of his flesh clearly does not mean physical execution since the church had no such calling. It therefore surely means turning the man over to Satan and back to a sinful, body-destroying way of life, far from the healthy influences of Christian fellowship, facing spiritual death in order that he might come to his senses and repent. From this extreme form of sexual sin that cannot be permitted in the life of the church, Paul develops a whole theology of communal holiness, obviously based on Leviticus, with concern for the church's witness to the pagan world.

Against Wolterstorff, who concludes that texts like Leviticus 18:18 are no longer applicable for Christians today, Paul clearly demonstrates—on the contrary—that the Levitical laws and even capital punishments were still in effect, though in this altered spiritual form. This is clear in what Paul says in 1 Corinthians 6:9, where he lists the sins that will merit exclusion from the Kingdom of God—excommunication, the ultimate expression of spiritual capital punishment. Similarly, the sins of Romans 1:26–32, which begins with homosexuality, are worthy of death (Rom. 1:32): "God's righteous decree [demands] that those who practice such things deserve to die." This is doubtless a reference to the capital punishments of the Levitical laws. Paul uses the term "righteous decree" [τὸ δικαίωμα, *to dikaiōma*], the same term as that used in the Greek translation of Leviticus 25:18, strengthening Paul's intentional connection with Old Testament law.

In the way Paul dealt with incest, showing that Leviticus was still invoked for spiritual discipline, it is clear that if there had been an active case of homosexual practice in the Corinthian church, he would have invoked Leviticus 18:18. "You shall not lie with a male as with a woman; it is an abomination…both of them shall surely be put to death" (Lev. 20:11). But he does not have to, because, by God's grace, he can say: "And such were some of you. But you were washed, you were sanctified, you were justified in the name of the

Lord Jesus Christ and by the Spirit of our God" (1 Cor. 6:9–11).

Amazingly, in the godless city of Corinth, whose very name became identified with wanton sexual licence, Paul is able to say that, apart from the case previously mentioned, there were no notable, unrepentant and ongoing sinners. Their sins had been confessed, renounced, and washed in the blood of Christ. But the warning of punishment should not be missed. Not inheriting the kingdom of God is a way of speaking of excommunication and of final damnation. To be denied entrance into the kingdom is to be given over, παραδοῦναι (*paradounai*), to Satan (1 Cor. 5:5). It is surely significant that on three occasions in Romans 1 (verses 24, 26 and 28), Paul again uses a form of the same verb, "give over," παρέδωκεν (*paredōken*), once with regard to idol-worshipers and twice with regard to those practicing homosexuality. They are "given over," παρέδωκεν (*paredōken*), by God to the woeful consequences of their actions, essentially given over to Satan. This is not a slip of the tongue. It is a serious warning that Paul repeats

to the Galatians: "I warn you, as I warned you before, that those who do such things [envy, drunkenness, orgies, and things like these] will not inherit the kingdom of God" (Gal. 5:21; Heb. 12:16–17); and to the Ephesians: "There is no inheritance in the kingdom of Christ and God for the sexually immoral or impure, or who is covetous [that is, an idolater]." He even says such issues as sexual immorality, all impurity or covetousness may never be entertained as part of public speech: "they must not even be named among you, as is proper among the saints" (Eph. 5:3–5).

Paul's standard for Christian believers is lovingly strict. This is why the list of sins and sinners that Paul gives in these various texts were never to be allowed as practices in the Christian community. He specifically lists sexual immorality, greed, swindling, drunkenness and idolatry as sins that should be "purged" from the churches. On the other hand, he insists that Christians must not cease to associate with unbelievers, which is not only impossible but undesirable, since God sends Christians into the world to speak the gospel (1 Cor. 5). The man charged with incest is an example of what must be done to all professing believers who openly practice forbidden sins. Anyone guilty of gross and persistent sin must be purged from the church body, doubtless using the prohibitions of Leviticus 18 in particular. The community must be cleansed of sinful leaven.

How far will evangelical "gay Christianity" stray from these moral foundations in the days ahead? Michael Brown describes the beliefs and practices of some leading gay theologians, well-esteemed in the gay-affirming Metropolitan Community churches. Such leaders affirm a number of orthodox beliefs, like the Trinity and the inspiration of the Bible.[2] However, Brown suggests that some of his readers might want to skip over one section of his book, so gross is the language and the practice therein described. Brown mentions in particular the books of a minister in the Metropolitan Community Church, Robert Goss, who has published such titles as *Jesus Acted Up: A Gay and Lesbian Manifesto* (HarperCollins, 1993) and *Queering Christ* (Pilgrim Press, 2002). In these books, the author describes in detail his erotic homosexual love of the naked Jesus on the cross, claims Jesus was gay, and develops "a Christology grounded in translesbigay experience," arguing that heterosexual ideology has "perverted Christianity."[3] Such so-called Christian theologians justify a sexual lifestyle devoid of any biblical norms, which are considered "homophobic." Such material is shocking (and I chose the least shocking) but it raises a serious question: once God's laws concerning sexual practice are abandoned in order to include monogamous gay marriage, what will arrest the slide of "evangelical gay Christian-

198

ity" into the extravagant, shocking belief and practice adopted by a radically liberal hermeneutic? Furthermore, what does an evangelical affirming church do with the "bi" lifestyle? For such a "bi" believer, should the church endorse polygamous marriage of a male and a female partner in order that the sexual and spiritual rights of bi's be respected?

Such thinking and practice is a universe away from Paul's strong call to early believers (and to us) to remember that Christ died for us "in order that the righteous requirement" [τὸ δικαίωμα, *to dikaiōma*] of the law might be fulfilled in us, who do not live according to the flesh but according to the Spirit" (Rom. 8:4). What will restrain "gay Christians" from full sexual expression? Paul exhorts the Corinthians to live lives of spotless holiness "cleanse[d] from every defilement of body and spirit, bringing holiness to completion in the fear of God" (2 Cor. 7:1). To the Philippians, Paul says:

> [I]t is my prayer that your love may abound more and more, with knowledge and all discernment, so that you may approve what is excellent, and so be pure and blameless for the day of Christ, filled with the fruit of righteousness that comes through Jesus Christ, to the glory and praise of God. (Phil. 1:9–11)

Is it conceivable in the light of such high moral requirements that a Christian could practice homosexuality as an acceptable expression of the holy people of God? Such lawless behaviour is also a universe away from the exhortation Moses gave to God's people before they entered the Promised Land:

> These are the commandments and the rules [δικαίωματα, *dikaiōmata*], that the LORD commanded through Moses to the people of Israel (Num. 36:13).

This day the LORD your God commands you to do these statutes and rules. You shall therefore be careful to do them with all your heart and with all your soul. ...[Y]ou are a people for his treasured possession ... you shall be a people holy to the LORD your God, as he promised. (Deut. 26:16–19)

What was true for Israel, remains true for the church. The people of God must maintain God's calling to be witnesses of his holy character and his image in human beings, to the pagan world. These moral ideals have never been rescinded, nor will they ever be. God's law still requires us to be a holy people, through the Spirit of power, whether faced by the pagans of Egypt, Mesopotamia, Canaan, the Greco-Roman Empire, or by those of the post-Christian, pagan Western empire of the twenty-first century.

In keeping God's law, we can hope for profound conversions like that of the recently converted lesbian, Emily Thomes, who says she "partied, slept around and, by fifteen...came out as a lesbian to some friends." Her view of God was one of benevolent all-acceptance. "God was chill with what you were cool with." Then she read 1 Corinthians 6:9–10:

Or do you not know that the unrighteous will not inherit the kingdom of God? Do not be deceived: neither the sexually immoral, nor idolaters, nor adulterers, nor men who practice homosexuality nor thieves, nor the greedy, nor drunkards, nor revilers, nor swindlers will inherit the kingdom of God.

"That day it was like my eyes were really opened," she said. "It scared me really, really bad." But then Emily made the discovery that has transformed millions of lives the world over: she read the next verse: "and such were some of you. But you were washed, you were sanctified." The light of new hope went on in Emily's heart. "My whole life changed that day," Emily proclaims. "I grasped his hand by faith.... I was amazed at the grace he showed me."[4] Emily learned the joy of hearing the law of God as good news and understanding how life should be lived to God's glory in holiness.

Our life of holiness looks forward to a goal beyond this life. What the present unbelieving culture will say or do has no lasting effect. In the end, what remains is the righteousness, τὸ δικαίωμα (*to dikaiōma*) of Christ that is reproduced, as Revelation says, in the righteous deeds τὰ δικαιώματα (*ta dikaiōmata*) of the saints in order to bring praise to our thrice-holy God. These righteous deeds are thus our humble offering to our Savior that become the "fine linen, bright and pure" robes, with which the "saints" are clothed for the marriage supper of the Lamb (Rev. 19:7–8).

CHAPTER **11**

LOVE GOD? LOVE HIS NEIGHBOURS

Everyone agrees with Burt Bacharach that the world needs more love. Love is the reason people cite for wanting to include homosexual practice in the church. That is understandable. Christianity is a message of love for the world, so how can love ever be wrong? We've all seen over-indulgent parents who "love" their children into becoming lazy louts by doing everything for them. No doubt the mother who is advocating that her seven-year-old should be given medication to stall his puberty thinks she is loving him by respecting his declaration that sometimes he feels like a girl. But such "love" can be extremely harmful in the end.

Heart-wrenching stories and emotional appeals make any opposition to the agenda of homosexual love seem heartless and unchristian. Moving accounts of direct guidance from the loving

Jesus seem to silence every other consideration, including thought-through principles of those seeking to obey Scripture. Many Christians ask, How can the love of gay couples, joined in marriage, as the embodiment of commitment and fidelity, be wrong? But realistically, we must all agree that the "love" of sinful human beings—however well-meaning—can never be the standard for human action.

Things are not that simple. As finite and sinful persons, we cannot know everything; but, as Christian believers, we do know two things: 1. that God is love and the origin of human love, and 2. that in order to love rightly, we need the wisdom given in God's revealed Word. Love is a deep and powerful human emotion, but like all our emotions, it needs to be tested by the Word of God, which is not lacking in guidance in this area. Indeed, Scripture contains at least 551 texts that define what love is from God's perspective.

God's Love for His People in the Old Testament

In the Old Testament Scriptures, the first mention of love concerns neither our love for God nor our love for our fellow human beings, but God's love for us—for his friend Abraham (2 Chron. 20:7; Isa. 41:8; Jas. 2:23), for the longsuffering Joseph (Gen. 39:21), for his friend Moses, with whom he spoke "face to face as with a man" (Ex. 33:11), and for his children in general. The story of the Exodus is the story of God's love for his people, Israel. Moses sings to the Lord: "You have led in your steadfast love the people whom you have redeemed; you have guided them by your strength to your holy abode" (Ex. 15:13). Scripture shows us that God's love is prior to and defines human love. Since God is the Creator and precedes all things created, God's love is the model for human love. "I am the LORD who practices steadfast love, justice, and righteousness in the earth. For in these things I delight, declares the LORD" (Jer. 9:24).

Just as Scripture demands that we love God with all our heart, soul and strength (Deut. 6:5), so God says: "I will rejoice in doing them good, and I will plant them in this land in faithfulness, with all my heart and all my soul" (Jer. 32:41). So God says to Israel:

> It was not because you were more in number than any other people that the LORD set his love on you and chose you, for you were the fewest of all peoples, but it is because the LORD loves you and is keeping the oath that he swore to your fathers, that the LORD has brought you out with a mighty hand and redeemed you from the house of slavery, from the hand of Pharaoh king of Egypt. (Deut. 7:7–8)

One of the earliest Old Testament statements of God's love (the sixth occurrence of the term in the Bible) reads:

> I the LORD your God am a jealous God, visiting the iniquity of the fathers on the children to the third and the fourth generation of those who hate me, but showing steadfast love [דֶסֶח, hesed, meaning "faithfulness" or "loyalty"] to thousands of those who love me and keep my commandments. (Ex. 20:5–6; see also Ex. 34:6–7)

This statement occurs in the second commandment on idolatry: "You shall not make for yourself a carved image.... You shall not bow down to them or serve them" (Ex. 20:4). Notice that this early definition of God's love is given with the warning of divine jealousy. God is jealous of the purity associated with his being. Clearly, love here is not just a feeling or an emotion, but part of a moral response of the child of God to God's love.[1] The notion of "jealousy" interjects the divine person of God and shows that there is no love without righteous jealousy—no love without ultimate respect for God's moral, personal character. From this derives the exclusive love of God, expressed in the believer's love for his law, as noted above.

Though this *hesed* or "faithful love" is undeserving grace, as Deuteronomy 7:7ff recognizes, the Lord's steadfast love does not mean he will not punish the guilty. For God's law places requirements on his people:

> And now, Israel, what does the LORD your God require of you, but to fear the LORD your God, to walk in all his ways, to love him, to serve the LORD your God with all your heart and with all your soul (Deut. 10:12).

This is why those who truly love God keep his word (1 John 2:5). The Lord's covenantal unfailing love requires faithful, long-lasting love in return.

Love Shared with Others

God is the source of love, and that love must be shared with people. Leviticus 19:18 states: "You shall not take vengeance or bear a grudge against the sons of your own people, but you shall love your neighbour as yourself: I am the LORD." In the final phrase, "I am the Lord," God sets his own love as the standard for human love. Mere vengeance and selfish anger are not part of God's dealing with us, but neither is mere sentimentality. Love of neighbour compared to love of oneself is really a demand for absolute fairness, which is the way God deals with us. Love of the foreigner is comparable to love of the neighbour.

> You shall treat the stranger who sojourns with you as the native among you, and you shall love him as yourself, for you were strangers in the land of Egypt: I am the LORD your God. (Lev. 19:34; Deut. 10:19–20)

To sum it up, love in the Old Testament is God's prior covenantal, undeserved faithfulness to his people, in particular, maintaining the Davidic line and giving the people hope for ultimate salvation from destruction and death.[2] The other side of love demands that God's people live faithfully, in accordance with his covenantal law, which then shows the love of God to their neighbours. This is the default biblical position, from the lips of Solomon:

> My son, keep my words and treasure up my commandments with you; keep my commandments and live; keep my teaching as the apple of your eye; bind them on your fingers; write them on the tablet of your heart. Say to wisdom, "You are my sister," and call insight your intimate friend. (Prov. 7:1–4)

This kind of covenant love should make us hesitate before making an appeal to a "love" defined by emotions or subjective feelings, such as those expressed by the Christian "Mommy blogger," mother of three children, who left them and her husband for another woman, declaring "LOVE WINS." She is convinced she loves Jesus, but the self-sacrificial love Jesus shows puts into question this woman's self-serving "love." God's love comes with real definitions.

GOD'S LOVE FOR US AND OUR LOVE FOR HIM IN THE NEW TESTAMENT

Just as the Old Testament establishes the fact that God's love came first, yet requires a moral response, so in the New Testament the love of God is still the origin of human love. "We love because he first loved us" (1 John 4:19). But Christians have an amazing gift. We have the person of Jesus as the very historical incarnation of love. So the famous New Testament text on love that everyone knows, 1 Corinthians 13, can really be read as a description of the person of Jesus (e.g. patient, kind, humble, gracious, and full of truth).

Our understanding of love now centers on the fulfillment of God's promises realized in the person and work of Christ, the eternal Son. The Apostle Paul says: "May the Lord direct your hearts to the love of God and to the steadfastness of Christ" (2 Thess. 3:5). We love Christ, the divine Son, because he is the author of our salvation. The love he showers upon us surpasses knowledge (Eph. 3:19). "In this the love of God was made manifest among us, that God sent his only Son into the world, so that we might live through him" (1 John 4:9). "This is love," says the Apostle John, "not that we have loved God but that he loved us and sent his Son to be the propitiation for our sins" (1 John 4:10). Our response to the prior love of God is to love the God of the Old Testament and his moral character, now revealed in the Son.

In his earthly teachings, Jesus does not change the nature of the believer's love for God already shown in the Old Testament. Love is tied to our obedience to God's commandments. His show of love does not come without cost. So Jesus says, "If you love me, you will keep my commandments" (John 14:15), or again, "Whoever has my commandments and keeps them, he it is who loves me. And he who loves me will be loved by my Father, and I will love him and manifest myself to him" (John 14:21, 23). Also, as John 15:10 says: "If you keep my commandments, you will abide in my love, just as I have kept my Father's commandments and abide in his love." Specifically, the Apostle John warns that we cannot love God if we love the world (1 John 2:15). By the world, John means "the desires of the flesh and the desires of the eyes and pride of life" (1 John 2:16) which we must "overcome" (1 John 5:4), since the world "lies in the power of the evil one" (1 John 5:19).

The example of the love of Jesus, with his outstretched arms receiving sinners of all kinds, provides a moving example of how followers of Jesus must love their neighbours.

JESUS' LOVE FOR PAGAN NEIGHBOURS

Jesus comes in the flesh, the embodiment of the love of God the Father who initiated his saving plan for humanity. We are deeply embarrassed when we realize the selfless love of Jesus, for it makes us realize how unloving we often are. In loving our neighbours, Jesus is our ultimate example. "Seeing the people, he felt compassion for them, because they were distressed and dispirited like sheep without a shepherd" (Matt. 9:36). The term for "felt compassion" literally refers to one's innards,[3] a figurative reference to deep emotion. Jesus no doubt physically felt the symptoms of genuine caring—ones such as aching and nausea, when encountering the agony of people's struggles with sin and hardship. When he saw Mary and others weeping for the deceased Lazarus, "He was deeply moved in spirit and was troubled" (John 11:33) and wept with them (John 11:35). This was a fulfilment of prophecy, "He himself took our infirmities and bore our diseases" (Matt. 8:17).

LOVE FOR CAPRICIOUS CROWDS

John McArthur captures the Lord's deep compassion in noting the response of Jesus to the crowd without bread: "When he (Jesus) saw the crowds, he had compassion for them, because they were harassed and helpless, like sheep without a shepherd." After Jesus had been in a boat following the death of John the Baptist, crowds sought him and he "felt compassion for them and healed their sick" (Matt. 14:14). Shortly after that, Jesus told the twelve disciples of his concern for the masses who had no food on hand (Matt. 15:30–32). But our Lord's omniscience saw an infinitely greater need in people's lives—the profound, pervasive nature of their sin and their desperate plight of spiritual blindness and lostness. Of this horrific condition he was most compassionate of all.[4]

He was also concerned to teach his disciples to exercise that same compassion. Thus he said: "therefore pray earnestly to the Lord of the harvest to send out labourers into his harvest" (Matt. 9:38). Immediately after his temptation in the wilderness, doubtless still weak from a forty-day fast, Jesus goes about healing the sick and teaching the crowds that flock around him, teaching for hours such sermons as the Sermon on the Mount (Matt. 5–7). Later, we are told that great crowds gathered about him and that he told them many things in parables (Matt. 13:2–3). Jesus loved people by patiently teaching them.

In the Sermon on the Mount, he tells his disciples, "You are the salt of the earth… the light of the world." Therefore, he says, "let your light shine before others, so that they may see your good works and give glory to your Father who is in heaven." For this function of light-bearing and "salty" living, he makes the startling declaration: "[U]ntil heaven and earth pass away, not an iota, not a dot, will pass from the Law until all is accomplished" (Matt. 5:13–18).

By engaging in questions of the fulfillment of the Law, Jesus once more gives us the example of a life of love; the Old Testament law becomes a living reality for the production of "light." His interpretation of Moses' Law actually intensifies it. Moses taught about love, but Jesus deepens it.

> You have heard that it was said, "You shall love your neighbour and hate your enemy." But I say to you, "Love your enemies and pray for those who persecute you, so that you may be sons of your Father who is in heaven. For he makes his sun rise on the evil and on the good, and sends rain on the just and on the unjust." For if you love those who love you, what reward do you have? (Matt. 5:43–46)

Though divine judgment was meted out on those who opposed God's people, Moses never taught hatred of enemies. However, since some interpreted Moses that way, Jesus makes it clear that God's providential love for all people ought to make Christians concerned to show love to all fellow human beings made in God's image, even those who persecuted them.

One teaching of Jesus that sounds very loving is Matthew 7:1 "Judge not, that you be not judged." This may well be the most quoted text in the Bible, supporting the belief that judging someone can never be loving. But Jesus was not saying, "Never judge." Even today's progressives, who claim to be free of judgmentalism, make judgments every day, finding racism, sexism, or homophobia even in off-handed expressions their opponents use. This text actually warns us against self-righteousness and hypocrisy, and invites us to exercise care before engaging in judgments we would not apply to ourselves. The context is important. Watch out, says Jesus in the next verse, "For in the way you judge, you will be judged; and by your standard of measure, it will be measured to you" (Matt. 7:2). Jesus did not mean that we should never make a judgment about moral issues. He wants us to avoid hypocrisy, which he attacks head-on in the next verse: "Why do you see the speck that is in your brother's eye, but do not notice the log that is in your own eye?" (Matt. 7:3). It can certainly be a loving thing to call out sin, especially since in Matthew 18:15–17 Jesus recommends a system for confronting a sinner (see also 1 Cor. 5:1–7; Gal. 6:1). But it is scandalous to commit the very sin you condemn in others, while refusing to see or acknowledge the same sin in yourself.

THE ROMAN CENTURION (MATTHEW 8:5–13)

Imagine a socially impressive man, possibly in dress uniform, in charge of between 100 and 1,000 legionnaires. The officer has won his appointment due to his displays of valor: the first over the enemy wall, the one who rushes into the thick of battle to rescue a fellow soldier. This hardened man had seen a thing or two. He is also wealthy, earning a salary seventeen times greater than that of the soldiers in his command. Jesus treats this powerful pagan with tenderness. In spite of his high rank, the centurion speaks with affection about his sick servant, who is "lying paralyzed at home, suffering terribly." The servant was probably at death's door. In responding in love, Jesus had one condition—faith. Jesus sees in this centurion enormous humility and great faith, for he, without concern for his status in the eyes of the Romans or the Jews (who would see him as an unclean sinner), publicly makes his appeal to this controversial Jewish teacher. Seeing the man's heart, Jesus declares: "Truly, I tell you, with no one in Israel have I found such faith." So Jesus dismisses him to his home with the words: "Go; let it be done for you as you have believed.... And the servant was healed at that very moment."

Jesus shows love to a pagan sinner because the man has a simple faith in him. We never hear of him again, but doubtless his meeting with Jesus transformed his whole life. Other centurions appear throughout the New Testament. The one in charge of the crucifixion of Jesus, when he saw the earthquake and "what took place," was filled with awe and said, "Truly this was the Son of God!" (Matt. 27:54). Later, in Joppa, another centurion, Cornelius, "an upright and God-fearing man," was baptized by the Apostle Peter into the Christian faith and received the Holy Spirit (Acts 10:17–48). The love of Jesus had begun to infiltrate the pagan military forces of Rome. Paul even speaks of believers in "Caesar's household" (Phil. 4:22). We will never know the extent of that reach of love until that day when we will meet in person all those who responded to Paul's preaching.

THE CANAANITE WOMAN (MATTHEW 15:21–28)

Similarly, Jesus shows open arms of love and respect to a Canaanite woman, whom today we might call an Arab or a Palestinian. While his disciples want Jesus to send her away because of her bothersome insistence, she cries out: "Have mercy on me, O Lord, Son of David; my daughter is severely oppressed by a demon." Jesus' dialogue with her seems at first glance to be a rejection, but he has seen her heart of faith and draws it out in all its force, for all to see, as she courageously "argues back" in fervent boldness. He then tenderly heals her daughter. As with the centurion, the love Jesus gives is not mere emotion but demands serious, believing faith.

THE UNJUST TAX COLLECTOR (LUKE 19:1–10)

I love this guy, even though he's someone you just *could not even like*. But Jesus loves him. He was a rich tax collector, a known crook, and perhaps almost a dwarf (see Lev. 21:20). Doubtless he had been bullied in school by much bigger kids. As an adult, he was a little man with a big chip on his shoulder, determined to get revenge on those who had mistreated him. Everyone would have despised and feared Zacchaeus, who worked for the Romans and took for himself a heavy cut out of the taxes he collected. This man had no friends among the Jews, whom he consistently defrauded, nor among the Romans, with whom his relationship was purely business. Jesus does not avoid this sinner, but rather invites himself to Zacchaeus's house for a pot of tea, as we English say. This action promotes much murmuring from the onlookers, who were "saying, he was gone to be guest with a man that is a sinner." How amazing is Jesus, who sees through the outward situation and affirms the value of this miserable man with a gesture of love and respect. The result is amazing. The social outsider, Zacchaeus, says to Jesus: "Behold, Lord, the half of my goods I give to the poor; and if I have taken anything from any man by false accusation, I restore him fourfold." Zacchaeus understood in some way the cost of the love of Jesus, for he understood what Jesus said: "For the Son of man is come to seek and to save that which was lost." In point of fact, Jesus was on his way to Jerusalem to die for sinners like Zacchaeus.

THE PROSTITUTE (LUKE 7:37–50)

The amazing, daring love of Jesus is shown in his love of sinners, vividly demonstrated in the case of his acceptance of, as the text says, "a woman of the city, who was a sinner," probably a prostitute. Luke recounts this shocking scene, where the woman "brought an alabaster flask of ointment, began to wet his feet with her tears and wiped them with the hair of her head and kissed his feet and anointed them with the ointment." This expression of love is daring because it happens in the home of Simon, a notable moralistic Pharisee, or legal expert, who immediately accuses Jesus of breaking the law by allowing himself to be touched by this "unclean" person. Jesus points out the self-righteousness and hypocrisy of Simon and says to the woman: "Your sins are forgiven.... Your faith has saved you." Her clear faith shown in intended repentance is met by the love of Jesus.

In an encounter with another woman who anoints him (Matt. 26:12–13 and elsewhere),[5] Jesus says: "she has done it to prepare me for burial. Truly, I say to you, wherever this gospel is proclaimed in the whole world, what she has done will also be told in memory of her." This woman understood the love of Jesus and recognized that Jesus' love would come at the cost of his atoning death.

TWO ADULTEROUS WOMEN (JOHN 4:1–29; JOHN 8:3–11)

Two similar events recounted in the Gospel of John make the same point. Imagine a voluptuous pagan (Samaritan) woman with no trouble inviting unsavory male attention, now alone in one more compromising situation with another male, Jesus, conversing at a public well. A "wiser" man would have avoided her, but not Jesus. He could see through her exterior to her deepest needs, and reached out to her. Here is another public sinner, shunned even by her own people, a woman who must come alone in the heat of midday for water to avoid contact with her neighbours. Jesus sees her deep human needs and talks to her about her inner thirst for living water "welling up to eternal life." In addition, Jesus points out her sinful life, and she replies with profound faith in Jesus as the Messiah: "Sir, give me this water." Radically changed, she returns to her village as an evangelist, publicly proclaiming herself to be a repentant, forgiven sinner, and declares that Jesus is the Christ. This love of Jesus loves the person but does not affirm the sin; indeed, the sin is identified and forgiven.

Later in the Gospel of John, we see the account of the woman caught in adultery (all by herself, amazingly!). This is the third or fourth time Jesus is in contact with a sexually compromised woman. Though this section of the Gospel of John does not appear in the earliest Greek manuscripts, it is an account so typical of Jesus that it could be considered authentic. Again, the legal authorities want to catch Jesus in some kind of moral compromise, so they cite the law requiring the stoning of adulterers. Jesus, who had already defined "lust" as an expression of adultery (Matt. 5:27–28) (which would ultimately mean that anyone who lusts deserves to be stoned), says to the Pharisees, "He that is without sin among you, let him first cast a stone at her." At that, every one of the Pharisees, accused in his conscience, slinks away. The perfect Saviour, in a tender expression of deep love, forgives the woman and, in mercy, commands her: "go, and sin no more." In both these accounts of adulterous women, Jesus does not ignore human sin. Rather, he forgives it and restores sinners to a life of holiness, pleasing to God. His outgoing love does not condone sin but carries it to the cross.

In his dealing with all kinds of unworthy people, Jesus puts into practice what he teaches about love: "He who loves me will be loved by my Father, and I will love him and manifest myself to him" (John 14:21). God's love for us and our love for God are always defined in terms of respect for God's holy requirements, deep repentance, and faithful obedience. There is much deep emotion, but no mere sentimentality. Love is always defined in relationship to the moral character of God. When we ask: "What would Jesus do?" The answer is, he showed love without condoning sin.

Always and everywhere, we see Jesus' heart reaching out to suffering and sinful people, bringing the healing balm of forgiveness and moral purity. A key verse for understanding how to show love to homosexuals is this: "By this we know that we love the children of God, when we love God and obey his commandments" (1 John 5:2). Our love for our neighbour is demonstrated by our love for God and what he commands. In other words, the only true love we can show for human beings is when they are caught up in our love for God. This kind of love is hardly present in Jen Hatmaker's declaration to the LGBT community: "[Y]our life is worthy and beautiful. There is nothing 'wrong' with you. Jesus still loves us beyond all reason and lives to make us all new, restored, whole. Yay for Jesus!"[6] Jesus did not say to the adulterous woman, "There is nothing wrong with you. Stay in your adulterous ways, you are restored and whole. Yay for adulterers!" David Gushee employs the same fake good news in claiming to "follow the way of Jesus"[7] while normalizing homosexual activity. According to the Jesus of Scripture, the way we love fellow human beings is by loving God. In all these texts we have examined, what stands out is that our love for God and for what he requires comes first, just as Jesus said when he called loving God "the first and greatest commandment." The results of that love for God constitute any genuine love for our fellow human neighbours.

NEW TESTAMENT TEACHING ON THE LOVE OF NEIGHBOUR

The Jesus we have seen loving sinners is the one who can teach us about love. He is our model in loving our neighbour. In the Gospel of John, Jesus gives "a new commandment," based on Leviticus 19:18 ("that you love your neighbour as yourself"): "Just as I have loved you, you also are to love one another" (John 13:34). Paul cites Leviticus 19:18 again in Romans 13:9, and then says: "Love does no wrong to a neighbour therefore love is the fulfilling of the law" (Rom. 13:10). In Galatians, Paul is even more insistent on the Old Testament principle: "For the whole law is fulfilled in one word: 'You shall love your neighbour as yourself'" (Gal. 5:14). Elsewhere in the New Testament, this love is called "brotherly" or *philadelphia* love."[8] This is the key to life in the body of Christ: "above all these, put on love, which binds everything together in perfect harmony" (Col. 3:14). Love is "the message from the beginning" (1 John 3:11). It is still standing when everything else has gone: "So now faith, hope, and love abide, these three; but the greatest of these is love" (1 Cor. 13:13). As long as we can be sure what genuine love is, we must make it superior to "prophecies, tongues, and knowledge" (1 Cor. 13:13) or to any forms of mystical practices.

Believers need to have this view of "neighbour-loving" as we deal with the delicate issue regarding the theological status of the homosexual agenda and, more especially, as we deal with our homosexual friends and acquaintances, many of whom, doubtless like most of us, have never thought theologically about the significance of their sexual practice. For too long, believers have tended to treat homosexuals as untouchable enemies. The infamous phrase of Westboro Baptist Church of Topeka, KS, "God hates fags," seemed to sum up for many the sole approach of the Christian church toward homosexuals. But a faithful Christian response is to joyfully follow the compassion of our Savior, who was never sparing in extending love to sinners. He has extended that incredible love to us and we can extend it to all those we know or meet. So we ask: Who is my neighbour?

CHAPTER 12

WHO IS MY NEIGHBOUR?

Jesus tells the lawyer who inquires how to inherit eternal life that he must fulfill the law by loving God (Deut. 6:5) and loving his neighbour as himself (Lev. 19:18). Hoping he'll come out clean, the lawyer asks, "Who is my neighbour?" A piercing question, indeed, and one we must all ask! It is true that the "neighbour" in Jesus' parable of the Good Samaritan is the Samaritan man (v.36-37), but it takes two to be "neighbours;" the neighbour was also the Jew, lying battered and bruised on the side of the road, in need of care and compassion.

As we think of our neighbours who consider themselves gay and who experience sexual desire for their own sex, we must remember that in spite of their pride demonstrations, these neighbours are often in need of real compassion. A number (though not all) of those calling themselves homosexuals have been led into homosexuality through abuse or dysfunctional relationships at home. Confused and deceived, teens turn to homosexuality, grasping for love and attention. The Fall affects us all in our natural sinful state, sometimes by sins committed against us, as well as by our own willing participation. This is the case for every human being in all of our relationships and choices.

Rosaria Butterfield, as she reflected on the notion of 'gay pride,' came to realize that gays were not "suffering in hell because we were gay but because we were proud." She asks: "[W]hose dictionary [for defining pride] did I trust? The one used by the [LGBT] community I helped create, or the one that reflected the God who created me?"[1] She is right to put her finger on pride. The prophet Isaiah shows us what our human pride produces. In Isaiah 47:10, the prophet shows unfaithful Israel her true self: "You felt secure in your wickedness [πονηρίας, *pornias*]. You said, 'No one sees me'; your wisdom and your knowledge led you astray, and you said in your heart, 'I am, and there is no one besides me.'" In this Old Testament text, we see the "wisdom and knowledge" of those who take sexual licence as their right. They are so filled with pride that they even assume divinity. The phrase, "I am, and there is no one besides me," is a clear reference to God's name, revealed to Moses in Exodus 3:14: "I AM WHO I AM." Paul's solemn warning to the New Testament church sees the refusal of the image of God in human male-female sexuality as a prideful form of pagan idolatry.

Evangelical churches must hear Paul's warning. It is not loving to encourage other Christians to accept or practice homosexuality. Paul makes his instructions abundantly clear in 1 Thessalonians 4:3–6: "For this is the will of God, your sanctification: that you abstain from sexual immorality; that each one of you know how to control his own body in holiness and honor, not in the passion of lust like the Gentiles who do not know God; that no one transgress and wrong his brother in this matter." The acceptance and practice of sexual immorality wrongs our brothers in Christ, leading God's people to a prideful denial of God himself, the Father, Son and Holy Spirit. When Christian leaders cave to worldly pressure, they are not only collapsing in their own faith but influencing and corrupting the consciences of those who love and follow them.

Our desires must be mastered by God's Spirit of power, for it is pride in all of us that rejects God's design for us as male and female. A homosexual may not be aware of the origin of his misplaced desires and may wish intensely to change them, without possessing the power to do so. Others rebel against God's law deliberately and consciously, choosing to engage in an active homosexual lifestyle for all kinds of selfish reasons. Both are guilty of rebellious pride in their rejection of God's image within us. Both need a demonstration of Christian love.

That demonstration must avoid a patronizing superiority. Homosexuals are at the mercy of a false view of existence that draws them into a life of unnatural homosexual distortion. Their false view is often created or reinforced by the reigning and very public upbeat message that one is born gay[2] and can only find happiness and fulfilment by a total embrace of the homosexual lifestyle. According to the LGBT philosophy, homosexuality should be accepted and entered into as an authentic identity. This message has captured the admiration of the general public and made moral and cultural heroes out of those who have risked public shame by boldly and courageously "coming out." The American Psychological Association (APA) has also bolstered a general acceptance of this opinion by their statements since 1975 that declare homosexuality to be normal and natural. Under heavy politically correct pressure, this professional association calls on psychologists to take the lead in removing the stigma of mental illness that was historically associated with lesbian, gay and bisexual practice. Critics (including the APA's own ex-president, psychologist Nicholas Cummings) accuse the association of becoming so ideological that it is no longer open to competing ideas. Yet few professionals are willing to speak up. "The career cost is simply too high."[3]

Though some teens, under social pressure or due to confusion, may experiment with sexual identity, deliberately deciding to try out another lifestyle, often homosexuals say they have had homosexual desires without ever seeking them. Yet, having a desire does not mean we must act on it. Homosexuality may be attributed both to our sinful natures due to the Fall and to our moral choices. But we cannot say that God created the homosexual condition as good. Scripture is clear that God created the human couple, male and female, in order to reflect his image as Trinity (Gen. 1:27–28) and that he instituted male/female marriage in order to reflect his image as Savior (Gen. 2:24). This union God declared to be "very good" (Gen. 1:31). Indeed, the absence of normal heterosexual relationships was declared "not good" (Gen.2:18). Thus, the appearance of homosexuality is part of the curse of the Fall, which came through human sin. We all feel those effects in diverse ways. We are all sinners, and we all know it. However, in the case of homosexuality, no study has ever shown that it is a natural, genetically determined condition. People are not born homosexual.

THE PROGRESSIVE VIEW OF HOMOSEXUALITY

The proportion of homosexuals in a population is nearly impossible to determine. Radical sexual libertarians tend to inflate the number for political purposes. Nevertheless, the 10% figure proposed by

1960s "sexologist"[4] Alfred Kinsey has been discredited. In 2013, the *National Health Interview Survey*, part of the government agency of the Center for Disease Control and Prevention (CDC), established that 1.6% of the population was gay and 0.7% bisexual.[5] This small proportion of citizens stands in need of Christian care, love and understanding. They have often not only been preyed upon but also deceived by the idealization of a homosexual lifestyle. They have been deeply injured through an ideologically driven promotion of same-sex practice that often dooms them to a lifetime of harmful and unnatural sexual relationships.

In the name of individual rights and civic freedoms, progressive and very public voices affirm that same-sex activity is a perfectly normal and valid human expression. Indeed, one psychological theory posits that homosexuality is nothing more or less than a natural "biological predisposition to gender nonconformity."[6] In other words, homosexuality is one harmless, biological expression among many. The American Psychiatric Association (APA) concludes that since homosexuality is not a psychological aberration, it doesn't need therapy.[7] The message is, "You're just fine. You don't need help." What a message to give to those who are drowning in loneliness, sorrow, and (often) drug-addicted hopelessness!

Many of those in the homosexual lifestyle are eager to abandon it but feel completely trapped. Powerful pressure from LGBT radicals is exerted on anyone who offers counseling or therapy to such people. This reduces their chance of getting the help they need. There may indeed exist heavy-handed, outlandish, and useless therapies that promise unrealistic results. But surely, wise and godly counsel—designated as harmful, even hateful, by such organizations as the CDC and the APA—is not something that should ever be withheld from a person eager to find freedom in Christ. When the

APA appointed a committee to report on "reparative therapy," it failed to take into consideration ex-gays who are entirely free from their old sinful habits. The light of joy and freedom in the faces of these men and women is beautiful to see.[8]

Not all ex-gays find freedom due to a paid counseling service or organization, however. More often than not, they have had Christian influence in their earlier lives and/or come across warm, welcoming Christians whose informal counseling extends over time, and whose faithful love never flags. Rosaria Butterfield describes the power of such an influence in her life. She was not seeking help, although, as she puts it, "questions [about life] sat quietly in the crevices of my mind." A Christian pastor wrote her a letter opposing things she had said in an interview. "I met a most unlikely friend," she recounts, who sent "the kindest letter of opposition that I had ever received." The pastor and his wife knew "that I had values and opinions too, and they talked with me in a way that did not make me feel erased."[9] Rosaria tells of conversations she had with them for two years, over countless meals in their home. As she puts it, "The teaching, the prayers, and the friendships the Lord has given to me through the Body of Christ have blessed me richly."[10]

Christians who understand the strident ideological convictions behind the normalization of homosexuality (an ideology that claims to know the "true self") will understand that many homosexuals are being misled about the source of their orientation and denied helpful counsel. Some are even encouraged by Christian ministers to accept and practice their "chosen" lifestyle. If this is the case, then part of loving the suffering neighbour means bringing the light of truth to the situation, with the kind of grace and hospitality shown to Rosaria Butterfield by the pastor and his wife. The warmth of those meals was not due only to the food and friendship but also to a steady diet of truth.

Dr. Joseph Nicolosi attempted to bring clarity to the discussion. In response to those who, like the APA, maintain that homosexuality is "natural," he indicates a number of "unnatural" elements present in the formation of homosexual orientation. He points to causes such as: a lack of needed approval and affection from males, especially fathers; a sense of loneliness, boredom, or curiosity; a sense of adventure; a need for money; an inability to resist peer pressure; a desire to express hostility against male peers; a general sense of rebellion; or the need to re-enact an early trauma of sexual molestation by another male—this time in a controlling role.[11] One objective study he cites found that 46% of homosexual men (compared with just 7% of heterosexual men) reported homosexual molestation. The same study also found that 22% of lesbians reported homosexual molestation compared with just 1% of heterosexual women.[12]

Granted the many successful results of sensible therapy, as witnessed by hundreds of ex-gay people, this unconscionable suppression of the truth in the name of "science" causes untold suffering. In an article entitled "Why I Am Not a Neutral Therapist," Nicolosi affirms without hesitation: "The body tells us who we are, and we cannot 'construct'—assemble or disassemble—a different reality in which gender and sexual identity are out of synchrony with biology.... Our belief is not a 'phobia' or pathological fear."[13] This clarity of thinking is a sound form of neighbourly love.[14]

David Pickup, a marriage and family counselor, publicly declared in January 2018 that *every week* he sees men delivered from homoerotic feelings. This is love for suffering humanity in the name and power of Christ. This, he adds, is what the homosexual agenda does not want to admit, since they believe that one is born that way, thus making therapy not only impossible, but cruel and illegitimate.

The constant emphasis on the sexual non-binary in everyday life is a sign not of civil rights but of religious indoctrination. The idea that God and the creation are distinct, as are male and female, must be obliterated from society's memory, according to the juggernaut of today's pro-homosexual consensus.

Physical and Psychological Consequences

Charles Socarides, a Life Fellow of the American Psychiatric Association, member of the American Psychoanalytic Association, and Clinical Professor of Psychiatry at Albert Einstein College of Medicine, took on the scandalous description of homosexuality by the American Psychiatric Society as "normal," by noting:

> This psychiatric nonsense and social recklessness has brought with it many individual tragedies.... Gayness is a "freedom too far,"...a fictive freedom that does not really exist, for it is a freedom that flies in the face of the reality of the male/female design, in the face of evolution itself—it is a freedom that cannot be given.[15]

Suppressing and misrepresenting the causes of homosexuality from easily influenced young people deprives them of any genuine possibility of deliverance and, in effect, refuses genuine neighbourly love. In addition, they are not warned about the negative physical and psychological consequences that stem from the choice of homosexuality.

"Gay identity" is depicted as a civil rights and self-determination issue, obscuring the serious physical, mental, and spiritual risks of such practice. The American College of Pediatricians stated unambiguously that "there are serious medical consequences to same-sex behaviour."[16] This is no longer a popular opinion, as Dr. Paul Church discovered, to the detriment of his career. Dr. Church,

228

for many years a doctor at Beth Israel Deaconess Medical Center in Boston, was summarily dismissed from his post because he stated that the high risk sexual practices in the homosexual community led to a disproportionate incidence of sexually transmitted diseases (STDs), HIV/AIDS, hepatitis, parasitic infections, anal cancers, and psychiatric disorders.[17] Further disorders include anxiety, depression, suicide, and substance abuse.[18] The progressive political and popular press portrays homosexuality as normal, respectable, and without harm. Yet in 2017, a dossier of 697 pages of knowledge was collected from numerous medical and psychological experts to show that "disproportionate physical illness and psychological dysfunction… accompany homosexuality," making homosexual practice "a serious public health issue."[19]

The danger is not only physical but psychological, as shown in two common practices often associated with the identity issues in the homosexual populace: 1. Gay people are seven times more likely to take illegal drugs,[20] and 2. Most (male) homosexuals live with impossible-to-satisfy promiscuous desires for the perfect male, which leads them to an obsessive worship of impersonal sex, lived out by cruising for anonymous sex in "bath houses" and at "gay parades." Sometimes the truth comes out. In his book I Was Gay Once, an Italian Roman Catholic, Luca Di Tolve recounts his search for identity. His compulsive drive for satisfaction in homosexual relationships left him empty and pushed him to despair:

> The deep motivation that drives homosexual behaviour is always the same: the search for the male traits, which cannot be expressed in one's self…. I could never find peace in sex with men…. A man and a woman see in difference how much they complement each other to form the foundation of a family, a whole. Two men or two women can never reach this perfection.[21]

An off-Broadway producer and film director Fred Caruso—an open homosexual who created homosexual-themed plays and movies— committed suicide June 13, 2016, at the age of 41, having suffered for years and having thought often of ending his life. "For...most of my life," he wrote in his suicide note, "I have been absolutely miserable.... I truly don't think I have any idea what love or happiness is."[22]

Promiscuity does not bring mental or physical health. Indeed, such uncontrollable behaviour suggests what Scripture says: God gives over such practitioners to their own harmful desires (Rom. 1:26). In a vast number of cases, homosexual relationships are severely unstable. Homosexual author Gabriel Rotello wrote in 1997 that gay rights was founded on "a sexual brotherhood of promiscuity."[23] According to the Center for Disease Control, in the early 1980s typical gays had had relations with 1,100 partners and some with as many as 20,000.[24] The American College of Pediatricians published a telling statistic: 60% of gay couples admitted to sexual infidelity after only one year in a relationship; after five years, the percentage rose to 90%.[25] Why so? Andrew Sullivan, a well-known gay journalist, openly admitted that male homosexual marriage needs "extramarital outlets...[because] the homosexuals' push for same-sex marriage does not mean they either want or are prepared to be monogamous."[26] This infidelity is fed by "the easy availability of homosexual pornography" which has produced an addiction that has "reached epidemic proportions"[27] (as has alas, heterosexual pornography).

Such inevitable promiscuity seems to be borne out by the fact that in spite of the Supreme Court decision normalizing same-sex "marriage," only 10% of LGBT Americans took advantage of the new law to marry their same-sex partner. Was something else happening in the Obergefell decision? Many homosexuals admit something that fooled many "straight" Americans who naïvely favor "marriage equality": the goal of legal same-sex "marriage" was not so much for the benefit of recognizing long, faithful commitments by homosexuals but rather to undermine the place of traditional marriage in the culture.[28] The normalization of homosexuality has made any and every sexual expression available and accepted.[29] All forms of sexual immorality are now becoming "moral."

The long-term results are sad. Seventy-five percent of homosexuals, as they age, are likely to live "alone and unhappy" without family or the support that family brings.[30] These are the words of two pro-gay spokesmen, Kirk and Madsen, in their book After the Ball,[31] which did so much to normalize homosexuality. Alas, after the ball—most of the time—there is no ball.

TRANSGENDER FALSEHOODS

We are reliving the same phenomenon with regard to transgender[32] issues. We have rushed to an immediate affirmation of transgender civil rights without consideration of the real dangers, both physical and psychological, of chemical and surgical modifications. Though less dangerous, complications of bathroom arrangements, shared living quarters, and inclusion in sex-separated sports teams are causing upheaval in society and leading to many costly court cases and other difficulties.

Intersex or hermaphroditism has long been seen by the medical establishment as a rare *biological* disorder of physical sexual development. This involves the malformation of sexual organs, or genetic anomalies that at birth create physical sexual ambiguity. A Christian worldview sees intersex hermaphrodite conditions as part of the Fall, where the introduction of sin brought about brokenness in all things, including our bodies. We need to have great empathy for those who have had a complicated and confusing childhood, and who sometimes have to live with choices their parents made at their birth. Such states are not the "fault" of the person born with such conditions.

But these physical intersex conditions are not evidence of multiple genders inherent within our human biology, so that transgender males (females who seek to become males) and transgender females (males who seek to become females) are perfectly normal. Olympic male gold-medalist Bruce Jenner's transformation into Caitlyn was purely psychological and cosmetic and had nothing to do with being born intersex. In spite of the cosmetic changes (and they can be stunning), genetically he is 100% male.[33] Under the lipstick, his chromosomes are still male-identified XY.

The transgender agenda serves the same ideology as the normalization of homosexuality: the belief that there is no such thing as a creation-based binary between male and female, which is an essential element of biblical orthodoxy. Thanks to this transgender ideology, great spiritual and physical harm has been done to children who feel that they straddle the gender line. Child psychologists tell us that most children take time to figure out the complexities of growing into adult sexuality and gender. But children unsure of their gender are now asked to declare definitively that they are the opposite of who they are biologically, at which point steps are taken to modify their biology with steroids or even with definitive surgical interventions that mutilate their bodies tragically for the rest of their lives— without ever changing their sex. In my opinion, administering such unnecessary medical treatment should be called child abuse, whether it is foisted on the child by parents or professionals. Like abortion, it is an expression of the worship of Moloch. Walt Heyer, a former transsexual, said: "Like others who elect to live the transgender life, I painfully discovered it was only a temporary fix to deeper pain."[34]

Clearly, the need to love the hurting homosexual or transgender neighbour requires far more than an affirming nod to what homosexual and the pagan culture advocates. I hope this book will help the church to understand that the legitimization of homosexuality will lead Christians into religious paganism. Nevertheless, the church *must show love* to homosexuals. We are not loving our friends well if we affirm and Christianize their every sexual choice. Deep love refuses to approve and encourage behaviour that is induced by deception and leads to destruction. It may seem like love, but it is approval of "the lie" (Rom. 1:25) and a refusal to extend a hand of rescue. Deep love understands how our homosexual friends have been injured, what they are suffering, and how we can embrace them in an expression of selfless love. Sexually dysfunctional people, whatever their history, are our neighbours, so Christians may not dismiss them as unworthy of our attention until they change their lives. As we saw in chapter 11, this was not the way Jesus acted with sinners. He did not say, "Clean up your act and then I will speak to you." He approached sinners, conversed with them, forgave those who confessed, healed them and then charged them to "sin no more." "It is God's kindness that leads to repentance" (Rom. 2:4).

Our homosexual neighbours, like all our neighbours, need to hear the same "bad news/good news" message that all Christians have had to hear. The bad news Is that in our lives of self-absorption, we are "given over" to the implications of both our fallen state and to our choices against God (Rom. 1:24, 26, 28). The very good news? God "did not spare his own Son but gave him over [same verb] for us all, and "with him will graciously give us all things" (Rom. 8:32). Telling people this message of divine, forgiving love and living it out with our homosexual friends is the greatest form of costly, neighbourly love we can ever show. It may cost us our jobs, and one day, even our lives, but we cannot refuse this kind of love to hurting people to bring them to know the love of God.

CHAPTER 13

A ROSETTA STONE FOR HUMAN IDENTITY: OLD TESTAMENT

Pierre-François Bouchard was an unremarkable soldier in Napoleon's army when, much to the pleasure of Brits everywhere, the British Royal Navy defeated the French in Egypt at the Battle of the Nile in 1798. Bouchard made his name in history not for bravery in war but because he stumbled across a strange black object inscribed with various forms of writing. He had discovered the Rosetta Stone. Alongside the Egyptian hieroglyphics on the object was a classical Greek translation, allowing scholars who knew Greek to decipher a previously untranslated language. Bouchard's discovery opened a vast treasure of Egyptian history and culture, although it did not help the French beat the British!

A NEW ROSETTA STONE?

With all the theories, practices, and experiences associated with contemporary sexual identity, it is reassuring to have a divinely inspired ancient text to serve as a spiritual and cosmological Rosetta Stone. The Bible brings clarity and sanity to a very emotional debate. Recently, however, some have claimed that the biblical texts justify homosexual practice in the church.[1] Frank Bruni, a radical journalist of the *New York Times*, echoes what many Christians are beginning to believe: "There's a rapidly growing body of impressive, persuasive literature that looks at the very traditions and texts that inform many Christians' denunciation of same-sex relationships, and demonstrates how easily those points of reference can be understood in a different way."[2] Apparently, a new Rosetta Stone has been discovered. Jen Hatmaker, popular blogger and evangelical conference speaker, believes that

> [g]odly, respectable leaders have exegeted the Bible and there is absolutely no unanimity on its interpretation. There never has been. Historically, Christian theology has always been contextually bound and often inconsistent with itself; an inconvenient truth we prefer to selectively explain.[3]

Hatmaker is no church historian and shows little evidence of having read recent works on the subject, in particular, a definitive study by Fortson and Grams, which we will see in the pages to follow.

In chapter 4, we examined some of the dubious methods Christian leaders use, and it is tempting to evaluate their exegetical work more closely, but two important books have already done this beautifully. Robert Gagnon's immense work, *The Bible and Homosexual Practice: Texts and Hermeneutics*,[4] is an exhaustive consideration of biblical and early Jewish evidence (200 BC–AD 200). No one else handles the ancient literature the way Gagnon does,[5] and his wise discussion of the key biblical texts is without peer. His unequivocal conclusion is that the Bible defines same-sex intercourse as sin, and that there are no valid interpretative principles that override what the Bible affirms.[6]

The other work, mentioned earlier, is an equally comprehensive achievement, *Unchanging Witness: The Consistent Christian Teaching on Homosexuality in Scripture and Tradition*,[7] authored by two Reformed scholars, S. Donald Fortson, Professor of Church History and Practical Theology at Reformed Theological Seminary, and Rollin G. Grams, Associate Professor of New Testament at Gordon-Conwell Theological Seminary. Fortson and Grams closely examine the texts dealing with the issue from Jewish sources before and during the New Testament period; from sources in the Early and Medieval church; from sources in modern Judaism; and from sources covering the scope of church history. After 385 pages, these scholars conclude that, in all its 2,000-year history, the Christian church has never wavered in its judgment that homoerotic practice always breaks the law of God. Their findings are in accord with that of one of the leading mainline New Testament scholars of our time, Richard Hays, who states that all the biblical texts give to homosexuality an "unambiguous...univocal... unqualified disapproval."[8]

The book by Fortson and Grams has the further advantage of showing that the present attempt to argue for homosexual inclusion has only occurred in the last few years and is thus profoundly *novel*, to say the least. This new, pro-homosexual approach to Bible interpretation corresponds with the major cultural changes that we examined and documented above, namely the appearance in the West both of a new outbreak of the practice of homosexuality and of the recent emergence of the practice of ancient pagan spirituality. As we have noted, some evangelicals naïvely desire to conform biblical teaching to the reigning pagan culture of the day, but this can surely never be a criterion for interpreting the Bible. As Paul exhorts us, "Do not be conformed to this world" (Rom. 12:2).

This new approach to the old texts convinced a traditionally Reformed and evangelical church, City Church in San Francisco, to allow full participation for practicing homosexuals. The elders produced an explanatory letter to their membership:

> Asking questions about what the Scriptures say on this issue must always be coupled with asking why the Scriptures say what they do and what kind of same-sex activity is being addressed. Scholars and leaders who have previously been united in their interpretations are coming to different conclusions. This does not mean that your view must change, but it does counsel humility with how we each hold our views. Given the status and variety of these opinions, what has become clear to us is that there is no longer clear consensus on this issue within the evangelical community.[9]

Apparently, we should be just as puzzled as those scholars of ancient Egypt before they had access to the Rosetta Stone. Is our current confusion about what the Bible says sufficient reason for making significant decisions about essential issues like human sexuality and its place in the church? Affirming authors say that the Bible only has six "pesky verses" or "clobber texts" against homosexuality. Such texts, they argue, have been "twisted, distorted, and inflated out of all proportion and out of context."[10] The passages are Genesis 19; Leviticus 18:22 and 20:13; 1 Corinthians 6:9–10; 1 Timothy 1:10; and Romans 1:26–28.

Some believe that since these texts are so few, they are relatively unimportant for the biblical writers. But, it may, on the contrary, show that such behaviour was so foreign to God's people, whether in Israel or in the New Testament community, that they didn't need to emphasize it. Ultimately, in questions of truth, numbers don't really matter. We only need two verses on incest (Lev. 18:6, 1 Cor. 5:1ff) to know it is wrong.

But it is also wrong to think that only six passages deal with homosexual practice. We may add texts concerning male cult prostitutes, as well as texts that use general categories, such as "abomination" תּוֹעֵבָה (tow'ebah) in the Old Testament, and "immorality," πορνεία (porneia) in the New Testament, to describe a wide variety of sexually immoral practices, including homosexuality, which is distinctly identified as belonging to such a category. Consider following texts: Deuteronomy 23:17–18; Judges 19:22–25;[11] 1 Kings 14:22–24; 22:43, 46; 2 Kings 23:4–7; Ezekiel 16:49–50; Galatians 5:19; Titus 1:16; Jude 1:4, 7, 19; and Revelation 21:27. These texts must be weighed in the context of 749 or so texts affirming the normativity of heterosexuality.[12]

Because this book focuses on cosmology, we will examine in depth only two key biblical texts—one in the Old Testament (Gen. 2:18–25) which has to do with the survival of civilization, and, in the next chapter, one in the New Testament (Rom. 1:26–28), written by the church's greatest theologian, the Apostle Paul, who shows explicitly the relationship between the doctrine of God the Creator and deviant sexuality—to see what light they shed on the Bible's view of homosexuality.

Genesis 2:18

"Then the LORD God said, 'It is not good that the man should be alone; I will make him a helper fit for him.'" This verse is part of a section that describes the institution of heterosexual marriage.

Gay-affirming authors appeal to this passage to justify same-sex homoerotic relationships by emphasizing the loving heart of God.[13] On the Oprah Winfrey Show[14] Rob Bell, ex-pastor of Mars Hill Church in Grand Rapids, Michigan, provides an emotive defence of same-sex "marriage" to the millions of viewers by reducing this foundational text to a statement from God about Adam's psychological anxiety of loneliness:

> One of the oldest aches in the bones of humanity is loneliness.... Loneliness is not good for the world. Whoever you are, gay or straight, it is totally normal, natural and healthy to want someone to go through life with. It's central to our humanity. We want someone to go on the journey with.[15]

On the basis of this text, Rob Bell claims that the Bible is, in principle, opposed to loneliness and thus inevitably in favor of all forms of "marriage." At the very least, this generalization fails to account for the teaching of Jesus on the validity of celibacy as a divine calling (Matt. 19:11–12). Matthew Vines also relies on emotive arguments, but goes beyond Bell by calling Jesus' teaching in Matthew 7:15–20 a denial of "romantic love and intimacy," which produces "unnecessary suffering." It is "bad fruit" and thus the source cannot be a "good tree."[16] The valid calling to singleness endorsed and lived out by Jesus is dismissed as "bad fruit!"

New Testament scholar James Brownson also seeks to defend the normalization of homosexuality in the church.[17] In spite of the mention of Adam and Eve's nakedness (Gen. 2:25) and that "one-flesh" union was for sexual intimacy (Gen. 2:24), Brownson reasons that we should not "overgenitalize or oversexualize this passage,"[18] because the goal is not sexuality but "human community and fellowship."[19] For him, the text opens a superior theme of overcoming

242

"isolation" and "the problem of aloneness" and does not refer to procreation. This observation fits his intention of justifying same-sex, non-procreating relationships. I believe he is wrong; heterosexuality and procreation are here essential.

A closer look at Genesis 2:18 reveals three key terms —"alone," "good," and "helper," which need to be examined.

ALONE (בַּד, *BAD*)

In English the adjective "alone" can have a connotation of emotional suffering, but in Hebrew, "alone" *never* expresses psychological or emotional loneliness. So it does not have this meaning in any of the 204 places where it is used in the Hebrew Old Testament. For Rob Bell, who was once a minister and professional interpreter of Scripture at Mars Hill Church, his peculiar interpretation is careless, at best.

In Scripture, the term "alone" refers to something or someone distinguished from something or someone else. In the story of Joseph and his brothers, for example, we read: "They [the servants] served him [Joseph] by himself ["alone"] and [the brothers] by themselves" ["alone"] (Gen. 43:32). That is, they did not eat together. The brothers were "alone," not in the sense of "loneliness," since they were in a group! The same Hebrew word is used in Exodus 24:2, where we read: "Moses *alone* shall come near to the LORD, but the others shall not come near, and the people shall not come up with him." Alone" is also an expression of Old Testament monotheism: "O LORD, the God of Israel, enthroned above the cherubim, you are the God, you *alone*, of all the kingdoms of the earth; you have made heaven and earth" (Ex. 22:20; 2 Kgs. 19:15). The force of this use is to set God apart as unique, not as "lonely." Here also, in Genesis 2:18, "alone" is used to mark the uniqueness of Adam.

At the moment God was about to establish marriage, Adam was the only human being God had made. Adam was not suffering from emotional isolation, for he had God as his intimate companion and could have envisaged a life of meaningful celibacy had God not had other plans. Adam was alone because *he was the only human being* on the face of the earth. So this is really a statement of brute fact.

GOOD (ב֑וֹט, *TOWB*)

Seven references to "good" are placed in the creation account, one after each major creative act of God. What makes everything good is the divine act of "separation"—light and darkness, seas and dry land, the many "kinds" of plants and animals—all are distinguished from each other and all produce a functioning, creative symphony of unity in difference. Where there is no separation, it is not good. The cosmos, "void and formless" (Gen. 1:2), needed separation into useable forms. When such distinctions are in place, God declares them "good."

This goodness of separation and distinction has cosmic significance. Twoness describes the relationship of God to creation: two distinct kinds of being, the Creator and his creatures, are united in a common purpose. Indeed, God as Trinity is Twoist in this sense, because in God there is both unity and distinction of persons. Little wonder that structures of distinction serve as God's model for his creative work, making distinct things, like day and night, and male and female. He unites them in a common purpose to maintain life.

But something holds back the final, overwhelming expression of goodness in the created order; something is lacking, something is *not* yet good. In context of the story of creation, there was more God was going to do. Adam could not function the way he was meant to function, granted the creational mandate he was given, until God finished his plan and rested from his labours. Something/someone was yet to come in God's creative project. Adam was not a lonely, emotional wreck, but God had something better than "good." He had "very good" coming. It is the "not good" of the "not finished." The process awaits its crowning moment. Adam is still "alone."

In the final act of creation "God created man...male and female.... And God saw everything that he had made, and behold, it was *very good*" (Gen. 1:27, 31). When male and female are in place, as the pinnacle of this distinction-making creative process, the "not good" disappears and everything is not only good, but *very good*. As soon as Eve appears, "the mother of the living" (Gen. 3:20), God's agents on the newly formed earth will live and reproduce, and everything becomes "very good." The heterosexual binary that God establishes constitutes the wholesome key to a functioning, God-honouring, moral, gospel-revealing cosmos.

In this pre-Fall situation, it is hard to see how Adam might have suffered loneliness. There was no sin or suffering in the world, yet the situation was "not good." Indeed Adam could not possibly feel psychologically or spiritually alone, since he had direct communion with God. The situation was not good because the process of creation had not yet been completed. A carpenter who is constructing a three-legged stool might well say after completing two legs that the stool is not (yet) good as a functioning, dependable stool. There is more to be done: one essential leg is required. For the moment, Adam was not yet effective in the role for which he was designed. The situation was not good because it was not yet functional.

A perfect example of this principle of ineffectiveness of function is found in the ministry of Moses as judge of the people, recounted in Exodus 18:14–23. Interestingly, this text contains two of our key words, "not good" and "alone." Jethro, Moses' father-in-law, sees him

245

toiling and not accomplishing his task. The text reads:

> When Moses' father-in-law saw all that he was doing for the people, he
> said, "What is this that you are doing for the people? Why do you sit
> alone, and all the people stand around you from morning till evening?"
> ...Moses' father-in-law said to him, "What you are doing is not good."
> (Ex. 18:17)

Notice that it is the inefficiently exercised function that is "not
good." That Moses is alone and unaided prevents him from doing
his job correctly—with "not good" results. He is not psychologically
lonely; indeed, there are too many people, making him unproductive
and exhausted. Jethro adds:

> You and the people...will certainly wear yourselves out.... You are not
> able to do it alone.... [L]ook for able men from all the people...and let
> them judge the people at all times.... God will direct you, you will be
> able to endure, and all this people also will go to their place in peace.
> (Ex. 18:17–18)

With the right structure and the right people in place, Moses could
offer satisfactory legislation for the people.

HELPER (עֵזֶר, 'EZER)

Moses got help from able men, suited to the task of judging the
people. In Genesis 2:18, Eve is identified specifically as a "perfectly
fitted helper" (`ezer) for Adam. She is not one possible answer to a
loneliness problem that could have been met by another man. She is
specifically—as *woman*—an irreplaceable, perfectly suited helper for
Adam's creational vocation.

In other places in the Old Testament, this term *ezer* is used for
God as "helper," not for emotional support against loneliness but for

military assistance in the life and death defence of Israel from her enemies (Deut. 33:26–29). As Moses stated in naming his son, "The God of my father was my *help*, and delivered me from the sword of Pharaoh" (Ex. 18:4). To this God, the mighty deliverer, the prophet Samuel raised a monument, an *eben-ezer* "a stone of help" (1 Sam. 7:12). *'Ezer* is also used to express needed assistance for a specific task, as in 1 Chronicles 15:26, which states that "God *helped* the Levites who were carrying the ark of the covenant of the LORD."

In the same way, to provide an "appropriate helper" for Adam's temporary ineffectiveness, God goes to the trouble of creating not another able-bodied male friend to help Adam with various tasks of husbandry and animal care, or to solve the problem of loneliness, but a new human being in female form. She is an incredibly specific complement to Adam, perfectly fitted for him, but in many ways different from him, enabling him to do the specific job he was called to do. The verb in Genesis 2:18 translated "perfectly fitted" also carries the meaning of "made," "manufactured," or "prepared." God makes a "helper" specifically prepared for his needs, presented "to him" or, as Gerhard Von Rad, the German Old Testament specialist translates, "as his opposite."[20] The helper, a special creation by God (Gen. 2:21–22), is a woman – different, but perfectly complementary. The task given to Adam *required* heterosexuality, not same-sex, loneliness-ending companionship. Indeed, if we only had the latter, there would be no one reading (or writing) this book!

The same term used in the Genesis 2:18 text with regards to Eve is used two verses later and reads as follows: "The man gave names to all livestock and to the birds of the heavens and to every beast of the field. But for Adam there was not found a helper (*'ezer*) fit for him" (Gen. 2:20). This reference to animals is omitted by Brownson. He states: "After a series of failures to overcome the isolation, at last a helper suitable to him has been found."[21] He fails to take into account that when compared to the animals and what they could offer, Eve's "help" takes on a very specific sexual function that neither an animal nor another man could fill. The help intended was not to lift Adam's endless sense of loneliness (though companionship is a wonderful secondary aspect of marriage) but to take up the massive task of the creation mandate, formally given to Adam and Eve in Genesis 1:28: "Be *fruitful and multiply* and fill the earth and subdue it, and have dominion over the fish of the sea and over the birds of the heavens and over every living thing that moves on the earth." You cannot make human babies with either animals or other men. To solve the "not good" situation, God completes the "very good" heterosexual structure of marriage, in which man and woman are perfectly *fitted*:

> [T]he LORD God caused the man to fall into a deep sleep; and while he was sleeping, he took one of the man's ribs and then closed up the place with flesh. Then the LORD God made a woman from the rib he had taken out of the man, and he brought her to the man. The man said, "This is now bone of my bones and flesh of my flesh; she shall be called 'woman,' for she was taken out of man." That is why a man leaves his father and mother and is united to his wife, and they become one flesh. (Gen. 2:20–24)

The future of the human race does not appear as an essential factor for those interpreters of Scripture seeking to defend same-sex "marriage." In their desire to relativize the male/female distinction, and to justify homosexuality, they argue, as Vines does, that the unique thing about Eve was not that she was a woman but that that she was a human, thus enabling a human relationship. Says Vines, "Adam and Eve's sameness, not their gender distinction was what made them suitable partners."[22] But the text is clear; God did not create another male. Eve's essential role is not the elimination of solitude by any kind of human companionship, good though that was, but the heterosexual companionship of physical marriage that produces babies, according to the cosmic formula: egg + sperm = civilization. Both Adam and Eve have the same calling: "be fruitful and multiply" (Gen. 1:28) but contribute in different, sexually distinct ways.

Ironically, this biblical text does not prove the correctness of same-sex "marriage" or maintain that Adam's real problem was loneliness. On the contrary, it gives *unequivocal support* for God-designed, cosmically essential, heterosexual marriage. God, the Creator of the human race, is not concerned as such with *human loneliness*, but with ongoing *human survival*. The text is describing the *physical* creation of the human race via heterosexual marriage. The uniquely "suitable help" that Eve brings is sexual. In this sense, the text cannot be "oversexualized."

The Genesis passage shows the intention of God in creating sexuality—explicitly heterosexuality. By obvious implication, it denies that God ever intended any other form, which at that time would have been without sense. It is part of the creation narrative that reveals a Creator committed to the procreation and survival of humanity in which the history of redemption would be played out.

The focus on God the Creator and on the male/female distinction carries into the New Testament, and it is probably in Paul's discourse in Romans 1 where the most ink was spilt insofar as the issue of homosexuality is concerned. It is to this stunning New Testament text that we now turn our attention.

CHAPTER 14

A ROSETTA STONE FOR HUMAN IDENTITY: NEW TESTAMENT

Romans 1:26–28 comes from the pen of the Apostle Paul, one of those essential, original witnesses called by God to lay the foundations of the church (1 Cor. 3:10). This key passage shows how the gospel relates both to creation and redemption. Paul says he is called as an inspired apostle of Christ to explain "the mystery" of God, not only as Redeemer but also as Creator (Eph. 3:9 and 1 Cor. 4:1). This is why we must take seriously the specific text that explicitly repudiates the validity of homosexual practice and explicitly re-states the deep relationship between creation and sexuality. Unlike Genesis 2:18, which describes positively why God created heterosexuality for the sake of human survival, Romans 1 describes negatively how we sinful beings, through our sexuality, "worship and serve" not God and his plans for the world, but the creation and our own lusts and desires. Paul is most specific in Romans 1:26–28:

> For this reason God gave them up to dishonourable passions. For their women exchanged natural relations for those that are contrary to nature; and the men likewise gave up natural relations with women and were consumed with passion for one another, men committing shameless acts with men and receiving in themselves the due penalty for their error. And since they did not see fit to acknowledge God, God gave them up to a debased mind to do what ought not to be done.

One must not miss the context in which these verses are found. Beginning with the bridge phrase ("for this reason"), verses 26 to 28 tie together everything Paul has been saying in the previous verses. In other words, these descriptions of same-sex activity follow immediately and directly from one of the most essential verses in the Bible: Romans 1:25. This verse sets out what might be considered the most succinct and significant programmatic statement on the nature of existence that one can find in the entire Scripture. It is strange that Matthew Vines would dismiss this passage as "not of central importance to Paul's message in Romans."[1] This verse states: "they exchanged the truth about God for the lie and worshiped and served the creature rather than the Creator, who is blessed forever! Amen." Rosaria Butterfield could not disagree more with argumentation like that of Vines. As she puts it, "Romans 1, especially verses 24–28, are the most frightening lines in Scripture to anyone struggling with sexual sin."[2]

In one sentence of just twenty-five Greek words, Paul defines the only two religious systems available to human beings throughout all of time and space. We worship and serve either the creation/nature—in a thousand different ways—or the eternal Creator, who is blessed forever. The first system, Oneism, eliminates the existence of a transcendent Creator, worships and deifies matter, and favours sameness. The second, Twoism, recognizes the Creator as distinct from the creation, the only God to whom alone, according to Scripture, worship is due. This second option thus recognizes two kinds of existence in reality: 1. the sovereign, all-powerful, uncreated Creator God and 2. everything else, which is created and which is totally dependent on the Creator. This text affirms two separate kinds of reality—God, and that which he created. The God who is distinct from his creation knits distinctions into it as he determines the nature of the world and sets in place the structures of the cosmos. These are the structures necessary for human flourishing, as well as for the good of nature and the animals.

A TWOIST MESSAGE FOR ALL TIME

Vines misses the immense implications of this text by downgrading it: "Romans 1:18–32 cannot be understood as a narrative about sameness and difference."[3] In seeking to normalize "homo" (same), Vines fails to see the fundamental Twoist or the "hetero" (different) structure written into the cosmos, the greatest of which is the distinction between the Creator and the creature.

Moses brought this amazing "hetero" message to the pagan nations of his day. He took to the pagan Egyptians and Canaanites (who believed in the divinity of nature) the unrecognized fact that "in the beginning" there was no nature, only a personal Creator God, who "created the heaven and the earth" (Gen. 1:1). It is the same message that Paul announced to the pagans of his day, and it constitutes the essence of the biblical gospel that we are called to proclaim in our day.

This fact has been recognized by many scholars of the past. The French philosopher Alexis De Tocqueville (1805–1859) said:

> Not content with the discovery that there is nothing in the world but a creation and a Creator, he [man] is still embarrassed by this *primary division of things* and seeks to expand and *simplify his conception by including God and the universe in one great whole.*[4]

"One great whole" deserves the term Oneism! Herman Bavinck, the great Dutch theologian of the nineteenth century, observed the same basic phenomenon:

> Irrespective, however, of what form the idolatry may take, it represents always a worship of the creature instead of the Creator. The distinction between God and the world is lost. The holiness of God, that is, His distinction from, and His absolute transcendence of, every creature—it was that which was lost to the Gentiles.... [T]he line between Creator and creature has been erased, and therefore the boundary between world and man, soul and body, and heaven and hell has nowhere been rightly drawn.... In the absence of a sense of the holiness of God there is a corresponding absence of a sense of sin.[5]

Colin Gunton (1941–2003), considered one of the most important British theologians of his generation, stated in different but parallel philosophical terms:

> There are, probably, ultimately only two possible answers to the question of origins, and they recur at different places in all ages: [either] that the universe is the result of creation by a free personal agency, or that in some way or other it creates itself. The two answers are not finally compatible, and require a choice, either between them or an attitude of agnostic refusal to decide.[6]

Editors always circle in red words like "it" and "these," and scribble in the margin: "Antecedent?" Romans 1:25, with its stunningly simple description of two possible worldviews,[7] uses many clear antecedents to unify the entire passage. Verse 25 is the key text in the middle of the passage that dictates, both logically and grammatically, the meaning of all the verses around it. Verse 25 shows the result of the behaviour described in the previous verses (Rom. 1:23–24). The antecedent of "they" or "such ones" who "worship creation" in verse 25 are those who (in verse 24) allowed their lust to bring them to impurity and to dishonour their bodies among themselves. Verse 26 begins with the transition phrase "for this reason," which should immediately prompt us to ask, "Which reason?" The "reason" mentioned in verse 26 refers back to their two previous exchanges: the glory of God for images (verse 23) and the truth about God for the lie (verse 25). Verse 25 also introduces the third exchange in verse 26: natural for unnatural sexual relations. Why do people give themselves to homosexuality? Verse 26 has an answer: "For this reason," namely that "they worship and serve the creation." We conclude that homosexual practice is both 1. the result of the idolatrous worship of creation and 2. the sexually embodied display of it.

This inner logic of Paul's thought is encased in a larger theological structure in Romans 1, as well as the even larger structure of the whole argument of Romans. We are in the presence of a remarkable theological mind.

Romans 1:1–16 introduces the theme of the gospel culminating in the verse that created the Protestant Reformation:

> For I am not ashamed of the gospel, for it is the power of God for salvation to everyone who believes, to the Jew first and also to the Greek. For in it the righteousness of God is revealed from faith for faith, as it is written, "The righteous shall live by faith." (Rom. 1:16–17)

For the gospel to be good news, however, there is necessarily bad news, namely the presence of human sin. This is the subject of the first three chapters of Romans, beginning with Romans 1:18–32, which exposes *the sin of the pagan world*. In Romans 2, Paul exposes *the sin of God's people, the Jews,* and in Romans 3, he makes the general statement that *all have sinned*: "as it is written: 'None is righteous, no, not one!'" (Rom. 3:10). In Romans 4–8, Paul works out the truth of justification; in Romans 9–11, the history of salvation, and in Romans 12–16, the practical implications of the gospel for believers.

In most of Romans 1, Paul deals in logical fashion with the sin of paganism, defined as the rejection of God the Creator. The sin of paganism is not the rejection of God the Savior but rather a rejection of God the Creator, whom *all know* because "what can be known about God is plain to them, because God has shown it to them" (Rom. 1:19).

Pagans refuse to honour God as transcendent Creator and, in their foolishness, "they exchanged the glory of the immortal God for images resembling mortal man and birds and animals and creeping things" (Rom. 1:23). Such rejection is the classic Oneist sin of all pagan ideas and religions throughout history and always comes down to worship of creation, not the Creator, as Paul says in Romans 1:25.

PAUL'S COHERENT COSMOLOGY

Paul's brilliant and comprehensive theological reasoning defines the three related elements of human existence, in both their rightly worshipful and their foolishly idolatrous forms:

1. *Theology*, which suppresses the knowledge of the true God, whose power and divine nature are evident as the Creator of this world (Rom. 1:25);

2. *Spirituality*, which turns adoring worship and praise of God, the only genuine object, onto idols, or images resembling "mortal man and birds and animals and creeping things" (Rom. 1:23), thus worshipping the creation rather than the Creator;

3. *Behaviour*, which in its deepest and most intimate physical expression finds manifestation in sexual acts "contrary to nature" (Rom. 1:26–28) and which develops and approves many full-blown associated expressions of "hatred of God" (Rom. 1:29–32).

These three intricately woven elements of human existence are not the only signs that we are in the presence of a carefully worked-out argument from a highly organized mind. The specific vocabulary also proves it. These three "exchanges" emphasize the determined pagan upending of the theological truths they see and know by living in the world God made. But here Paul uses a vocabulary word which he never uses elsewhere in his epistles:

- In theology—"they *exchanged* [μετήλλαξαν, *metēllaxan*] the truth for the lie" (Rom. 1:25);
- In spirituality—"they *exchanged* [ἤλλαξαν, *ēllaxan*][8] the glory of the immortal God for images resembling mortal man" (Rom. 1:23);[9]
- In sexuality—"they *exchanged* [μετήλλαξα, *metēllaxan*] *natural relations for those that are contrary to nature*" (Rom. 1:26).

Having seen the use of these identical verbs, can we possibly doubt that Paul saw these three acts of rebellion as deeply and organically connected?[10]

Another repeated phrase ties all three elements together. It is the three temporal divine judgments that God pronounces on the disobedient. Three times, God the Judge "gives them over" to consequences that prefigure the final judgment: in Romans 1:24, "God gave them over [παρέδωκεν, *paredōken*] to impurity, to the dishonoring of their bodies among themselves"; in Romans 1:26 "God gave them over [παρέδωκεν, *paredōken*] to dishonourable passions"; and, in Romans 1:28, "God gave them over [παρέδωκεν, *paredōken*] to a debased mind."

There are other deep connections to be noted in this short text between pagan worship and pagan sexuality. Failing to honour God by the practice of religious idolatry (Rom. 1:21) is a parallel with failing to honour their bodies by practicing dishonourable sexual acts (Rom. 1:26).[11] Also, spiritual idolaters have become fools (Rom. 1:22), just as those engaged in homosexuality have acquired debased minds (Rom. 1:28).[12] Without unnecessary repetition, the connections are everywhere. We no doubt only scratch the surface of Paul's deep, biblical thinking, but we see in the structure and vocabulary of this passage a coherent theological discussion of the doctrine of creation and of the implications of its rejection, particularly as it applies to sexuality.

ECHOES OF THE GENESIS CREATION ACCOUNT

This text brings us a coherent development of the biblical doctrine of creation as well as the pagan attempt to advocate a theory of nature as God.

References to Creator and Creature

Specific vocabulary focuses on the creation doctrine. God is defined as "Creator" (Rom. 1:25), author of "the creation of the world." Paul's emphasis on Genesis rolls through this passage in a preponderance of words like "creation," "Creator," "the creation of the world," and "the things that have been made" (Rom. 1:20).

Romans 1:23 uses the Greek terms "image," εἰκόνος (*eikonos*) and "likeness," ὁμοιώματι (*homoiōmati*), which appear here just as they do in the Septuagint in Genesis 1:26: (Let us make man) in our image, after our likeness" [κατ᾽ εἰκόνα ἡμετέραν καὶ καθ᾽ ὁμοίωσιν, *eikona ēmeteran kai kath homoiōsin*]. This point is well made by Robert Gagnon.[13] Paul is not expressing mere personal opinion or homophobic sentiments to produce one or two "pesky verses."

Terms of Male and Female

Paul employs specialized terms for "females" and "males" in Romans 1:26–27. He does not use the general terms, "woman" [γυνή, *gunē*], from which we get "gynecology," or "man" [ἄνθρωπος, *anthrōpos*], from which we get "anthropology." These well-known Greek words for man and woman are used hundreds of times in the Bible. But here Paul uses the *unusual* terms "females, "θήλειαι (*thēleai*) and "males," ἄρσενες (*arsenes*)—unusual because they are used only once by Jesus and only twice by Paul—here and in Galatians 3:28, as a term to include all humanity.[14] Jesus uses these terms in Matthew 19:4, when he replies to the Pharisees in a debate about marriage and the original creation: "Haven't you read that at the beginning the Creator made them *male and female* [ἄρσεν καὶ θῆλυ, *arsen kai thēly*]?" Both Jesus and Paul employ the technical terms for male and female found in Genesis 1:27. This foundational text describes heterosexuality as the only possible sexual form of God's creation: "So God created man in his own image, in the image of God he created him; *male and female* he created them, ἄρσεν καὶ θῆλυ ἐποίησεν αὐτούς" (*arsen kai thēly epoiēsen autous*). That Paul and Jesus both insist on these unique terms, which occur in the Genesis account, shows that they are both using the same inspired reference point of the original creation.

Idolatry

Another echo from Genesis is found in the upside-down nature of dominion. God granted Adam and Eve dominion over "the fish of the sea and over the birds of the heavens and over the livestock and over all the earth and over every creeping thing that creeps on the earth" (Gen. 1:26). In Romans 1:23, these terms are picked up again, but now fallen man is worshipping animals and submitting himself to them: "they exchanged the glory of the immortal God for images resembling mortal man and birds and animals and creeping things."

The Truth and the Lie

Another hint of the Eden account is found in the reference to "the Lie" (Rom. 1:25), the original lie, whispered by the Tempter to Eve. Most modern English translations oddly have "a lie." However, the original Greek includes the definite article and should be translated "the lie," [τῷ ψεύδει, *tō pseudei*], as it is in the King James Version, as well as in many foreign language translations.[15] Jesus identified the devil as the original liar, who plied his trade at the beginning. Jesus says to the Jewish authorities:

> You are of your father the devil, and your will is to do your father's desires. He was a murderer from the beginning, and does not stand in the truth, because there is no truth in him. When he lies, he speaks out of his own character, for he is a liar and the father of lies. But because I tell the truth, you do not believe me. (John 8:44–45)

Likewise, the Apostle John states: "the devil has been sinning from the beginning. The reason the Son of God appeared was to destroy the works of the devil" (1 John 3:8). In Revelation, it is said that Satan is "the deceiver of the whole world—he was thrown down to the earth, and his angels were thrown down with him" (Rev. 12:9). In other words, Paul is describing the original struggle between *the truth and the lie*, a struggle that began in the Garden of Eden and still troubles the world to this day.

Unnatural

Romans 1:26–27 states: "They exchanged *natural relations* for those that are *contrary to nature*; and the men likewise gave up *natural relations*." Gay-affirming modern scholars attempt to dismiss the terms "natural" and "unnatural" as mere conventional standards set by the social customs of the day.[16]

A contemporary of Paul, Josephus, well understood the apostle's meaning when he declared, "The Law recognized no sexual connections except for the natural (κατὰ φύσιν) union of man and wife."[17] The New Testament scholar, Rollin Grams, has discovered a use of these terms to describe the natural state in many ancient writers, especially Plato, who describes heterosexuality and homosexuality in these terms. In his *Laws* (1.636c), Plato says,

> And whether one makes the observation in earnest or in jest, one certainly should not fail to observe that when male unites with female for procreation the pleasure experienced is held to be due to nature [*kata physin*], but contrary to nature [*para physin*] when male mates with male or female with female, and that those first guilty of such enormities were impelled by their slavery to pleasure.[18]

Romans 11:24 gives a clear understanding of what Paul means by these terms: "For if you have been cut from what is 'by nature' [κατὰ φύσιν, *kata physin*] a wild olive tree and grafted, contrary to nature [παρὰ φύσιν, *para physin*], into a cultivated olive tree, how much more will these natural [κατὰ φύσιν, *kata physin*] branches be grafted back into their own olive tree." Paul is certainly speaking of how things work in nature, not what is customary.[19] Paul refers in this chapter to the Gentiles who are "by nature children of wrath," and then applies it to everyone: "like the rest of mankind." This not a passing custom; this is the way all people are.

Matthew Vines, in his influential book *God and the Gay Christian*, argues that the term "nature" or "natural," merely means "customary," and "customs," which, unlike moral values, change from one culture to the next.[20] He refers to Paul's use of "nature" in 1 Corinthians 11:15: Does not *nature* itself teach you that if a man wears long hair it is a disgrace for him (1 Cor. 11:14)? Vines posits that Paul could not be referring to a fixed principle in the essence of creation, but rather to the custom of short hair for males in the Greco-Roman world. But this is superficial equivocation. Whatever one thinks about Paul's view of male/female roles or how hair styles reflect gender differences, there is no doubt what he means by "nature" here. The immediate context speaks of the creation God established and the relation of men and women within it. Thus Paul says:

> For a man ought not to cover his head, since he is the image and glory of God, but woman is the glory of man. For man was not made from woman, but woman from man. Neither was man created for woman, but woman for man. That is why a wife ought to have a symbol of authority on her head, because of the angels. Nevertheless, in the Lord woman is not independent of man nor man of woman; for as woman was made from man, so man is now born of woman. And all things are from God. (1 Cor. 11:7–12)

Paul here appeals not to mere social custom but to the very essence of the creational meaning of male and female as it reflects the Trinitarian nature of God (1 Cor. 11:3) and bears witness to God in the pagan world. "Does not nature itself teach you that if a man wears long hair it is a *disgrace* for him?" (1 Cor. 11:14). Paul uses the same term "disgrace" in Romans 1:26: "For this reason God gave them up to dishonourable [disgraceful] passions. For their women exchanged natural relations for those that are contrary to nature." The apostle's use of "disgrace" and "contrary to nature" highlights a failure in our culture to recognize the theological meaning of the physical sexual practice. To exchange natural relations for unnatural ones is to share in the disgrace of those who reject the God of Scripture, as Psalm 83:17–18, describes it: "Let them [the pagan enemies of Israel] be put to shame and dismayed forever; let them perish in *disgrace*, that they may know that you alone, whose name is the LORD, are the Most High over all the earth." This is so important that Paul invokes the presence of angels (1 Cor. 11:10), and states, with full apostolic authority: "If anyone is inclined to be contentious, we have no such practice, nor do the churches of God" (1 Cor. 11:16). For Paul, the unchanging character of human sexuality and sexual roles, whatever the various cultural details, reflects aspects of the very being of God and his creative work, and must be honoured in the body of Christ.[21]

Two Further Objections

Those who wish to persist in condoning the practice and affirmation of homosexuality in the church usually deny the clear meaning of the Romans 1 text by using two arguments: 1. Paul is only referring to the horrendous situation of sexual and spiritual abuse in Roman society, and/or 2. Paul was ignorant of "sexual orientation."

The first argument holds that, in Romans 1:26–28, Paul was referring exclusively to the sexual scene in the Rome of his day: that of cult prostitution or pederasty (man-boy love) and obligatory master/ slave relations. David Gushee believes Paul is alluding to the sexual debauchery and the extreme expressions of sexuality found in the Roman imperial court.[22] Therefore, we can only apply Paul's description to that dissolute pagan culture.

Against this argument, a number of considerations must be taken into account. We can fairly assume that Paul is not describing forced sex or pederasty because he presents the same-sex relationships as occurring between two willing (doubtless adult) men of equal standing. He speaks of men "consumed with passion for one another" (Rom. 1:27), wording that suggests a relationship between equals. There is no hint here of slaves forced into sex for the pleasure of their masters or of young boys abused against their will. Had Paul meant pederasty, he could have used well-known terms that specifically designate those practices, such as *erastes* (the older lover) and *eromenos* (the younger, usually teenage male). He uses terms that clearly define lustful homosexual relationships.

There is no hint, either, of religious ritual or payment, which was the case in homosexual or heterosexual religious prostitution where *mutual* pleasuring was not a part of the arrangement. Even more to the point, Paul includes lesbianism, which in the ancient literature never includes slavery, pederasty, temple prostitution, or violent abuse. If Gushee's theory is correct, why would Paul include lesbian relationships in his rejection of homosexual activity?[23] In light of these considerations, surely Ken Wilson's judgment is wrong when he says that "a plain and simple reading [of Romans 1] suggests that the language of these texts is best suited to violent, degrading, sex-as-domination practices. Whether it also refers to all same-sex relationships is the matter in dispute."[24] There is surely no "dispute," for without any hint of special cases and with the inclusion of lesbianism (which makes Paul's teaching apply to both men and women), we should conclude that a "plain and simple reading" of Paul's teaching is to receive it as a general denial of *all forms* of same-sex practice. To take any other approach assumes an ability to read into the mind of Paul an approval of the very thing he is denouncing. All the evidence points to a clear condemnation of lesbian and homosexual practice.

The second argument tries to show that Paul did not know the phenomenon of "sexual orientation." Matthew Vines puts this argument starkly: "What Paul is describing is fundamentally different from what we are discussing."[25] Others have advanced variations on this argument. New Testament scholar Walter Wink has a very peculiar take on this passage:

> No doubt Paul was unaware of the distinction between sexual orientation, over which one has apparently very little choice, and sexual behavior. He apparently assumes that those whom he condemns are heterosexual, and are acting contrary to nature, "leaving," "giving up," or "exchanging" their regular sexual orientation for that which is foreign to them. Paul knew nothing of the modern psychosexual understanding of homosexuals as persons whose orientation is fixed early in life, persons for whom having heterosexual relations would be acting contrary to nature, "leaving," "giving up" or "exchanging" their usual sexual orientation.[26]

Nicholas Wolterstorff does not argue that Paul's reference is to heterosexuals who are going "against nature" in order to take part in homosexual acts, but he does seem to imply that orientation is an immutable reason for his friends declaring themselves to be homosexuals:

> Romans 1 depicts a truly appallingly wicked people. Can we generalize

from this passage and say that Paul is saying that God says homosexual activity is always wrong? There is a night-and-day difference between what Paul describes and the same-sex couples I know.[27]

This is perhaps the strongest argument raised against the normativity of Paul's teaching for the church of today; it is "strong" because it is appealing. However, an argument based only on emotional appeal is decidedly weak, as are all arguments from silence. Is it believable to think that natural human behaviour has changed so drastically that we can now create a heretofore unknown form of sexual behaviour called "natural orientation"?[28]

It is safe to assume that Paul knew about long-term homosexual relations of affection, since such relationships were part of the pagan culture of his day, though they were not loaded with today's specialized medical or psychological terminology. Technical language cannot create a novel sexual category, unknown in the past history of sexuality. As New Testament scholar N.T. Wright puts it:

> [The ancient Greeks and Romans] knew a great deal about what people today would regard as longer-term, reasonably stable relations between two people of the same gender. This is not a modern invention; it's already there in Plato. The idea that in Paul's day it was always a matter of exploitation of younger men by older men or whatever...of course there was plenty of that then, as there is today, but it was by no means the only thing. They knew about the whole range of options.[29]

Robert Gagnon opens his competent, in-depth study of the phenomenon with the statement: "Even on the surface of it, the notion that mutually caring same-sex relationships first originated in modern times sounds absurd."[30] He recounts that in Greece long-standing relationships of homosexual soldiers was believed to make unbeatable armies.[31] In Plato's *Symposium*, one of the speakers,

Pausanius, believes in good homosexual relationships that "remain throughout life."[32] If the Scriptures considered these to be a valid form of sexual relationships, why is there is no hint of such an attitude in Paul's writings? Why does he not make an exception for a loving, life-long commitment between homosexuals?

Paul knew about mutual and long-term same-sex relationships because the ancients knew of homosexual orientation.[33] Alexander the Great, for example, had a long-term, intimate same-sex relationship with Hephaestion, head of his army, a friendship that lasted throughout their entire lives. This was not a slave/master or a pederastic relationship. Aristotle, Alexander's teacher, described such friendships as "one soul abiding in two bodies," which seemed to be the case with Alexander and Hephaestion. When his "lover" died, Alexander lay on his body for a whole day, was so distraught that he did not eat for days, and had Hephaestion's physician killed. This argument that "orientation" was unknown in Paul's day should be described as "amateurish and unworthy of a scholar."[34]

Plato did believe that there was a third (homosexual) sex, what we might call "orientation" today. But even if Paul had seen sexual orientation as a "psychological" phenomenon, he would *not* have accepted it. As a highly trained rabbi in Old Testament law, Paul believed that all human beings are born either male or female. And, by the way, for many believers today that belief is still the case. They see orientation as a sad implication of the curse from the Fall.

The modern argument that Paul did not know the kind of homosexuality we know today sounds like a case of special pleading to avoid the obvious implications of Romans 1. "Loving" forms of homosexuality, like "loving" expressions of incest or prostitution, would not convince Paul of its value. He could only see such arrangements as a form of Gnosticism, rejecting the physical works of the good Creator. To this, in his entire theology, Paul was adamantly opposed.

Vines and Wolterstorff are unable to imagine that evangelical gays could ever be included in the ranks of God-denying idolaters, so they conclude that Paul does not have such people in mind. This is not good exegesis, and it fails to see how theological trends can develop. Alas, belief and practice move in a circle. Your belief affects your practice and your practice affects your beliefs. Wherever you enter the circle, you will eventually end up on the other side. Homosexual practice is both the *result* of the idolatrous worship of creation and an embodiment of it. In spite of anyone's good intentions, continual homosexual practice, without repentance, will finally lead to apostasy. Evangelicals who accept homosexuality as normative will almost inevitably slide into some form of paganism.

DEEP SIGNIFICANCE

The deep significance of this issue is drawn out in the work of Richard Hays, professor at Duke Divinity School, who posits that the apostle "portrays homosexual behavior as a 'sacrament' (so to speak) of the anti-religion of human beings who refuse to honor God as Creator. When human beings engage in homosexual activity, they enact an outward and visible sign of an inward and spiritual reality—the rejection of the Creator's design… [homosexuality is] a particularly graphic image of the distortion of creation."[35]

The Apostle Paul describes heterosexuality as a "*mystery* hidden in ages past," now revealed in the gospel. In both Oneism and Twoism, sexuality plays a deeply symbolic and embodied role in constructing a worldview. Paul provides the profound "reason" (Rom. 1:26) for same-sex practice: anti-creational, unnatural practice carries with it a religious significance because it is organically, logically, and inevitably tied to apostate theology and idolatrous spirituality, which always rejects God the Creator.

Paul's numerous references to Genesis are key, granting the very force of his argument. By mentioning creation, Paul is simply telling the reader to go back to Genesis and see that there are only two 'natural,' created sexes: heterosexual males and females. It is impossible to stretch Paul's theology to say that, if he had only known about orientation, he would have ordained practicing homosexuals as pastors and encouraged them to marry. For Paul, as for all the biblical writers, and those who have faithfully believed the Scriptures during the long history of Christian tradition, the gospel of Christ is built upon the original good foundation of divine creation. The Christ who died for us is he by whom "all things were created, in heaven and on earth, visible and invisible, whether thrones or dominions or rulers or authorities—all things were created through him and for him. And he is before all things, and in him all things hold together" (Col. 1:16–17). To deny the value and meaning of creation is theologically unthinkable.

A Serious Warning

With the following paragraphs I come to the conclusion of this chapter and of this book, and it comes in the form of a warning. It is becoming evident that the LGBT agenda is the twenty-first century's version of Gnosticism, the great early heresy that almost took over the church of the second century. Gnosticism is not simply the preference of spirituality over things physical. It is the deliberate rejection of the being of God the Creator.[36] Though Gnosticism often claimed to be Christian, it fundamentally undermined the Christian faith. God was identified as the evil creator who had made all things material. He would receive what he deserved. The Gnostic goddess, Zoë, breathed upon "the face of God [Jahweh] and her breath became an angel of fire…and threw him down into Hell under the abyss."[37]

Robert Reilly, a senior advisor to the United States Secretary of Defense, in his book *Making Gay Okay: How Rationalizing Homosexual Behaviour Is Changing Everything* (2014), clarifies the issues involved in the acceptance of homosexuality. He argues that if the definition of morality is based on mere desire, eventually described as love, "no moral distinctions can be made between heterosexuality, homosexuality, adultery, or even incest. Sexuality has to have meaning outside of the mere act."[38]

Our culture applies this Gnostic view of sexuality to everything, making into a human right what Paul describes as "unnatural" (Rom. 1:26). For Paul, homosexuality is "unnatural" not only for believers but for everyone, because it is out of order with the physical cosmos as God the Creator made it. Engaging in homosexuality is thus both a rejection of the real, natural world and of God himself, who is both moral judge and the intelligent Creator of all things, whose image human beings are meant to reflect. To deny the authority and goodness of God's created design is serious heresy and will lead to social implosion.

In the face of these social pressures, the church urgently needs to assure people both in the world and in the church that the stand for biblical truth is not immoral, unworthy, or unnecessary, but crucial for this world and for the next. Our gay friends, including those who claim to be Christian, need to be made aware of the theological and cosmological implications of the embrace of homosexuality. What is at stake are *essential* issues regarding the ultimate nature of the meaning of existence, and of how God created the world. Sexuality is not the result of outmoded customs, personal choices, or individual feel-

270

ings. It reflects the image of God as a Trinitarian being. Do evangelicals, understandably moved on a purely emotional level to accept the homosexual lifestyle, see the immense cosmological consequences of such an ideologically embodied practice? Do they see the coming disaster of imposing such a practice onto the Christian community of Bible- and God-honouring churches? In endorsing homosexuality as an expression of pastoral love and concern, do they see the coming dominance of a gay culture that eventually will seek to wipe out the truth of the gospel?

William Love, Anglican Bishop of Albany, in a heart-wrenching and passionate appeal to his church, writes:

> The Episcopal Church and Western Society have been hijacked by the "Gay Rights Agenda" which is very well organized, very strategic, very well financed, and very powerful. Satan is having a heyday bringing division into the Church over these issues and is trying to use the Church to hurt and destroy the very ones we love and care about by deceiving the leadership of the Church into creating ways for our gay and lesbian brothers and sisters to embrace their sexual desires rather than to repent and seek God's love and healing grace.[39]

Surely, it can only create catastrophic theological and spiritual perplexity when a sinful practice that throughout time and space has expressed the doctrine of pagan Oneism is imposed on churches long nurtured in the Bible's doctrine of creation. Individual congregations and whole denominations are being ripped in two as the implications of this wrong-headed argumentation become evident.

I fear that sooner or later many "gay evangelicals" will follow their mentor, David Gushee, out of evangelicalism and—though I pray I am wrong—out of Christianity altogether. Ken Wilson, whose careful but mystical approach we discussed earlier, has had a great influence on evangelicals through his book *Letter to My Congregation*. He has now appointed a lesbian co-pastor, Emily Swan, to his staff at Blue Ocean Faith church in Ann Arbor. Wilson and Swan published a book, *Solus Jesus: A Theology of Resistance*, which they describe as "post-evangelical—even post-Protestant," and they now reject the traditional view of the atonement. The book is enthusiastically endorsed by Gushee.

PRACTICE AND BELIEF

No one can live for long in the tension between practice and belief. Either your practice will conform to your belief, or your belief to your practice. We see what has so often happened to those calling themselves "progressives." Eventually, their practice will conform to their changing beliefs. Alas, you can call yourself a "progressive," as Gushee does,[40] but liberal progressivism finally rejects Scripture, denies God as Creator, embraces interfaith fellowship, and opens itself to all pagan religions and to their methods of moral discernment— all modern forms of ancient idolatry. We must pray for David Gushee and for all those who will doubtless follow him. Homosexuality is not a superficial issue, it is the engine leading many "progressive" evangelicals into God-denying heresy. It is a logical progression. Liberalism, in spite of its claims to be "Christian," has embraced a Oneist apostasy that causes people to abandon the biblical truth of Twoism. Within a generation, such a move, in the name of love, will lead many currently professing believers into paganism, where homosexuality is defined and practiced as a kind of pagan religious sacrament. As the Apostle John reminds the church: "Little children, keep yourselves from idols."[41] Those who justify their sexual practice in the name of love should remember the words of the prophet Jonah: "Those who cling to worthless idols turn away from God's love for them" (Jon. 2:8).

Finally, we return to the demand of Jesus to love God first, and then, in second place, our neighbours. We cling to the promise of Scripture: "let all who take refuge in you rejoice; let them ever sing for joy, and spread your protection over them, that those who love your name may exult in you. For you bless the righteous, O LORD; you cover him with favor as with a shield" (Ps. 5:11–12).

In Scripture, the rainbow is a sign of God's covenant with the earth, and his promise never again to destroy it with flood:

> And God said, "This is the sign of the covenant that I make between me and you and every living creature that is with you, for all future generations: I have set my bow in the cloud, and it shall be a sign of the covenant between me and the earth. When I bring clouds over the earth and the bow is seen in the clouds, I will remember my covenant that is between me and you and every living creature of all flesh. And the waters shall never again become a flood to destroy all flesh. When the bow is in the clouds, I will see it and remember the everlasting covenant between God and every living creature of all flesh that is on the earth." God said to Noah, "This is the sign of the covenant that I have established between me and all flesh that is on the earth." (Gen. 9:11–17)

This Noahic covenant restates Genesis 1:27 ("male and female he created them") five times (Gen. 5:2; 6:19; 7:2, 9, 16), underlining the importance of the male/female distinction both for humans and for animals. The distinction is clearly part of God's plan for the preservation of human life. This promise is of sheer grace because mankind is so evidently sinful (Gen. 6:11–12). It also restates the portion of the original covenant (Gen. 1:27) that man is made, male and female, in God's image (Gen. 9:6).

The bow of peace in the clouds affirms that the Creator God

is in control, watching with care over his handiwork. The rainbow also prophesies a day when the God who "laid the foundation of the earth in the beginning, and the heavens are the work of your hands (Heb. 1:10) will create a new heavens and earth where "righteousness dwells" (2 Pet. 3:13). The bow is "the light of grace which shines over the threatening waters of the wrath of God."[42]

We need to share with our homosexual neighbors the good news that "the steadfast love of the LORD never ceases; his mercies never come to an end; they are new every morning; great is your faithfulness" (Lam. 3:22–23) and "that our Lord is a great and awesome God, who keeps covenant and steadfast love with those who love him and keep his commandments" (Dan. 9:4).

Here is the Rosetta Stone of cosmic meaning, the rainbow hope of a God full of justice and mercy. The God of Scripture is the unique source of wisdom and grace. God did all that was necessary to save sinners who could do nothing to save themselves. He sent his Son to live a perfect life of righteousness, in which he fulfilled all of God's Law. The Son then went willingly to the cross, taking the condemnation we deserved so that we could be received into heaven. Indeed, as Scripture so clearly and movingly says: "For our sake [God] made [Jesus] to be sin who knew no sin, so that in him we might become the righteousness of God (2 Cor. 5:21). There is no greater love story in human history.

Whose Rainbow? has sought to share with anyone the good news that God, our loving Father, set the rainbow in the sky as his own reminder of grace and mercy for us. The one who created and owns the rainbow is the source of all beauty. He owns both the multi-coloured beauty of his rainbow sign of care for the cosmos, and also the beauty he invested in every human being, made gloriously in his own image. To understand this is to hold the Twoist key to the ultimate meaning of existence. Though we are mere creatures surrounded by the physical and temporal immensity of the cosmos, yet—in union with Christ and in our male and female identities—we reflect the very person of God himself.

POSTSCRIPT

If you are reading this book because you experience strong same-sex attraction, which you have resisted or even given in to…if you feel helpless and hopeless in its power, I would plead with you to consider the end of those who have abandoned their beliefs in order to appease their desires. To compromise the truth of God's clear revelation for what you think will make you happier will not end well. Though the road is hard, faithfulness in loving God first is worth it in the end. He will bring you safely home to ultimate intimacy with him, even if he calls you to self-sacrifice in this life. He is able to forgive and to heal wrong desire and give us the "mind of Christ."

If you are a pastor or Christian leader, I beg you to consider how you will affect those who come to you for advice and counsel. Will you contravene the clear message of the gospel and thus "wrong" those who look up to you and eagerly follow your advice (1 Thess. 4:3–6)? Or will you boldly declare God's design for sexuality and marriage? As an ordained minister of the gospel myself, I realize the seriousness of the job God places upon us. I pray that we will stand firm on the immutable Word of our Creator and Redeemer—in humility and with great love.

REFERENCES

Preface

1. Jena McGregor, "Chick-fil-A CEO Dan Cathy steps into gay marriage debate," *Washington Post*, last modified July 19, 2012, https://www.washingtonpost.com/blogs/post-leadership/post/chick-fil-a-president-dan-cathy-bites-into-gay-marriage-debate/2012/07/19/gJQACrvzvW_blog.html.

Chapter 1

1. David B. Calhoun, *The Glory of the Lord Risen Upon It: First Presbyterian Church, Columbia, South Carolina, 1795–1995* (Columbia, SC: First Presbyterian Church, 1995), 133.
2. See https://en.wikipedia.org/wiki/Harvey_Milk. See also "Should Harvey Milk Have Been a Registered Sex-Offender?" *Politics Forum*, last modified March 22, 2012, https://www.politicsforum.org/forum/viewtopic.php?t=137713.
3. Another book whose title contains the rainbow should be noted, Scott Lively's, *Redeeming the Rainbow: A Christian Response to the "Gay" Agenda* (Springfield, MA: Veritas Aeterna Press, 2009). I only discovered this book as my own text was going to press—which I regret—but an overview indicates the enormous importance of Lively's thoughtful work. His goal is to expose "in the strongest possible terms, the homosexual movement and its destructive agenda for social change (p.1)." My own work seeks to show the theological and cosmological implications of human sexuality, both in its "natural" and "unnatural" forms, for the church and its witness.
4. According to Wikipedia, the history of the LGBT flag is somewhat fortuitous, meandering through versions with as many as eight or nine coloured stripes. Only in the original eight-stripe version created by Gilbert Baker were the colours given any more specific meaning than a general sense of diversity. Baker gave colors the following significance: Sex, Life, Healing, Sunlight, Nature, Magic/Art, Serenity and Spirit. See https://en.wikipedia.org/wiki/Rainbow_flag_(LGBT_movement).
5. Steven D. Smith, *Pagans and Christians in the City: Culture Wars from the Tiber to the Potomac* (Grand Rapids: Eerdmans, 2018). This book confirms what the present author has been seeking to show during the last twenty-five years or so, in publications such as The Gnostic Empire Strikes Back: An Old Heresy for the New Age (Phillipsburg, NJ: P & R, 1992), and Spirit Wars: Pagan Revival in Christian America (Escondido, CA: Main Entry Editions, 1998).
6. Smith, *Pagans and Christians*, 111–12. Internal quotations are taken from

Jan Asmann, *The Price of Monotheism*, trans. Robert Savage (Stanford University Press, 2010), 39; emphasis Smith's.

7. Smith, *Pagans and Christians*, 46, citing Emile Durkheim, The Elementary Forms of Religious Life, trans., Karen E. Fields (New York: Free Press, [1912] 1995), 1.

8. Smith, *Pagans and Christians*, 46, 218.

9. Quotes in this paragraph are from Smith, *Pagans and Christians*, 124, citing Kyle Harper, *From Shame to Sin: The Christian Transformation of Sexual Morality in Late Antiquity* (Cambridge, MA: Harvard University Press, 2013), 94.

10. See Nancy Pearcey, *Love Thy Body: Answering Hard Questions about Life and Sexuality* (Grand Rapids: Baker Books, 2018), 11. Pearcey shows very practically how a secular view does not fit the real universe. "Secular" and "pagan" ultimately describe, from different perspectives, the same ways of thinking. I recommend reading this fine book, which deals with both contemporary and popular philosophical issues as well as Scriptural teaching, showing in very practical ways that "the body has a built-in telos, or purpose" (29).

11. Brian McLaren, *The Great Spiritual Migration* (New York: Convergent, 2016), 103.

12. McLaren, *Spiritual Migration*, 222.

13. Peter Jones, *One or Two: Seeing a World of Difference* (Escondido, CA: Main Entry Editions, 2010). This book is a sustained reflection on Paul's argument in Romans 1.

14. The Nashville Statement is an evangelical and biblical statement of faith concerning sexuality and gender roles. Sponsored by the Council on Biblical Manhood and Womanhood, it was made public August 2017. See https://cbmw.org/nashville-statement.

15. Cited in Peter Jones, *The God of Sex: How Spirituality Defines Your Sexuality* (Escondido, CA: Main Entry Editions, 2006), 13.

16. See the very wise articles by Rosaria Butterfield, refusing the identity of "Gay Christian" implicit in the Side B option: "What is Wrong with Gay Christianity? What is Side A and Side B Anyway?" Rosaria Champagne Butterfield, accessed July 14, 2020, https://rosariabutterfield.com/new-blog/2018/2/14/what-is-wrong-with-gay-christianity-what-is-side-a-and-side-b-anyway. See also her helpful books: *The Secret Thoughts of an Unlikely Convert: An English Professor's Journey into Christian Faith* (Pittsburgh, PA: Crown & Covenant, 2012), and *The Gospel Comes with a House Key: Practicing Radically Ordinary Hospitality in Our Post-Christian World* (Wheaton, IL: Crossway, 2018).

17. Merriam-Webster defines "cisgender" as: "of, relating to, or being a person whose gender identity corresponds with the sex the person had or was

identified as having at birth."

18. Cited in Albert Mohler, "Torn Between Two Cultures? Revoice, LGBT Identity, and Biblical Christianity," *Aquila Report*, last modified October 10, 2019. https://www.theaquilareport.com/torn-between-two-cultures-re-voice-lgbt-identity-and-biblical-christianity/.

19. Peter Jones, "Revoice: Sliding into Heresy," *truthXchange*, last modified August 3, 2018, https://truthxchange.com/2018/08/revoice-sliding-in-to-heresy/ and "Slouching to Ancient Rome," last modified August 31, 2018, https://truthxchange.com/2018/08/slouching-to-ancient-rome.

20. See 1 Corinthians 6:9–10 where the Greek term *malakos* or "soft" distinguishes effeminacy from male sexual intercourse. See the correct translation: "nor effeminate, nor abusers of themselves with men" (ERV). As Tim Bayly notes, "[T]he gay Christian who says he isn't going to have gay intercourse is counting on the Christians to give him a pass on his effeminacy…that the Bible does not condemn his homosexual desires or identity…. This is directly contrary to the teaching of Scripture." See Tim Bayly, Joseph Bayly and Jurgen von Hagen, *The Grace of Shame: Seven Ways the Church Has Failed to Love Homosexuals* (Bloomington, IN: Warhorn Media, 2017), 63–4.

21. Side B advocates should resist the temptation to normalize nonpracticing homosexuality as pleasing to God (which the 2018 Revoice conference suggested). Homosexual desire is the result of the Fall and, in itself, expresses Oneism, even in its celibate form.

22. Mohler, "Torn Between Two Cultures?"

Chapter 2

1. Ken Myers, *All God's Children and Blue Suede Shoes: Christians and Popular Culture* (Wheaton, IL: Crossway, 2012), 104.

2. Peter Collier and David Horowitz, *Destructive Generation: Second Thoughts about the Sixties* (Los Angeles: Second Thoughts Books, 1989/1990/1995), 81, 85.

3. See Saul Alinsky, *Rules for Radicals* (New York: Random House, 1971). Collier and Horowitz, *Destructive Generation*, 361.

4. Supported by George Soros, his justice includes the liberation of most of the criminals from local prisons. Lloyd Billingsley, "Son of Two Unrepentant Terrorists Wins DA San Fran Race." *FrontPage*, last modified November 11, 2019, frontpagemag.com/fpm/2019/11/son-two-unrepentant-terrorists-wins-da-san-fran-lloyd-billingsley.

5. Elizabeth Fox-Genovese, *Women and the Future of the Family* (Grand Rapids: Baker Books, 2000), emphasis mine. At the end of her life Fox-Genovese converted to Roman Catholicism. "I believed in Christ Jesus and

accepted him as my Lord and Savior, and that that Jesus had died for my sins." She also saw the selfishness of abortion, and said of her earlier radical friends: "there but for the grace of God go I." Elizabeth Fox-Genovese, "A Conversion Story," *First Things*, last modified April 2000, https://www.firstthings.com/article/2000/04/a-conversion-story.

6. Smith, *Pagans and Christians*, 111–12, 114.

7. Jones, *The God of Sex.*

8. Christian De La Huerta, *Coming Out Spiritually* (New York: Penguin Putnam, 1999), xi.

9. Kristin Luker, "Sex, Social Hygiene, and the State: The Double-Edged Sword of Social Reform," in *Theory and Society*, Vol. 27, No. 5 (Oct. 1998), pp. 601-634. http://www.jstor.org/stable/657941.

10. Robert VerBruggen, "How We Ended Up With 40 Percent of Children Born Out of Wedlock," *Institute for Family Studies*, last modified December 18, 2017, https://ifstudies.org/blog/how-we-ended-up-with-40-percent-of-children-born-out-of-wedlock.

11. Paul Kengor, *Takedown: From Communists to Progressives: How the Left Has Sabotaged Family and Marriage* (WND Books, 2015), 202–3.

12. Kengor, *Takedown*, 205.

13. Kris Fraser, "SIC Scraps Safer Sex Night," *Oberlin Review*, last modified April 5, 2014, https://oberlinreview.org/5357/uncategorized/5357.

14. https://adaringexistence.wordpress.com/2017/08/30/the-nashville-statement-a-plain-language-translation. As of press time this source is no longer available.

15. See Peter Jones, *Stolen Identity: The Conspiracy to Reinvent Jesus* (Colorado Springs: Victor Books, 2006), 33.

16. Benjamin Wiker, "From a Moral-Historical Perspective, This Crisis is Worse Than You Realize," *National Catholic Register*, last modified August 30, 2018, http://www.ncregister.com/blog/benjamin-wiker/from-a-moral-historical-perspective-this-crisis-is-worse-than-you-realize.

17. It later became evident that Kinsey was also preparing the way for full acceptance of homosexuality.

18. The information on Hefner and Kinsey is drawn from Michael Brown, "What Alfred Kinsey and Hugh Hefner had In Common," *Christian Post*, last modified October 10, 2017, and from Judith Reisman, *Kinsey: Crimes and Consequences: The Red Queen and the Grand Scheme* (Crestwood, KY: Institute for Media Education, 2001); Susan Brinkmann, *The Kinsey Corruption* (Charlotte, NC: Ascension Press, 2004); Michael Jones, *Degenerate Moderns: Modernity as Rationalized Sexual Misbehaviour* (Charlotte, NC: Ignatius Press, 1993).

19. Alfred C. Kinsey, Wardell B. Pomeroy, and Clyde E. Martin, *Sexual Behaviour in the Human Male* (Philadelphia: W.B. Saunders Company),

1948.

20. Alfred C. Kinsey, Wardell B. Pomeroy, Clyde E. Martin and Paul H. Gebhard, *Sexual Behaviour in the Human Female* (Bloomington, IN: Indiana University Press, 1953).

21. Jonathon Van Maren, "Alfred Kinsey was a pervert and a sex criminal," *Lifesite News*, last modified August 25, 2014, https://www.lifesitenews.com/news/alfred-kinsey-was-a-pervert-and-a-sex-criminal.

22. *The Lancet*, vol. 337, March 2, 1991, 547. See also Robert H. Knight, "How Alfred C. Kinsey's Sex Studies Have Harmed Women and Children," *Free Republic*, last modified July 11, 2011, http://www.freerepublic.com/focus/f-news/2803975/posts.

23. "The Truth Behind Alfred Kinsey," *Zenit*, last modified May 15, 2005, https://zenit.org/articles/the-truth-behind-alfred-kinsey.

24. Van Maren, "Alfred Kinsey was a pervert."

25. Jones, *Degenerate Moderns*, 87ff.

26. Tom Kershaw, "Hugh Hefner." *Hollowverse*, last modified December 10, 2012, https://hollowverse.com/hugh-hefner.

27. James Wilkinson, "Playboy founder Hugh Hefner dies of natural causes aged 91 surrounded by loved ones at his infamous $100million Beverly Hills mansion," *Daily Mail*, last modified December 14, 2017, http://www.dailymail.co.uk/news/article-4927948/Hugh-Hefner-dies-aged-91.html#ixzz4tzMHJJIt.

28. Wilkinson, "Hugh Hefner dies."

29. Piers Morgan, "Farewell to the Hef, the King of Sex and an unlikely champion of freedom, equality and everybody's right to some fun," *Daily Mail*, last modified September 29, 2017, http://www.dailymail.co.uk/news/article-4929898/PIERS-MORGAN-Hef-King-Sex-champion-freedom.html#ixzz4tzsnKELr.

30. Brown, "What Alfred Kinsey and Hugh Hefner had in Common."

31. See Kathryn Lopez, "Sex, Hefner, and Hookup Culture," *Town Hall*, last modified September 30, 2017.

32. Adolescents and Young Adults," *Center for Disease Control*, last modified December 7, 2017, https://www.cdc.gov/std/life-stages-populations/adolescents-youngadults.htm.

33. Robert Schwarzwalder, "Hugh Hefner's True Legacy," *The Stream*, last modified October 1, 2017, https://stream.org/hugh-hefners-true-legacy/.

34. Fox-Genovese, *Women and the Future of the Family*, 17.

35. Melanie Phillips, *The World Turned Upside Down: The Global Battle over God, Truth, and Power* (New York: Encounter Books, 2010), 290.

36. Gabriele Kuby, *The Global Sexual Revolution: Destruction of Freedom in the Name of Freedom* (Kettering, OH: Angelico Press, 2015, German 2012).

37. Kuby, *Global Sexual Revolution*, 7.

38. Kuby, *Global Sexual Revolution*, 8.

39. Kuby, *Global Sexual Revolution*, 9.

40. Philip Rieff, *The Triumph of the Therapeutic: Uses of Faith after Freud* (Intercollegiate Studies Institute; 1st edition, 2006). See the useful analysis of Rieff by Rod Dreher, "Sex after Christianity," *The American Conservative*, last modified April 11, 2013, www.theamericanconservative.com/articles/sex-after-christianity.

41. Cited in Dreher, "Sex after Christianity."

42. *Gay Liberation Front: Manifesto*. See https://sourcebooks.fordham.edu/pwh/glf-london.asp. Printed by the Russell Press Ltd., 45 Gamble Street, Nottingham NG7 4ET and revised 1979 and reprinted by Gay Liberation Information Service, 5 Caledonian Road. London N1. Paul Buhle, "Marxism, the United States, and the Twentieth-century," *Monthly Review* (May, 2009), 61 optimistically states: "The realities of a collapsing ecosystem are as fearful as the threats of nuclear war in the first decade of *Monthly Review*'s existence. Still, there are lots of prospects in front of us and around the corner. Marxism, always unfinished, is going to be a big help in figuring out what they are and what to do about them."

43. MassResistance describes itself as: "A leading pro-family activist organization, MassResistance provides the information and guidance people need to confront assaults on the traditional family, school children, and the moral foundation of society. Based in Massachusetts, we have supporters and activists in all 50 states, Puerto Rico, and several foreign countries." https://www.massresistance.org/AboutUs.html.

44. "MassResistance-Texas Parents Present Shocking Facts on LGBT & Sex-Ed Agenda in Elementary Schools," *Mass Resistance*, last modified September 7, 2017. http://www.massresistance.org/docs/gen3/17c/MR-TX-Library-Meeting_081217/meeting.html.

45. See Andrew T. Walker and Albert Mohler, *God and the Transgender Debate* (Centralia, WA: The Good Book Company, 2017).

46. Rebecca Bromwich, "Consider Research when it Comes to Polyamory," *Law Times*, last modified September 18, 2017, https://www.lawtimesnews.com/archive/consider-research-when-it-comes-to-polyamory/262707.

47. Bromwich, "Consider Research."

48. Harry Pettit, "The Man with the Ph.D. in Threesomes," *Daily Mail*, last modified October 18, 2017, http://www.dailymail.co.uk/sciencetech/article-4992062/The-British-man-PhD-threesomes.html #ixzz4vs7vOmMb.

49. See Anjana Sreedhar, "74% of Millennials Support Gay Marriage," *PolicyMic*, last modified March 25, 2013, https://www.mic.com/articles/30916/74-of-millennials-support-gay-marriage.

50. Byron York, "An Evangelical Surrender in the Marriage Wars?" *Portland Press Herald*, last modified December 12, 2017, https://www.pressherald.

com/2014/04/02/an-evangelical-surrender-in-the-marriage-wars/.

51. Simon Lewis, "Same-Sex Marriage Ban Lifted in Vietnam But a Year Later Discrimination Remains," *Time*, last modified January 19, 2016.

52. "U.S. Public Becoming Less Religious," *Pew Research Center*, last modified November 3, 2015, http://www.pewresearch.org/fact-tank/2017/05/04/though-still-conservative-young-evangelicals-are-more-liberal-than-their-elders-on-some-issues/. See also http://www.pewforum.org/2015/11/03/u-s-public-becoming-less-religious.

53. Benoit Denizet-Lewis, "The Scientific Quest to Prove Bisexuality Exists," *The New York Times Magazine*, last modified March 20, 2014. http://www.nytimes.com/2014/03/23/magazine/the-scientific-quest-to-prove-bisexuality-exists.html.

54. Judith Butler, *Gender Trouble: Feminism and the Subversion of Identity* (New York: Routledge, 2006).

55. Denizet-Lewis, "The Scientific Quest."

56. Simone de Beauvoir, *Le Deuxième Sexe* (Gallimard, 1949, 2004).

57. Butler, *Gender Trouble*, 6.

58. Elwood Watson, "Pornography Addiction Among Men is On The Rise," *Huffington Post*, last modified December 9, 2014, https://www.huffingtonpost.com/elwood-d-watson/pornography-addiction-amo_b_5963460.html.

59. Jochen Peter and Patti Valkenberg, "Adolescents and Pornography: A Review of 20 Years of Research," *Annual Review of Sex Research*, special issue, 509–31, last modified March 20, 2016, https://www.tandfonline.com/doi/full/10.1080/00224499.2016.1143441.

60. Robert Weiss, "The Prevalence of Porn," *Sex and Intimacy in the Digital Age*, last modified March 28, 2018, https://blogs.psychcentral.com/sex/2013/05/the-prevalence-of-porn.

61. "Porn-Induced Erectile Dysfunction," *Your Brain on Porn*, last modified 2014, https://www.yourbrainonporn.com/videos/porn-induced-erectile-dysfunction-2014.

62. Von Baader says that man was originally an androgynous being. Neither man nor woman is the "image and likeness of God" but only the androgyne.

63. Jonathan Goldberg, *Reclaiming Sodom* (New York: Routledge, 1994), is a collection of essays by gay authors who refuse "to imagine a social movement founded on the 'stigma' of Sodom."

64. June Singer, *Androgyny: The Opposites Within* (New York: Nicholas Hays, 2000), 86.

65. Mary Eberstadt, *How the West Really Lost God: A New Theory of Secularization* (West Conshohocken, PA: Templeton Press, 2013), 172.

66. Eberstadt, *How the West Really Lost God*, 175.

67. Fox-Genovese, *Women and the Future of the Family*, 17.
68. Collier and Horowitz, *Destructive Generation*.
69. Phillips, *The World Turned Upside Down*, 290.
70. Kristin Luker, *When Sex Goes to School: Warring Views on Sex—and Sex Education—Since the Sixties* (New York: Norton, 2006), 7.

Chapter 3

1. Mohamad Omar, "Meanwhile In Canada, Peel Regional Officers Meditate In A Temple," *Huffington Post*, last modified April 13, 2016, http://www.huffingtonpost.ca/2016/04/13/peel-police-meditation_n_9684274.html.
2. For the demise of secular humanism and the rise of postsecularism, see Peter Jones, *The Other Worldview: Christianity's Greatest Threat* (Bellingham, WA: Kirkdale Press, 2015), which traces in detail both the cultural demise of biblical faith and atheistic rational humanism.
3. Paul Heelas and Linda Woodhead, *The Spiritual Revolution: Why Religion is Giving Way to Spirituality* (Oxford: Blackwell, 2005).
4. Jones, *The Other Worldview*, 162–70.
5. John Oswalt, *The Bible among the Myths: Unique Revelation or Just Ancient Literature?* (Grand Rapids: Zondervan, 2009), 47.
6. Douglas R. Groothuis, *Unmasking the New Age* (Downer's Grove, IL: InterVarsity Press, 1986), 15–16.
7. David Buchdahl, "American Realities: Anthropological Reflections from the Counterculture," PhD thesis, 1974, cited in McLaren, *Great Spiritual Migration*, 249.
8. Cited in John P. Dourley, *The Illness that We Are: A Jungian Critique of Christianity* (Toronto: Inner City Books, 1984), 158.
9. June Singer, *Androgyny: Toward a New Theory of Sexuality* (Norwell, MA: Anchor Press, 1977), 207.
10. Singer, *Androgyny*, 333.
11. "Drag Queens Read To Kids At Chula Vista Library Complete With Cops And Free Speech Zones," *GOPUSA*, last modified September 12, 2019, http://www.gopusa.com/drag-queens-read-to-kids-at-chula-vista-library-complete-with-cops-and-free-speech-zones.
12. Robert Knight, "Hubris on Marriage Laws not Limited to Unelected Judges," *The Washington Times*, last modified May 26, 2014, https://www.washingtontimes.com/news/2014/may/23.
13. Heelas and Woodhead, *Spiritual Revolution*.
14. Samuel P. Huntington, *Who Are We? The Challenges to America's National Identity* (New York: Simon & Schuster, 2004), xvii.
15. Huntington, *Who Are We?* 171.
16. Huntington, *Who Are We?* 171.

17. Among the many recent books documenting the success of this ideological revolution on the university campuses, see Heather Macdonald, *The Diversity Delusion: How Race and Gender Pandering Corrupt the University and Undermine our Culture* (New York: St Martin's Press, 2018), 2; and Scott Greer, *No Campus for White Men: The Transformation of Higher Education into Hateful Indoctrination* (WND Books, 2017), xi. MacDonald speaks of generalized "contempt for Enlightenment values and due process." Greer documents the view of the campus progressives, endorsed by weak administrations, namely that "the views of the majority must be stamped out."

18. Huntington, *Who Are We?* 175.

19. Colin Campbell, *The Easternization of the West: A Thematic Account of Cultural Change in the Modern Era* (London: Paradigm, 2007), 39–41.

20. Philip Goldberg, *American Veda: How Indian Spirituality Changed the West* (New York: Harmony Books, 2010).

21. Goldberg, *American Veda*, 5.

22. Goldberg, *American Veda*, 344.

23. Huntington, *Who Are We?* 109.

24. Even Plato's system is based on oneness. His divine being/creator is not outside and separate from him but something in which he participates in a chain of being. Since God is not triune, the divine is a singularity, finally dependent on a derivative chain of being. See A. H. Armstrong, *An Introduction to Ancient Philosophy* (Ottawa: Rowman and Allanheld, 1983), 49.

25. Madan Lal Goel, "Oneness in Hinduism," *Boloji*, last modified August 13, 2006, http://www.boloji.com/articles/1528/oneness-in-hinduism.

26. Christine Chandler, *Enthralled: The Guru Cult of Tibetan Buddhism* (CreateSpace Independent Publishing Platform, 2017).

27. Chandler, *Enthralled*, 36.

28. Chandler, *Enthralled*, 37.

29. Chandler, *Enthralled*, Preface.

30. Peter Jones, *The Gnostic Empire Strikes Back: An Old Heresy for the New Age* (Phillipsburg, NJ: P & R, 1992).

31. James Robinson, *The Nag Hammadi Library in English* (New York: Harper Row. 1977).

32. See Jones, *The Other Worldview*, 29–41.

33. Edward Conze, "Buddhism and Gnosis," in Ugo Bianchi's, *Origins of Gnosticism: Colloquium of Messina*, 13–18 (Leiden: Brill, 1967) and Stephan A. Hoeller, *Gnosticism: New Light on the Ancient Tradition of Inner Knowing* (Wheaton, IL: Quest Books, 2012).

34. Ron Charles, in a review of Elaine Pagels, *Why Religion?* observes that Pagels kept "studying the Gospels, the letters of Paul, the Gnostic texts and the insights of Buddhism." See Charles, "After her Son and Husband

Died, Elaine Pagels Wondered Why Religion Survives," *Washington Post*, last modified November 6, 2018, https://www.washingtonpost.com/entertainment/books/after-her-son-and-husband-died-elaine-pagels-wondered-why-religion-survives/2018/11/06/83e2fb24-e1da-11e8-8f5f-a55347f48762_story.html

35. Robinson, *The Nag Hammadi Library*, 1–3.

36. See Robert Reilly, "The New Gnosticism and the Homosexual Movement," *The Catholic World Report*, May 12, 2015. See also Robert P. George, "Gnostic Liberalism," *First Things*, last modified December, 2016. George states: "And all of this explains, of course, why contemporary liberal ethics endorses same-sex marriage. It even suggests that marriage can exist among three or more individuals in polyamorous sexual (or non-sexual) groups. Because marriage swings free of biology and is distinguished by its emotional intensity and quality—the true 'person' being the conscious and feeling self—same-sex and polyamorous 'marriages' are possible and valuable in the same basic ways as the conjugal union of man and woman." https://www.firstthings.com/article/2016/12/gnostic-liberalism.

37. Jones, *Stolen Identity*, 99–102.

38. One ancient Gnostic group, called the Naasenes (worshippers of Naas, "serpent" in Hebrew), believed that the serpent actually had homosexual sex with Adam. This is reported by Hippolytus, an anti-Gnostic church father in his book Haer. 5:26.22–3.

39. Cox, *Future of Faith*, 135.

40. Cox, *Future of Faith*, 184.

41. Cox, *Future of Faith*, 178.

42. Cox, *Future of Faith*, 87.

43. Cox, *Future of Faith*, 178.

44. See Peter Jones, "The Pauline Canon and Gnosticism," *Unio Cum Cristo* (April, 2016), 35–7.

45. Joachim Jeremias, *The Eucharistic Words of Jesus* (New York: Scribner, 1966), 100–2.

46. See the Amazon review section of Cox's book, *Future of Faith*.

47. Carl Teichrib, *Game of Gods: The Temple of Man in the Age of Re-enchantment* (Nashville: Thomas Nelson, 1982, repr. White Mudhouse, 2018), 147.

48. Richard Rohr, *The Enneagram: A Christian Perspective* (with Andreas Ebert, 1995), reissued by Crossroad, 2002).

49. Richard Rohr, *The Divine Dance: The Trinity and Your Transformation* (New Kensington, PA: Whitaker House, 2016), 111, see also Teichrib, *Game of Gods*, 164.

50. David Crumm, *ReadtheSpirit.com* (Mar, 2013).

51. Mike King, *Postsecularism: The Hidden Challenge to Extremism* (Cam-

bridge: James Clarke, 2009).

52. For other contemporary scholars who use the term "Postsecular" see James K. A. Smith, "Secularity, Globalization and the Re-enchantment of the World," *After Modernity? Secularity, Globalization and the Re-enchantment of the World* (Waco, TX: Baylor University Press, 2008), 10 et passim.

53. King, *Postsecularism*, 45, 47.

54. Ross Douthat, "The Return of Paganism," *New York Times*, last modified December 12, 2018, https://www.nytimes.com/2018/12/12/opinion/christianity-paganism-america.html. I highly recommend Ross Douthat's work.

55. Steven D. Smith, *Pagans and Christians in the City: Culture Wars from the Tiber to the Potomac* (Grand Rapids: Eerdmans, 2018).

56. See Jones, *The Other Worldview*, which contains a description of postsecularism.

57. Robert Knight, "Having a merry pagan Christmas," *Washington Times*, last modified December 16, 2018, https://www.washingtontimes.com/news/2018/dec/16/americas-culture-war-now-includes-paganism-an-old-/.

58. See my blog, "Anti-Gay? Get Out of the Way," *truthXchange*, last modified December 14, 2018. https://truthxchange.com/2018/12/anti-gay-get-out-of-the-way/.

59. Robert Sokolowski, *The God of Faith and Reason* (Washington, DC: Catholic University of America Press, 1982, 1995), x.

60. If this is true, how does one relate to Rabbinic Judaism and Islam? Both Judaism and Islam have a defective view of biblical Twoism and are biblical heresies. Both deny the Trinity and thus end up with an impersonal god, a singularity that must depend on human beings for personhood. Such dependence is a fundamental element of Oneism, in which God and the world are the same. Rabbinic scholar, Abraham Heschel (1907–1972), rightly critiques Islam for seeing God as "unqualified Omnipotence," who can never be "the Father of mankind," and thus is radically impersonal. See Abraham Heschel, *The Prophets* (New York: Harper, 1962), 292 and 311. The medieval Jewish rabbi, Maimonides, believed in an "absolutely transcendent God who is independent of humanity." See the contemporary Jewish scholar, Reuven Kimelman, "The Theology of Abraham Joshua Heschel," *First Things*, last modified December 2009, https://www.firstthings.com/article/2009/12/the-theology-of-abraham-joshua-heschel. Judaism and Islam share the same dilemma. Kimelman notes that Heschel commits the opposite error to that of Maimonides (and Islam) of making God dependent on man in a covenantal relationship that both need. Heschel adopts the rabbinical concept that it is human witness that makes God real. Once more, God is dependent upon humanity. This is the classic Jewish dilemma that is only resolved in the doctrine of the divine Trinity.

61. Sokolowski, *God of Faith and Reason*, xi, agrees: "The pagan religious and philosophical attitude is always with us and is not a point of view proper to a particular period of human development."

62. David Tacey, *The Spiritual Revolution: The Emergence of Contemporary Spirituality* (London and New York: Routledge, 2004), 11.

63. Tacey, *Spiritual Revolution*, 11.

64. Readers who know a little Greek will note that Paul uses the definite article, "the" before both "truth" (*hay alaythea*) and "lie" (*to pseudos*). English translators mysteriously leave out the definite article but other translations, as in French and German, include it. Also the parallelism is worth noting— "the Creation," "the Creator," "the Truth," and "the Lie.

Chapter 4

1. George Conger, "Derby Cathedral shows erotic films but bans evangelical preacher," *Anglican Ink*, last modified November 28, 2018, http://anglican.ink/2018/11/28/derby-cathedral-shows-erotic-films-but-bans-evangelical-preacher.

2. Ben Glaze, "Tory Cabinet Minister Piles Pressure on Religious Leaders to Let Gay Couples Marry in Church," *The Daily Mirror*, last modified July 23, 2017.

3. "Gay activist Says it's Time to Target Christians: Time to 'punish the wicked,'" *The Blaze*, last modified July 19, 2017, http://www.theblaze.com/news/2017/07/19/gay-activist-says-its-time-to-target-christians-time-to-punish-the-wicked.

4. Al Mohler, "God, the Gospel, and the Gay Challenge—A Response to Matthew Vines," *Albert Mohler*, last modified April 22, 2014, https://albertmohler.com/2014/04/22/god-the-gospel-and-the-gay-challenge-a-response-to-matthew-vines.

5. Mohler, "God, the Gospel, and the Gay Challenge."

6. Stoyan Zaimov, "Gay Marriage Support Among White Evangelicals Has Doubled, but 59 Percent Still Oppose: Pew," *The Christian Post*, last modified June 27, 2017, http://www.christianpost.com/news/gay-marriage-support-white-evangelicals-doubled-but-59-percent-still-oppose-pew-189762/. See also Jeff Diamant, "Though still Conservative, Young Evangelicals are More Liberal than their Elders on Some Issues," *Pew Research Center*, last modified May 4, 2017, https://www.pewresearch.org/fact-tank/2017/05/04/though-still-conservative-young-evangelicals-are-more-liberal-than-their-elders-on-some-issues/.

7. Al Mohler, "The Agonizing Ordeal of Eugene Peterson — You Might be Next," *Albert Mohler*, last modified July 19, 2017, https://albertmohler.com/2017/07/17/eugene-peterson.

8. Leslie Scanlon, "PC(USA) Releases 2018 Statistical Report," *The Presbyterian Outlook*, last modified April 24, 2019, https://pres-outlook.org/2019/04/pcusa-releases-2018-statistical-report.

9. "Episcopal Church Domestic Fast Facts," *The Episcopal Church*, last modified 2020, https://episcopalchurch.org/research/episcopal-church-domestic-fast-facts.

10. Maike Hickson, "Cardinal Schönborn Receives Public Honor for His Synod Role," *Free Republic*, last modified April 2, 2016, www.freerepublic.com/focus/f-religion/3417101/posts.

11. http://rorate-caeli.blogspot.com/2013/04/conservative-cardinal-once-again.html.

12. Pete Baklinski, "Sacrilegious: Pro-gay Group in Malta Archdiocese Uses Rainbow Flag as Altar Cloth," *LifeSite News*, last modified June 5, 2017, https://www.lifesitenews.com/news/sacrilegious-pro-gay-group-in-malta-archdiocese-uses-rainbow-flag-as-altar.

13. Dave Urbanksi, "Famed Catholic university reportedly approves 'Gender and Sexuality' dormitory," *The Blaze*, last modified January 8, 2018, http://www.theblaze.com/news/2018/01/08/famed-catholic-university-reportedly-approves-gender-and-sexuality-dormitory.

14. Pete Baklinski, "Cardinal Cupich: Amoris laetitia Is a Call for an 'Adult Spirituality' Where We 'Discern' What Is True," *LifeSite News*, last modified June 9, 2017, https://www.lifesitenews.com/news/cardinal-cupich-amoris-laetitia-is-a-call-for-an-adult-spirituality-where-w.

15. Christine de Marcellus Vollmer, "More proof that Francis' pontificate has been 'hijacked' by the 'Gay Lobby'." *Lifesite News*, last modified January 12, 2018, https://www.lifesitenews.com/opinion/more-proof-that-francis-pontificate-has-been-hijacked-by-the-gay-lobby.

16. "Church of England fears gay rights talks could end global Anglican communion," *The Guardian*, last modified January 8, 2016, http://www.theguardian.com/world/2016/jan/08/church-of-england-fears-talks-on-gay-rights-could-end-global-anglican-communion.

17. Laurie Goodstein, "Largest Presbyterian Denomination Gives Final Approval for Same-Sex Marriage," *New York Times*, last modified March 17, 2015, https://www.nytimes.com/2015/03/18/us/presbyterians-give-final-approval-for-same-sex-marriage.html.

18. Ruth Gledhill, "German Evangelical Church Votes for Same-sex Marriage," *Christian Today*, last modified January 18, 2016, https://www.christiantoday.com/article/german-evangelical-church-votes-for-same-sex-marriarge/76974.htm.

19. Caleb Parke, "Finnish Politician under 'Hate Crime Investigation' for Sharing Bible Verse on Facebook," *Fox News*, last modified September 5, 2019, https://www.foxnews.com/world/bible-verse-lgbt-hate-crime-inves-

tigation.

20. Joshua Scheer, "An Open Letter from Concordia University, Portland. Queer Straight Alliance now Chartered as Club on Campus," *Steadfast Lutherans*, last modified January 19, 2018, https://steadfastlutherans. org/2018/01/news-an-open-letter-from-concordia-university-portland-queer-straight-alliance-now-chartered-as-club-on-campus.

21. Trevin Wax, "The Fault Lines Before the Evangelical Earthquake," *The Gospel Coalition*, last modified April 2, 2014, https://www.thegospelco-alition.org/blogs/trevin-wax/the-fault-lines-before-the-evangelical-earth-quake/.

22. "Steve Chalke's Church to Offer Same-sex 'Marriages'," *Christian Concern*, last modified May 7, 2016, https://www.christianconcern.com/our-con-cerns/same-sex-marriage/steve-chalkes-church-to-offer-same-sex-marriages.

23. James Brownson, *Bible, Gender, and Sexuality: Reframing the Church's Debate on Same-sex Relationships* (Grand Rapids: Eerdmans, 2013).

24. Ken Wilson, *A Letter to My Congregation* (ReadtheSpirit, 2014).

25. Matthew Vines, *God and the Gay Christian: The Biblical Case in Support of Same-sex Relationships* (New York: Convergent, 2014).

26. Wendy VanderWal-Gritter, *Generous Spaciousness: Responding to Gay Christians in the Church* (Grand Rapids: Baker, 2014).

27. David Gushee, *Changing Our Mind* (Canton, MI: David Crumm Media, 2014).

28. Eugene F. Rogers Jr, *Sexuality and the Christian Body: Their Way into the Triune God,* 1st ed. (Hoboken, NJ: Wiley Blackwell, 1999).

29. David Crumm, "Like Mister Rogers before her, Amy Julia Becker is Opening Doors Through Our Neighborhood's 'White Picket Fences,'" *ReadtheSpirit*, last modified December 2, 2018, https://www.readthespirit. com/explore/like-mister-rogers-before-her-amy-julia-becker-is-in-a-spirit-ual-quest-to-open-doors-through-our-neighborhoods-white-picket-fences. For Amy Julia's decision, see Amy Julia Becker, "Why I am Ditching the Label 'Evangelical' in the Trump Era," *Washington Post*, last modified October 18, 2017, https://www.washingtonpost.com/news/acts-of-faith/wp/2017/10/18/why-i-am-ditching-the-label-evangelical-in-the-trump-era/?noredirect=on.

30. Read more at Robert A.J. Gagnon, "What I Knew About Julie Rodgers Before She Resigned From Wheaton," *The Christian Post*, last modified July 22, 2015, http://www.christianpost.com/news/what-i-knew-about-ju-lie-rodgers-before-she-resigned-from-wheaton-1-2-141758/.

31. Julie Rodgers, "An Update on the Gay Debate: Evolving Ideas, Untidy Stories, and Hopes for the Church," *Huffington Post*, last modified July 23, 2016.

32. Michael Haverluck, "Christian College: Faculty Senate Resigns To

Support LGBT Professor", *GOPUSA*, last modified April 22, 2017, http://www.gopusa.com/christian-college-faculty-senate-resigns-to-support-lgbt-professor.

33. "Historic Baptist Church Hires Same-Sex Couple to Lead Congregation in DC," *Fox News*, last modified January 12, 2017, http://www.foxnews.com/us/2017/01/12/historic-baptist-church-hires-same-sex-couple-to-lead-congregation-in-dc.html.

34. David Crumm, "Maggie Rowe, Sin Bravely and Hollywood's New Compassion for Evangelicals," *ReadtheSpirit*, last modified April 17, 2017, http://www.readthespirit.com/explore/maggie-rowe-sin-bravely-and-hollywoods-new-compassion-for-evangelicals.

35. Trevin Wax, "Fault lines."

Chapter 5

1. Diana Butler Bass, *Christianity After Religion: The End of Church and the Birth of a New Spiritual Awakening* (New York: Harper One, 2013).

2. Bass, *Christianity After Religion*, 186.

3. Bass, *Christianity After Religion*, 186.

4. The original leader of the Emergent Movement, Brian McLaren, writes a glowing preface to David Schmelzer's book *Blue Ocean Faith* (Canton, MI: Front Edge Publishing, 2017), xiii-xv, describing it as a "new Jesus movement," and Schmelzer cites a number of "emergent" writers like Phyllis Tickle (*Blue Ocean Faith*, 102).

5. David Gushee, the once evangelical ethicist, has left evangelicalism over the gay issue, endorsing this new movement because of "its complete commitment to inclusion." See David Crumm, "'Changing Our Mind' and Finding the Courage to Stand with Vulnerable Minorities," *ReadtheSpirit*, last modified June 4, 2017, http://www.readthespirit.com/explore/changing-our-mind-and-finding-the-courage-to-stand-with-vulnerable-minorities.

6. Schmelzer, *Blue Ocean Faith*, 89, n. 77.

7. Schmelzer, *Blue Ocean Faith*, xxvi.

8. Schmelzer, *Blue Ocean Faith*, 17.

9. Schmelzer, *Blue Ocean Faith*, 13.

10. Schmelzer, *Blue Ocean Faith*, 94.

11. Schmelzer, *Blue Ocean Faith*, 101.

12. Schmelzer, *Blue Ocean Faith*, 23.

13. Schmelzer, *Blue Ocean Faith*, 19.

14. Schmelzer, *Blue Ocean Faith*, 14.

15. Schmelzer, *Blue Ocean Faith*, 43.

16. "Spiritual Direction," a common term in many churches, usually, though

not always, indicates a move away from biblically oriented training toward a more subjective spirituality. See Ken Wilson, *A Letter to My Congregation*, 26.

17. This is the saint who inspired Ignatius of Loyola, who in turn inspired Ken Wilson.

18. Cited in Richard Bennett, "Pope Francis the Fox," *Berean Beacon*, last modified May 30, 2017, https://bereanbeacon.org/pope-francis-the-fox/.

19. Schmelzer, *Blue Ocean Faith*, 93.

20. "Retired Soccer Star Abby Wambach Marries Christian Mommy Blogger, Nine Months after Divorcing from Her Husband," *Daily Mail*, last modified May 16, 2017, http://www.dailymail.co.uk/news/article-4508724/Retired-soccer-star-Abby-Wambach-marries-Christian-blogger.html#ixzz4hBrHxR4F.

21. Wilson, *Letter to My Congregation*, viii.

22. Schmelzer, *Blue Ocean Faith*, 93.

23. Wilson, *Letter to My Congregation*, 26.

24. Ken Wilson, "Response to Tim Keller's review of A Letter to My Congregation and God and the Gay Christian," *Third Way Newsletter*. See also Tim Keller, "The Bible and Same-sex Relationships: A Review Article," *Redeemer Report* (June, 2015).

25. When evaluating spiritual criteria for decisions about the legitimacy of homosexuality, it is important to understand exactly what constitutes that spirituality, especially that of one's "spiritual director." I was an observer at the Chicago Parliament of the World's Religions in 1993, which was a centenary celebration of the same event in 1893, when Hinduism was introduced to America. I watched Donald Postema, a Christian Reformed minister, lead thousands of representatives of all the world's religions in a kind of worship service. I later learned that Postema, for nearly a quarter century, was involved in the Snowmass InterSpiritual Dialogue founded by Fr. Thomas Keating, which practices interspirituality with world's religions. Keating, a Trappist monk, teaches Centering Prayer and was both past president of the Temple of Understanding, an interfaith organization with consultative status at the United Nations, and also president of the Monastic Interreligious Dialogue. Postema also studied spirituality for a semester with Dutch Roman Catholic priest Henri Nouwen at Yale. For some of this information see *Calvin College FORUM* (Spring 2014). Postema also attended the follow-up POWR in South Africa in 1966.

26. From the 1960s on, Roman Catholic interfaith mystics like Thomas Merton, Thomas Keating, William Menninger, Basil Pennington, and Henri Nouwen, as well as that of Protestants like Richard Foster, Robert Webber, Dallas Willard, Brian McLaren, Tony Jones, Phyllis Tickle, Richard Rohr, Ruth Haley Barton, and others, have been promoting the mystical path of

spiritual discernment.

27. Emily Swan and Ken Wilson, *Solus Jesus: A Theology of Resistance* (Canton, MI: Read the Spirit Books, 2018). In this book, Wilson adopts a thoroughly anti-Protestant, anti-evangelical theology; his co-author is a self-declared lesbian.

28. Ruth Haley Barton, with the help of Intervarsity Press, has sought to extend this thinking in the evangelical world. According to Barton, "Discernment is first of all a habit, a way of seeing that eventually permeates our whole life. It is the journey from spiritual blindness (not seeing God anywhere or seeing him only when we expect to see him) to spiritual sight (finding God everywhere, especially where we least expect it). Ignatius of Loyola, founder of the Jesuits and best known for developing a set of spiritual exercises intended to hone people's capacity for this discipline, defined the aim of discernment as "finding God *in all things* in order that we might love and serve God in all." Ruth Haley Barton, *Sacred Rhythms: Arranging Our Lives for Spiritual Transformation* (Downers Grove: InterVarsity, 2006), 111 (emphasis hers). I am indebted to Pamela Frost, a researcher with *truthXchange*, for this reference.

29. I recommend the excellent lecture by Pamela Frost, (13 Oct, 2018), "One Solution," presented at the 2018 *truthXchange* symposium in Escondido, CA. The DVD and/or audio are available at www.truthXchange.com. For clarity's sake, I would encourage Christian schools, churches and institutions to avoid the terms "Spiritual Formation," "Spiritual Guidance," or "Spiritual Direction" for their classes on Christian growth. Another good overview is found on the "Got Questions?" website: "What is the Spiritual Formation Movement?" *GotQuestions*, last modified 2020, https://www.gotquestions.org/spiritual-formation.html.

30. Wilson, *Letter to My Congregation*, 178.

31. Wilson, *Letter to My Congregation*, 179. See Gary Gilley, "The Dangers of Spiritual Formation (Part V – Spiritual Exercises of St Ignatius)," The Narrow Path (20 Apr, 2014), for a warning of the dangers of Ignatian spirituality. As for gradations of sin, see J. I. Packer, "All Sins Are Not Equal," *Christianity Today* (2005) and Robert A. J. Gagnon, "Is Homosexual Practice No Worse than Any Other Sin?" *Aquila Report* (Feb, 2018).

32. See chapter 4. Pastor Fred Harrell of City Church states: "In May of 2014 the Board asked me for a book that was clearly grounded in Scripture that we might study on pastoring our brothers and sisters in Christ who are part of the LGBT community. We read Ken Wilson's *A Letter to My Congregation*."

33. Wilson, *Letter to My Congregation*, 60. David Gushee sees Wilson's book as an example of "how the fully authoritative and inspired bible ought to be taken to mean in the life of the church today," which is, in Wilson's case,

ambiguously! (Wilson, *Letter to My Congregation*, viii).

34. Wilson, *Letter to My Congregation*, 7, 15.
35. Wilson, *Letter to My Congregation*, 186.
36. Wilson, *Letter to My Congregation*, 48.
37. Wilson, *Letter to My Congregation*, 28, 40.
38. Wilson, *Letter to My Congregation*, 48.
39. Wilson, *Letter to My Congregation*, 43.
40. Ken Wilson, "An Appeal to Evangelical Pastors Conflicted by the Gay Controversy," *Huffington Post*, last modified August 6, 2014, https://www.huffpost.com/entry/appeal-to-evangelical-pastors_b_5440341.
41. Wilson, *Letter to My Congregation*, 17.
42. Ken Wilson, "Starve the Gay Controversy," *Huffington Post*, last modified July 15, 2014, https://www.huffpost.com/entry/starve-the-gay-contro-vers_b_5325074.
43. Wilson, *Letter to My Congregation*, 122. As for "gay weddings," Wilson says: "Let pastors do what I have done for years when considering the request of divorced persons to remarry—understand their situation, wrestle with Scripture, pray about it, and trust the Spirit of the risen Jesus to lead. If your pastor decides to honour any couple's request to place Jesus at the center of their commitment to each other, let it be on his or her head, not yours."
44. Wilson, *Letter to My Congregation*, 19.
45. Wilson, *Letter to My Congregation*, 182.
46. "Scottish Bishop Defends Same-Sex Marriage: 'Love Means Love'," *The Guardian*, last modified October 3, 2017, https://www.theguardian.com/world/2017/oct/03/scottish-bishop-defends-same-sex-marriage-love-means-love.
47. "Unfundamentalist Christians," *Patheos*, last modified October 9, 2017, http://www.patheos.com/blogs/unfundamentalistchristians.
48. Gayla R. Postma, "Wolterstorff: Biblical Justice and Same-Sex Marriage," *The Banner*, last modified October 24, 2016, https://www.thebanner.org/news/2016/10/wolterstorff-biblical-justice-and-same-sex-marriage.
49. Chelsen Vicari, "Jen Hatmaker, Blurry Lines, and Transformative Truth," *Juicy Ecumenism*, last modified April 26, 2016, https://juicyecumenism.com/2016/04/26/35974.
50. Sarah Stites, "Famed Christian Mommy Blogger Throws Faith to the Wind to Marry Lesbian Partner," *Charisma News*, last modified May 18, 2017, http://www.charismanews.com/us/64992-famed-christian-mommy-blogger-throws-faith-to-the-wind-to-marry-lesbian-partner.
51. Fred Harrell, "A Letter from the Elder Board – March 13, 2015," *Grace Church SC*, https://gracechurchsc.org/wp-content/uploads/2016/11/A-Letter-from-the-Elder-Board-City-Church-SFO.pdf

52. Brian McLaren in his foreword to David P. Gushee, *Changing Our Mind* (ReadtheSpirit, 2014), xvi.

53. In addition to Denny Burk's article, see Os Guinness, *Impossible People: Christian Courage and the Struggle for the Soul of Civilization* (Downers Grove: InterVarsity Press, 2016). Guinness remarks: "Christian advocates of homosexual and lesbian revisionism believe in themselves and in the sexual revolution rather than the gospel. They therefore twist the Scriptures to make reality fit their desires rather than making their desires fit the truths of the Scriptures.".

54. Dan Winiarski, "Turning the CRC into an LQBTQ+ Ally," *Network*, last modified November 13, 2018, https://network.crcna.org/crcna-and-synod/turning-crc-lgbtq-ally.

55. Angie Chui, "Rob Bell Says Church will Become Increasingly Irrelevant if it Holds to Words of the Bible on Marriage," *Christian Today*, last modified February 19, 2015, https://www.christiantoday.com/article/rob-bell-says-church-will-become-increasingly-irrelevant-if-it-holds-to-words-of-the-bible-on-marriage/48377.htm.

56. David Wells, *No Place for Truth: Or Whatever Happened to Evangelical Theology?* (Grand Rapids: Eerdmans, 1994), 128.

Chapter 6

1. Heather Clark, "Tim Keller Staff Member Says Homosexuality Isn't Sin, Part of 'Church Plant' Behind Transgender Restroom Plan," *Christian News*, last modified May 16, 2016, https://christiannews.net/2016/05/16/tim-keller-staff-member-says-homosexuality-isnt-sin-part-church-plant-be-hind-transgender-restroom-plan/.

2. Joe Dallas, *The Gay Gospel: How Pro-Gay Advocates Misread the Bible* (Eugene, OR: Harvest House, 1997, 2007), 97.

3. John Barber, "The Gay Christian: The Unicorn in Our Midst," *BarbWire*, last modified June 9, 2017.

4. "Why is the Episcopal Church Near Collapse?," *BeliefNet*, last modified 2020, http://www.beliefnet.com/faiths/home-page-news-and-views/why-is-the-episcopal-church-near-collapse.aspx?

5. Jeffrey Walton, "Episcopal Church Still Skidding Downhill," *Juicy Ecumenism*, last modified September 21, 2017, https://juicyecumenism.com/2017/09/21/episcopal-membership. See also "Data from 2016 Parochial Reports now available," *Episcopal Church*, last modified September 21, 2017, https://episcopalchurch.org/posts/publicaffairs/data-2016-parochial-reports-now-available.

6. The following comments can be found in a different format in my blog, "Defining Orthodoxy in Our Modern World," *truthXchange*, last modified

September 7, 2017, https://truthxchange.com/2017/09/defining-ortho-doxy-modern-world/.

7. Jim Wallis, "Jim Wallis: Nashville Statement Damaging to People and to the Evangelical Witness," *Sojourners*, last modified August 30, 2017, https://sojo.net/articles/jim-wallis-nashville-statement-damaging-peo-ple-and-evangelical-witness.

8. Nadia Bolz-Weber, "The Denver Statement," *Patheos*, last modified August, 30, 2017, https://www.patheos.com/blogs/nadiabolzweber/2017/08/the-denver-statement.

9. "A Liturgists Statement," *The Liturgists*, last modified August 29, 2017, https://theliturgists.com/statement.

10. See http://www.christiansunitedstatement.org. As of press time this web-site has been taken down.

11. John Pavlovitz, "The Nashville Statement (A Plain Language Translation), *John Pavlovitz*, last modified August 30, 2017. https://johnpavlovitz.com/2017/08/30/nashville-statement-plain-language-translation.

12. These are the words of Wheaton College Professor of Psychology, Michael Mangis.

13. Deborah Jian Lee, *Rescuing Jesus: How People of Colour, Women, and Queer Christians Are Reclaiming Evangelicalism* (Boston: Beacon Press, 2015).

14. Kathleen Dupré, "Rescuing Jesus: How People of Color, Wom-en, and Queer Christians Are Reclaiming Evangelicalism." *Library Journal* 140 (17): 91. http://search.ebscohost.com/login.aspx?di-rect=true&site=eds-live&db=lfh&AN=110530418&custid=s6224580.

15. Carey Lodge, "Meet Allyson Robinson, the First Openly Transgender Bap-tist minister," *Christian Today*, last modified January 5, 2016, https://www.christiantoday.com/article/meet.allyson.robinson.the.first.openly.transgen-der.baptist.minister/75672.htm?internal_source=ct_related_news.

16. Frank Bruni, "Bigotry, the Bible and the Lessons of Indiana," *New York Times,* last modified April 3, 2015, https://www.nytimes.com/2015/04/05/opinion/sunday/frank-bruni-same-sex-sinners.html. Op-ed writer Frank Bruni, onetime Times restaurant critic and a gay activist, has written that Christians who hold on to "ossified," biblically based beliefs regarding sexual morality have no place at America's table and are deserving of no particular regard. In one fell swoop, Bruni trashes all believing Christians as "bigots," saying that Christians' negative moral assessment of homosexual relations is "a choice" that "prioritizes scattered passages of ancient texts over all that has been learned since—as if time had stood still, as if the advances of science and knowledge meant noth-ing."

17. S. Donald Fortson and Rollin G. Grams, *Unchanging Witness: The Consistent Christian Teaching on Homosexuality in Scripture and Tradition*

(Nashville: B&H Academic, 2016), 10, 348.

18. McLaren, *Great Spiritual Migration*, 92

19. McLaren, *Great Spiritual Migration*, 46.

20. McLaren, *Great Spiritual Migration*, 93.

21. McLaren, *Great Spiritual Migration*, 103.

22. McLaren, *Great Spiritual Migration*, 222.

23. Colby Martin, *UNclobber: Rethinking Our Misuse of the Bible on Homosexuality* (Westminster John Knox Press, 2016), 142–3.

24. Peijean T., "Untitled Review of Sojourn Grace Collective," *Yelp*, last modified July 17, 2014, https://www.yelp.com/biz/sojourn-grace-collective-san-diego?hrid=03Gasnftw5ZWIKk-tbOKBA&rh_type=phrase&rh_ident=sermon.

25. Martin, *UNclobber*, 178.

26. "Rob Bell, The Pastor Who Questioned Hell, Is Now Surfing, Working With Oprah And Loving Life In L.A.," *Huffington Post*, last modified December 2, 2014, http://www.huffingtonpost.com/2014/12/02/rob-bell-oprah_n_6256454.html.

27. Quoted by Kurt Rudolf, *Gnosis: the Nature and History of an Ancient Religion* (Edinburgh: T&T Clark, 1983), 14.

28. Hippolytus, *Refutation of All Heresies*, 5:9:10.

29. Joe Boot, "Goodbye to the Anglican Church of Canada," *Ezra Institute*, last modified July 13, 2016, http://www.ezrainstitue.ca/resource-library/blog-entries/goodbye-to-the-anglican-church-of-canada.

30. J. Gresham Machen, *Christianity and Liberalism* (Grand Rapids: Eerdmans, 1923), 62.

31. Fortson and Grams, *Unchanging Witness*, 143.

32. Matthew Schmitz, "Liberal Catholicism's Unexpected Crisis," *Catholic Herald*, last modified July 16, 2016, https://catholicherald.co.uk/liberal-catholicisms-unexpected-crisis/.

33. Michael Brown, *Can You Be Gay and Christian? Responding with Love and Truth* (Lake Mary, FL: Frontline, 2014), 193–5.

34. Brown, *Can You Be Gay and Christian?* 196.

35. Brown, *Can You Be Gay and Christian?* 193.

36. Brown, *Can You Be Gay and Christian?* 193.

37. Brown, *Can You Be Gay and Christian?* 197.

38. Don Kistler (ed.), *Sola Scriptura: The Protestant Position on the Bible* (Morgan, PA: Soli Deo Gloria Publications, 1995). See 2 Samuel 23:2–3; Isaiah 59:21; Jeremiah 1:9; Matthew 22:42–43; Mark 12:36; Acts 4:24–25, 28:25.

39. Mark 7:3–13; Galatians 1:13–14; Colossians 2:8, 20–23; 1 Peter 1:18.

40. Deuteronomy 13:1–3; Matthew 7:21–23, 24:24; Luke 16:27–31; 2 Thessalonians 2:9–10.

41. Deuteronomy 13:1–3; 18:20–22; Matthew 7:21–23; Galatians 1:8–9; 2:11–21.

42. Galatians 1:8.

43. Isaiah 8:19–20; 29:13–14; Jeremiah 8:5–9; 17:5; Matthew 22:23–33; Mark 7:3–13; Acts 17:10–12; 2 Timothy 4:3–4; Titus 1:13–14.

44. Acts 24:14; Galatians 1:11–12; Ephesians 3:2–5; I Corinthians 14:36–37; 1 Thessalonians 2:13; 1 Timothy 1:8, 11.

45. Jeffrey Walton, "As Losses Mount, Presbyterian Official Declares: 'We are not Dying. We are Reforming,'" *Juicy Ecumenism*, last modified May 24, 2017, https://juicyecumenism.com/2017/05/24/pcusa.

46. Joseph Rossell, "Islamic Prayer Stirs Controversy at PCUSA General Assembly," *Juicy Ecumenism*, last modified July 2, 2016, https://juicyecumenism.com/2016/07/02/islamic-prayer-stirs-controversy-pcusa-general-assembly.

47. David Gushee and Glen Stassen, *Kingdom Ethics: Following Jesus in a Contemporary Context* (Wheaton, IL: InterVarsity Press, 2003).

48. Joseph Rossell, "Evangelical Break-Up: David Gushee Is 'Done Fighting,'" *Juicy Ecumenism*, last modified May 16, 2017, https://juicyecumenism.com/2017/05/16/evangelical-david-gushee-done-fighting.

49. "2016 Wilbur Awards Program Book," *Religion Communicators*, last modified 2016, https://religioncommunicators.org/wp-content/uploads/2020/03/wilburawardsprogram2016.pdf.

50. Gushee, *Changing Our Mind*, 41.

51. Gushee, *Changing Our Mind*, 5.

52. Gushee, *Changing Our Mind*, 33.

53. David Gushee, "Telling the Story of My Departure from American Evangelicalism," *Religion News Service*, last modified May 9, 2017, https://religionnews.com/2017/05/09/changing-our-mind-still-christian/.

54. Gushee, *Changing Our Mind*, 96.

55. Gushee, *Changing Our Mind*, 94.

56. Gushee, *Changing Our Mind*, 98.

57. Gushee, *Changing Our Mind*, 81.

58. Denny Burk, "What David Gushee's Change of Heart Really Means," *Denny Burk*, last modified October 24, 2014, http://www.dennyburk.com/what-david-gushees-change-of-heart-really-means-jonathanmerritt-rns.

59. David P. Gushee, "On LGBT equality, middle ground is disappearing," *Religion News Service*, last modified August 22, 2016, http://religionnews.com/2016/08/22/on-lgbt-equality-middle-ground-is-disappearing.

60. Joseph Rossell, "4 Top Responses to David Gushee Leaving Evangelicalism," *Juicy Ecumenism*, last modified May 17, 2017, https://juicyecumenism.com/2017/05/17/4-top-responses-david-gushee-leaving-evangel-

icalism.

61. David Crumm, "'Changing Our Mind.'"
62. Denny Burk, "David Gushee: Our 'Differences are Unbridgeable,'" *The Aquila Report*, last modified May 15, 2017, http://theaquilareport.com/david-gushee-differences-unbridgeable.
63. Gushee, "Telling the Story."
64. #EmptyThePews #NashvilleStatement (29 Aug, 2017).
65. See Matthew Vines's endorsement of Gushee's book, *Changing Our Mind*. Vines is the author of a much-cited book in "gay Christian" circles, *God and the Gay Christian: The Biblical Case in Support of Same-Sex Relationships* (Convergent Books, 2014).
66. David Gushee, *Still Christian*, endorsements.
67. Vines, *God and the Gay Christian*, 2.
68. The exact text that was available on Facebook is no longer available. However, this post from Anne Lamott, written by Mark Yaconelli, contains similar content: https://www.facebook.com/AnneLamott/posts/a-letter-to-annies-sunday-school-class-on-the-bible-and-homosexualityhey-annies-/870968636366114. Last modified November 30, 2019.
69. Jeffrey Walton, "Nude Female 'Christa' Back at Episcopal Cathedral," *Juicy Ecumenism*, last modified October 6, 2016, https://juicyecumenism.com/2016/10/06/christa.
70. Shane Rosenthal, "Abandoning Evangelicalism?," *White Horse Inn*, last modified March 1, 2012, https://www.whitehorseinn.org/article/abandoning-evangelicalism/.
71. David Crumm, "Watch Diana Butler Bass at the National Cathedral," *ReadtheSpirit*, last modified January 25, 2016, http://www.readthespirit.com/explore/video-of-diana-butler-bass-at-the-national-cathedral/#sthash.z9k5mM0j.dpuf.
72. I do not use the term "intersex" here to refer to those who have genetic anomalies, making them physically intersex, but only as a term to define the "anything goes" sexual confusion of the day.
73. Carl Teichrib, *Forcing Change*, Vol. 9, Issue 10 (Oct, 2015).
74. J. Michael Clark, *Defying the Darkness: Gay Theology in the Shadows* (Pilgrim Press, 1997), 10.
75. Robert A.J. Gagnon, "A Response to Julie Rodgers' Reasons for Changing Her Mind about Homosexuality (Part 2 of 2)," *Defending Marriage*, last modified July 23, 2015, https://defendingmarriage.com/feed/article/498.
76. Wolfhart Pannenberg. "Revelation and Homosexual Experience: What Wolfhart Pannenberg Says about this Debate in the Church," *Christianity Today* (11 Nov, 1996).
77. "Scottish Archbishop Predicts Greater Hostility to Faith in United States Catholic Culture," *Free Republic*, last modified August 8, 2017, http://

www.freerepublic.com/focus/f-religion/3575640/posts.

Chapter 7

1. Christian de la Huerta, *Coming Out Spiritually: The Next Step* (New York: Penguin Putnam, 1999).
2. De la Huerta, *Coming Out Spiritually*, 3.
3. De la Huerta, *Coming Out Spiritually*, 4.
4. Jones, *The Other Worldview*, 99– 100.
5. According to de La Huerta, *Coming Out Spiritually*, 8. Eleanor Roosevelt was an early lesbian social activist.
6. See Jean Houston, *The Passion of Isis and Osiris: A Gateway to Transcendent Love* (New York: Ballantine, 1995), 2.
7. Jean Houston, *Passion of Isis and Osiris*, 338.
8. Jones, *The Other Worldview*, 85–129.
9. Eugene Monick, *Phallos: Sacred Image of the Masculine* (Toronto: Inner City Books, 1987), 120.
10. Marilyn Sewell, "The Emergence of the Feminine," *Huffington Post*, last modified August 27, 2013, https://www.huffingtonpost.com/marilyn-sewell/the-emergence-of-the-femi_b_3820310.html.
11. Marilyn Sewell, "The Emergence of the Feminine."
12. J. Michael Clark, "Gay Spirituality," in *Spirituality and the Secular Quest*, ed. Peter H. Van Ness (New York: Crossroads/Herder, 1996), 335.
13. M. Stanton Evans, *The Theme Is Freedom: Religion, Politics, and the American Tradition* (Washington, DC: Regnery Publishing, 1994).
14. Evans, *The Theme is Freedom*, 128.
15. John Oswalt, *The Bible among the Myths: Unique Revelation or Just Ancient Literature?* (Grand Rapids: Zondervan, 2009), 28.
16. Oswalt, *The Bible among the Myths*, 56–7.
17. Wilson, *Letter to My Congregation*, 182.
18. Fortson and Grams, *Unchanging Witness*, 20.
19. Clark, *Defying the Darkness*, 53.
20. Clark, "Gay Spirituality," 337.
21. Clark, "Gay Spirituality," 338.
22. Clark, "Gay Spirituality," 342.
23. Walter L. Williams, *The Spirit and the Flesh: Sexual Diversity in American Indian Culture* (Boston: Beacon Press, 1986).
24. See Jones, "Androgyny: The Pagan Sexual Ideal," *Journal of the Evangelical Theological Society*, 43 (September, 2000). This article is posted by permission at www.truthxchange.com. See also my review of Jenell Williams Paris's book, *The End of Sexual Identity: Why Sex Is Too Important to Define Who We Are* (Downers Grove, IL: InterVarsity, 2011) at https://truthX-

change.com/ 2011/05/heterosexuality-is-an-abomination.

25. Martti Nissinen, *Homoeroticism in the Biblical World: A Historical Perspective* (Minneapolis: Fortress Press, 1998), 28. I am greatly indebted to Nissinen's work, which is supported by Helmer Ringgren, *Religions of the Ancient Near East* transl. John Sturdy (Philadelphia: Westminster Press, 1973), 25. Ringgren speaks of naked "eunuchs" associated with the cult to the Sumerian goddess Inanna (Ishtar), which includes a *hieros gamos* rite. The priests dressed and made themselves up as women, expressing their "otherness" *via* their androgyny. Physically, they were men, but their appearance was either feminine or it had both male and female characteristics.

26. Nissinen, *Homoeroticism*, 30.

27. Nissinen, *Homoeroticism*, 32.

28. Mircea Eliade, "Androgynes," vol. vi, *The Encyclopedia of Religion* (New York: Macmillan, 1987), 277: also Mircea Eliade, *The Quest: History and Meaning in Religion* (University of Chicago Press, 1969), 134.

29. Mircea Eliade, *Mephistopheles and the Androgyne: Studies in Religious Myth and Symbol*, translated by J. M. Cohen (New York: Sheed and Ward, 1965), 12.

30. See Williams, *The Spirit and the Flesh*, 3, where he discusses the South American situation. He sees the role of the *berdache* as the elimination of dichotomies for the acceptance of ambiguity.

31. Eliade, *Mephistopheles*, 122.

32. Eliade, "Androgynes," 277.

33. Eliade, "Androgynes," 277.

34. Eliade, *Myths, Dreams and Mysteries* (New York: Harper and Row, 1975) 174–5.

35. Eliade, "Androgynes," 277, and *Patterns of Comparative Religion* (New York: New American Library, 1974) 420–1.

36. Mircea Eliade, *Shamanism: Archaic Techniques of Ecstasy* (Princeton: Princeton University Press, 1972), 352.

37. Franciscan Father Richard Rohr, an authority on the use of Contemplative Spirituality for many evangelical groups like Willow Creek, organized a women's conference led by Marianne Williamson, whose book, *A Return to Love: Reflections on the Principles of "A Course in Miracles"* (New York: HarperOne, 1996), was proposed as conference reading. Helen Schucman's *A Course in Miracles* (New York: Foundation for Inner Peace, 1975), now in the public domain, was a wildly successful New Age course that denied sin and encouraged initiates not to cling to the old rugged cross. Rohr teaches evangelicals that our awakened heart discovers that we, God, and all things are one. We must learn, like the mystics and holy people have learned, that non-dualistic thinking that either/or thinking is not

good.

38. Goldberg, *American Veda*, 344.

39. In *The Other Worldview* (29–41, 87–9), I show how Singer was implementing the vision of the radical pagan, Carl Jung.

40. June Singer, *A Gnostic Book of Hours: Keys to Inner Wisdom* (Nicolas-Hays, 2003).

41. By androgyny (the joining of male and female), Singer means homosexuality, since a homosexual couple has to play both the male and female roles in sexual expression.

42. Singer, *Androgyny*, 237.

43. Singer, *Androgyny*, 207.

44. Singer, *Androgyny*, 333.

45. The more overt pronouncements about homosexuality appeared in lectures by Jungian followers, and contemporaries of Jung who applied his theories to issues of bisexuality and homosexuality. Beatrice Hinkle applies the theories in her article "Arbitrary Use of the Terms Masculine and Feminine," *Proceedings of the International Conference of Women Physicians*, vol. III, *The Health of the Child* (New York: The Woman's Press, 1920). Constance Long also uses them in her article, "Sex as a Basis of Character," *Collected Papers on the Psychology of Phantasy* (New York: Moffat, Yard and Company, 1921), which is a positive affirmation of homosexual love. Jung's followers, like June Singer and Toby Johnson, develop Jung's thinking to include the full justification of homosexuality.

46. Jones, *The Other Worldview*, 99.

47. King, *Postsecularism*, 105.

48. Jones, *The Other Worldview*, chapter 2.

49. Dalai Lama, *Beyond Religion: Ethics for a Whole World* (Boston, MA: Houghton Mifflin Harcourt, 2011). See also Dalai Lama, *The Universe in a Single Atom: The Convergence of Science and Spirituality* (New York: Morgan Road Books, 2005). According to Robert Sharf, scholar of Buddhist studies at UC Berkeley: "Thanks to the work of the Dalai Lama and others, Buddhism can seem far friendlier to modern, scientifically-minded sensibilities than the Abrahamic religions." This alignment with science is strengthened by the widespread adoption of Mindfulness techniques—often derived from Buddhist and other contemplative practices—in domains like medicine and psychology: Adam Frank, "Buddhism, Science and the Western World," *NPR*, last modified May 11, 2017, http://www.npr.org/sections/13.7/2017/05/11/527533776/buddhism-and-science.

50. Jones, *The Other Worldview*, 100. King, *Postsecularism*, 45, 47.

51. Richard Tarnas, *Passion of the Western Mind: Understanding the Ideas That Have Shaped Our World View* (New York: Ballantine Books, 1991), 403-.

52. Wayne Teasdale, *The Mystic Heart* (Novato, CA: New World Library,

1999), 4.

53. See Mohler, "God, the Gospel, and the Gay Challenge."

54. Tony Campolo, "Why Gay Christians Should be Fully Accepted into the Church," *Premier Christianity*, last modified October 26, 2016, https://www.premierchristianity.com/Blog/Tony-Campolo-Why-gay-Christians-should-be-fully-accepted-into-the-Church.

55. Alisa Childers, "Three Beliefs Some Progressive Christians and Atheists Share," *The Gospel Coalition*, last modified September 9, 2019, https://www.thegospelcoalition.org/article/3-beliefs-progressive-christians-atheists-share/

56. Childers, "Three Beliefs."

57. Michael Haverluck, "Democrat Jerrold Nadler: Religious Rights Must Bow To LGBT," *GOPUSA*, last modified April 5, 2019, https://www.gopusa.com/democrat-jerrold-nadler-religious-rights-must-bow-to-lgbt/.

58. Peter Jones, "Equality=Legal Persecution of Christians?," *truthXchange*, last modified June 19, 2019, https://truthxchange.com/2019/06/equality-legal-persecution-of-christians.

Chapter 8

1. McLaren, *Great Spiritual Migration*, 56–7.

2. McLaren, *Great Spiritual Migration*, 92.

3. McLaren, *Great Spiritual Migration*, 103.

4. Matthew 4:8–10. Paul also has something to say about worship and service in Romans 1:25.

5. Anne Kennedy, "It Is About Love: A Commentary on the Anglican Condition," *Patheos*, last modified April 26, 2017, http://www.patheos.com/blogs/preventingrace/2017/04/26/love-commentary-anglican-condition.

6. Robert Sokolowski, *The God of Faith and Reason* (Washington, DC: The Catholic University of America Press, 1995), x.

7. See Jones, *One or Two*.

8. John Calvin, *Institutes* vol 1 Bk ll, chapter Xll, 4060.

9. This creed was probably written between the 5th and 7th centuries, after Athanasius's death. See R.C. Sproul's history of the Athanasian Creed: R.C. Sproul, "The Athanasian Creed," *Ligonier*, last modified August 1, 2007, https://www.ligonier.org/learn/articles/athanasian-creed.

10. From John Shelby Spong's book, *Escaping from Fundamentalism*, cited in "The War Comes Home: More Spontaneous Eruptions," Religion, *Time* (February 18, 1991), 62.

11. Michael Reeves, *Delighting in the Trinity: An Introduction to the Christian Faith* (Downers Grove: InterVarsity Press, 2012), 23.

12. Genesis 1:31. For a longer development of the creational process of separa-

tion and its holy character, see Jones, *The God of Sex*, 127–30.

13. On this, see the important work of Henri Blocher, *In the Beginning: The Opening Chapters of Genesis* (Downers Grove: IVP Books, 1984), 93.

14. James B. DeYoung, *Homosexuality: Contemporary Claims Examined in Light of the Bible and Other Ancient Literature and Law* (Grand Rapids: Kregel Publications, 2000), 31.

15. Reeves, *Delighting*, 59.

16. Blocher, *In the Beginning*, 92–3, shows that Genesis excludes the myth of the primitive androgyne, found in particular in Plato. He states that "the biblical text moves to the plural in order to leave no doubt: 'he created them.' The duality of the sexes implies the plurality of the persons."

17. See Reeves, *Delighting*, 37.

18. Raymond Brown, *The Semitic Background of the Term "Mystery" in the New Testament* (Philadelphia: Fortress Press, 1968), 65.

19. Cited in Michael Reeves, *Rejoicing in Christ* (Downers Grove: IVP Academic, 2015), 60.

20. Robert Gagnon, "Truncated Love: A Response to Andrew Marin's Love Is an Orientation, Part 1," cited in Michael Brown, *A Queer Thing Happened to America: And What a Long, Strange Trip It's Been* (Concord, NC: Equal Time Books, 2011), 342.

21. Doug Mainwaring, "Same-Sex Marriage vs. the Real Thing: A Gay Man's View of the Big Picture," *The Witherspoon Institute*, last modified September 19, 2016, https://www.thepublicdiscourse.com/2016/09/17513/. [Chapter 9 begins]

22. Even in the typical Christian manner of referring to God as "our Father," we must assume the normativity in created reality of the heterosexual origin of paternal love. The author of Hebrews uses earthly fatherhood to teach us about the nature of God's fatherhood (Heb. 12:9). Only in heterosexual relationships do childbirth, sonship and fatherhood have any meaning. It is true that in adoption and, beyond that—in "two father" male households—there is a notion of fatherhood, but both men depend on the creational norm of biological paternity.

23. Cornelius Van Til, *The Defense of the Faith*, 4th Ed. (Phillipsburg, NJ: P & R, 2008), 70–1.

Chapter 9

1. David Gushee in an interview with David Crumm, "'Changing Our Mind.'"

2. Gushee, "'Changing our Mind.'"

3. See also Linda Harvey, "Is 'LGBTQ' coalition balkanizing?" *WND*, last modified June 6, 2017, https://www.wnd.com/2017/06/is-lgbtq-coali-

tion-balkanizing/#D3ViXzG2YHAgP5ya.99.

4. Jake Meador, "On David Gushee's Dishonesty," *Mere Orthodoxy*, last modified August 24, 2016, https://mereorthodoxy.com/persistent-dishonesty-progressive-evangelicals-religious-liberty-debates.

5. Bekah Mason, "Finding My 'True Self' as a Same-sex Attracted Woman," *Christianity Today*, last modified June 23, 2017, https://www.christianitytoday.com/women/2017/june/finding-my-true-self-as-same-sex-attracted-woman-obergefell.html.

6. Superoctave, "All One Body Lecture," YouTube video, 1:31:39, October 13, 2016, https://www.youtube.com/watch?v=NkFE0sSF0fU. See Wolterstorff's thoughtful works: *Until Justice and Peace Embrace* (Grand Rapids: Eerdmans, 1983. 2nd ed. 1994); *Faith and Rationality: Reason and Belief in God*, ed. with Alvin Plantinga (University of Notre Dame Press, 1984); "Suffering Love," in *Philosophy and the Christian Faith*, ed. Thomas V. Morris (University of Notre Dame Press, 1988); Justice: Rights and Wrongs (Princeton University Press, 2008).

7. Superoctave, "All One Body Lecture."

8. This is the testimony of Dr. Willie Parker in Time (24 Apr, 2017), 56.

9. *The Code of Hammurabi*, translated by L. W. King, 1915, 251. *Internet Sacred Text Archive*, https://sacred-texts.com/ane/ham/ham07.htm.

10. See also Romans 6:15; 7:12, 14, 22; and 8:4; all passages that show that believers must not live as if the law no longer matters.

Chapter 10

1. See also Deuteronomy 22:30: "A man shall not take his father's wife, so that he does not uncover his father's nakedness."

2. While affirming certain tenets of orthodoxy the Metropolitan Community churches are open to interfaith relations. "While we are a Christian church who follows Jesus, we respect those of other faith traditions and work together with them to free all those who are oppressed by hate, disregard and violence," http://www.mccla.org/about-us/our-mission-beliefs-values-vision.

3. Brown, *A Queer Thing Happened to America*, 343–4.

4. David Qaoud, "From Lesbianism to Follower of Christ: An Interview With Emily Thomes," *Gospel Relevance*, last modified July 4, 2016, http://gospelrelevance.com/2016/07/04/interview-emily-thomes.

Chapter 11

1. Deuteronomy 11:1, 13; 13:4; Joshua 22:15; Psalm 25:10. Love is attached to keeping the commandments.
2. 1 Kings 3:6; 2 Chronicles 6:42–7:1. See also Isaiah 55:3: "Incline your ear, and come to me; hear, that your soul may live; and I will make with you an everlasting covenant, my steadfast, sure love for David," and Psalm 33:4–22: "Let your steadfast love, O LORD, be upon us, even as we hope in you."
3. The term, *esplangchnisthay*, ἐσπλαγχνίσθη (Matt. 9:36) comes directly from the Greek word for "guts" or "intestines," something deeply felt.
4. John MacArthur, *Truth for Today: A Daily Touch of God's Grace* (Nashville: Thomas Nelson, 2006).
5. Mark 14:3–9, Matthew 26:6–13 and John 12:1–8 probably refer to the same incident. The Luke 7 passage may recount a separate occasion involving a different woman. See the *Reformation Study Bible* notes on Matthew 26:6–13.
6. Chelsen Vicari, "Jen Hatmaker."
7. Gushee, *Changing Our Mind*, 41.
8. Hebrews 13:1. See also 1 Thessalonians 4:9; 1 John 4:21; James 2:8; 1 Peter 3:8.

Chapter 12

1. Rosaria Champagne Butterfield, *Openness Unhindered: Further Thoughts of an Unlikely Convert* (Pittsburgh, PA: Crown and Covenant, 2015), 23–5.
2. "Born gay" has been scientifically shown as unfounded, even by the pro-homosexual community. It is also now destabilized by the phenomenon of transgender and gender fluidity, which argues that gender is eminently changeable.
3. Joseph Nicolisi, "Psych Association Loses Credibility, Say Insiders," *Joseph Nicolisi*, accessed July 14, 2020, https://www.josephnicolosi.com/collection/psych-association-loses-credibility-say-insiders.
4. Judith A. Reisman, *Kinsey: Crimes and Consequences: The Red Queen and the Grand Scheme* (Institute for Media Education, 1998).
5. "Sexual Orientation in the 2013 National Health Interview Survey: A Quality Assessment," *US Health and Human Services*, last modified December 2014, http://www.cdc.gov/nchs/data/series/sr_02/sr02_169.pdf.
6. Daryl Bem, "Exotic Becomes Erotic: A Developmental Theory of Sexual Orientation," *Psychological Review*, vol. 103, #2 (1996), 320–35.
7. "The American Psychiatric Association does not believe that same-sex orientation should or needs to be changed, and efforts to do so represent a significant risk of harm by subjecting individuals to forms of treatment

which have not been scientifically validated and by undermining self-esteem when sexual orientation fails to change. No credible evidence exists that any mental health intervention can reliably and safely change sexual orientation; nor, from a mental health perspective does sexual orientation need to be changed." See "APA Reiterates Strong Opposition to Conversion Therapy," *American Psychiatric Association*, last modified November 15, 2018, https://www.psychiatry.org/newsroom/news-releases/apa-reiterates-strong-opposition-to-conversion-therapy.

8. See the work of the Changed Movement, which shows scores of testimonies from those who are free of same-sex attraction or a homosexual lifestyle, https://changedmovement.com.

9. Rosaria Champagne Butterfield, *The Secret Thoughts of an Unlikely Convert: An English Professor's Journey into Christian Faith* (Pittsburgh, PA: Crown and Covenant, 2012), 1, 9.

10. Butterfield, *Secret Thoughts*, 23.

11. Joseph Nicolisi, "The Meaning of Same-Sex Attraction," *Joseph Nicolisi*, https://www.josephnicolosi.com/the-meaning-of-same-sex-attrac.

12. E. Marie Tomeo, et.al., "Comparative Data of Childhood and Adolescence Molestation in Heterosexual and Homosexual Persons," *Archives of Sexual Behaviour*, vol. 30, No.5 (2001).

13. Joseph Nicolisi, "Why I am Not a Neutral Therapist," *Joseph Nicolisi*, https://www.josephnicolosi.com/why-i-am-not-a-neutral.

14. Some Christian theologians reject Nicolosi's therapy because it is not "Christ-centered." However, we do not discontinue chemotherapy if the administering doctor is not a Christian or the valid marriage counseling of a secular counselor. Nicolosi's books were dropped by Amazon, as were those by Restored Hope Network Executive Director Anne Paulk and pastoral counselor Joe Dallas because they were in "violation of our content guidelines." See Brandon Showalter, "Christian Authors Blast Amazon for Banning their Books, Selling Pedophilia Titles," *Christian Post*, last modified August 30, 2019, https://www.christianpost.com/news/christian-authors-blast-amazon-banning-their-books-selling-pedophilia-titles.html.

15. Charles W. Socarides, MD, "Thought Reform and the Psychology of Homosexual Advocacy," *Orthodoxy Today* (1995).

16. "About Us," Facts About Youth, accessed July 2020, http://factsaboutyouth.com/aboutus.

17. MassResistance, *The Health Hazards of Homosexuality: What the Medical and Psychological Research Reveals* (Waltham, MA: Mass Resistance, 2017), 53.

18. See the major study by Dr. Laurence S. Meyer and Dr. Paul. R. McHugh, ex-professors at the Johns Hopkins Medical School, "Sexuality and Gender: Findings from the Biological, Psychological and Social Sciences," *New*

Atlantis (Fall, 2016).

19. MassResistance, *Health Hazards*, 19.

20. Sarah Morrison, "Drug Use Seven Times Higher Among Gays," *The Independent*, last modified September 23, 2012, https://www.independent.co.uk/life-style/health-and-families/health-news/drug-use-seven-times-higher-among-gays-8165971.html.

21. Luca Di Tolve, *I Was Gay Once: I Found Myself In Medjugorje*, 1st English Ed. (Alla Lella & Stefano Giorgi Ambrosetti Group, 2019).

22. Kathy Ehrich Dowd, "Fred Caruso, Producer of The Big Gay Musical, Dies in Apparent Suicide, Posts Emotional Note on Facebook: 'I Have Been Absolutely Miserable,'" *Yahoo News*, last modified June 15, 2016, https://www.yahoo.com/news/fred-caruso-producer-big-gay-223231937.html.

23. Quoted in John R. Diggs, Jr., MD. "The Health Risks of Gay Sex," *Corporate Research Council* (2002); see also MassResistance, *Health Hazards*, 95.

24. MassResistance, *Health Hazards*, 97.

25. Facts About Youth.

26. Andrew Sullivan, *Virtually Normal: An Argument about Homosexuality* (New York: Alfred A. Knopf, 1995), 202–3.

27. Joseph Nicolosi, "Overcoming Gay Pornography: Identifying the Three Underlying Needs," *Joseph Nicolisi*, https://www.josephnicolosi.com/collection/overcoming-gay-pornography-identifying-the-three-underlying-needs. Alas this same result occurs with heterosexual users.

28. Joseph Nicolosi, "An Open Secret: The Truth about Gay Male Couples," *Joseph Nicolisi*, https://josephnicolosi.com/an-open-secret-the-truth-about. The decision of the Supreme Court in the *Obergefell* ruling was a travesty of justice, in the opinion of conservative jurists. "The *Obergefell* ruling, written by then-Justice Anthony Kennedy, was entirely a political ruling. It was utterly devoid of any reasoned legal analysis, any application of the history and tradition of American jurisprudence, and any meaningful reliance on legal precedents. Instead, it was a ruling based on emotion and empathy, an imposition of legal force because it's what a slim majority of justices felt was the right public policy for the country, rather than a policy mandated by the United States Constitution. The dissents in the *Obergefell* ruling are powerful and telling, an extraordinary rebuke of the majority opinion. The late Justice Antonin Scalia referred to the majority's ruling as "a naked judicial claim to legislative… power; a claim fundamentally at odds with our system of government." Justice Clarence Thomas said the opinion "exalts judges at the expense of the People from whom they derive their authority." Justice Samuel Alito wrote that it is "beyond dispute that the right to same-sex marriage" does not exist in the Constitution and is not "deeply rooted in this Nation's history and tradition." And Chief

Justice John Roberts wrote "the Constitution leaves no doubt" that the majority's 'pretentious' opinion is wrong." Taken from "Our Tattered Constitution," *National Organization for Marriage* website (18 Sep, 2019).

29. This includes bestiality, pedophilia, and sadomasochism, see Mass Resistance, *Health Hazards*, 182, 185. On page 158, *Health Hazards* gives a complete list of diseases associated with anal intercourse: "Anal cancer, Chlamydia, trachomatis, Cryptosporidium, Giardia lamblia, Herpes, HIV, Human papilloma virus, Isospora belli, Microsporidia, Gonorrhea, Viral Hepatitis, Syphilis." Many of these diseases are virtually unknown in the heterosexual community. See also pages 215 and 249–75. We have also seen the rise of scores of physical illnesses uniquely associated with anal sex.

30. Mass Resistance, *Health Hazards*, 467.

31. Marshall Kirk and Hunter Madsen, *After the Ball: How America Will Conquer its Fear and Hatred of Gays in the 90s* (Penguin, 1990), 317.

32. See Peter Jones, "Transgender: Transition to Nowhere," *Unio cum Christo* vol 4:2 (Oct, 2018), 27–48.

33. He won the gold medal in the men's decathlon at the 1976 Summer Olympics in Montreal and became an instant celebrity, proclaimed to be "the world's greatest [male] athlete."

34. Walt Heyer, "The National Geographic Transgender Cover Champions Child Abuse and Junk Science," *The Federalist*, last modified January 3, 2017. See also Tim Geiger, "Transgenderism: The Reshaping of Reality," *Harvest USA*, last modified 2016.

Chapter 13

1. See chapter 4, where I discuss the methodology of authors who propose this new exegesis. Works by authors normalizing homosexuality for Christians include: James Brownson's *Bible, Gender, and Sexuality*, Ken Wilson's *A Letter to My Congregation*, Jeff Chu's *Does Jesus Really Love Me?*, David Gushee's *Changing Our Mind*, and Matthew Vines' *God and the Gay Christian*.

2. Bruni, "Bigotry, the Bible and the Lessons of Indiana."

3. Jen Hatmaker, "World Vision, Gay Marriage and a Different Way Through," *Church Leaders*, last modified March 26, 2014, https://churchleaders.com/pastors/pastor-articles/173806-world-vision-gay-marriage-and-a-different-way-through.html.

4. Robert Gagnon, *The Bible and Homosexual Practice: Texts and Hermeneutics* (Nashville: Abingdon, 2001).

5. One can get what Gagnon calls "a revised synthesis" of his monograph in his 52-page contribution in *Homosexuality and the Bible: Two Views* (Min-

neapolis: Fortress, 2003). Another valuable study is Richard Hays, *The Moral Vision of the New Testament* (HarperSanFranciso, 1996).

6. Gagnon, *The Bible and Homosexual Practice*, 37.

7. Fortson and Grams, *Unchanging Witness*, 111.

8. Hays, *Moral Vision of the New Testament*, 389.

9. Harrell, "A Letter from the Elder Board."

10. Jay Michaelson, *God vs. Gays?* (Boston: Beacon Press, 2011), 55. See also Colby Martin, UnClobber.

11. See Daniel I. Block, *The New American Commentary: An Exegetical and Theological Exposition of Holy Scripture: Judges, Ruth* (Nashville: Broadman Holman, 1999), 515ff. After showing that Judges 19:22–24 is in almost every expression and detail a parallel and a reminder of the account of the threatened homosexual gang rape in Genesis 19:4–8, Block says, "Contemporary feminist approaches tend to see in this account evidences for the fundamental injustice of patriarchy. But this is to miss the point. Instead of asking why heterosexual rape is preferable to homosexual rape (as if it is good in any sense at all), we should be asking 'What is it about homosexual rape that makes it worse than heterosexual rape?....The Scriptures are consistent in affirming only heterosexual marriage" (543–4).

12. The Bible mentions husbands 142 times, wives 505 times, heterosexual marriage or marrying 75 times, weddings 16 times, bridegrooms 27 times, and brides 26 times. In these 796 occurrences not once is homosexuality ever in mind. Homosexuality is clearly not presupposed in the 682 mentions of children.

13. See a previous interpretation of this text in Peter Jones, "The Dreadful Loneliness of Life without Scripture," *truthXchange*, last modified March 5, 2015, from which I have extracted much of the argumentation.

14. Kristen and Rob Bell (ex-pastor of Mars Hill Church in Michigan) have moved from their evangelical roots (having met as students at Wheaton College). On the show, Kristen commented to Oprah that she now begins each day not with Scripture but with the Deepak/Oprah guided meditation method. Bell states: "The church will continue to be even more irrelevant when it quotes letters from 2,000 years ago as their best defense." See Stevie St. John, "WATCH: Oprah Asks if Christian Support for Marriage Equality is 'Moments Away'," *Advocate*, last modified February 17, 2015.

15. OWN, "Oprah Goes Soul to Soul with Rob Bell | SuperSoul Sunday | Oprah Winfrey Network," *YouTube video*, 4:20, November 3, 2013, https://www.youtube.com/watch?v=e4vhjXQwrUc.

16. Vines, *God and the Gay Christian: The Biblical Case in Support of Same-Sex Relationships* (Convergent Books, 2014), 15, 17, 29.

17. James Brownson, *Bible, Gender, and Sexuality: Reframing the Church's Debate on Same-sex Relationships* (Grand Rapids: Eerdmans, 2013), 89.

Brownson is Professor of New Testament at Western Theological Seminary in Holland, Michigan and is an ordained minister in the Reformed Church in America.

18. Brownson, *Bible, Gender, and Sexuality*, 87.
19. Brownson, *Bible, Gender, and Sexuality*, 88.
20. Gerhard von Rad, *Genesis: The Old Testament library* (Westminster Press, 1956), 80.
21. Brownson, *Bible, Gender, and Sexuality*, 87.
22. Vines, *God and the Gay Christian*, 46.

Chapter 14

1. Vines, *God and the Gay Christian*, 96.
2. Butterfield, *The Secret Thoughts*, 17.
3. Vines, *God and the Gay Christian*, 113.
4. Citing De Tocqueville, Ross Douthat, *Bad Religion: How We Became a Nation of Heretics* (New York: Free Press, 2012), 222.
5. Herman Bavinck, *Our Reasonable Faith*, (Grand Rapids: Eerdmans, 1956), 56–7.
6. Colin E. Gunton, *The Triune Creator: A Historical and Systematic Study* (Grand Rapids: Eerdmans, 1998).
7. Jones, *The Other Worldview*.
8. A simple form of the verb "exchange" is employed in the first instance, since Paul is doubtless citing Psalm 106:20, but in the other two usages he adds a preposition for emphasis, which are the only occurrences of this form in the Bible.
9. This verb is a form of the other two, which are unique in Paul's letters.
10. The Jewish *Testament of Naphtali* from the second century BC states: "But you will not be so, my children, you have recognized in the vault of heaven, in the earth, and in the sea, and in all created things, the Lord who made them all [THE CREATOR], so that you should not become like Sodom which *changed* the order of its *nature*." *The Apocryphal Old Testament*, ed. H. Sparks, trans. M. DeJonge (New York: Clarendon, 1984).
11. See Fortson and Grams, *Unchanging Witness*, 341.
12. Paul describes the pagan world in Ephesians 4:17–19. "Now this I say and testify in the Lord, that you must no longer walk as the Gentiles do, in the futility of their minds. They are darkened in their understanding, alienated from the life of God because of the ignorance that is in them, due to their hardness of heart. They have become callous and have given themselves up to sensuality (ἀσελγεία—which doubtless includes homosexuality), greedy to practice every kind of impurity."
13. Gagnon, *The Bible and Homosexual Practice*, 289ff.

14. In Galatians 3:28, Paul uses three pairs or merisms to describe the entire human race—male or female, *ouk eni arsen kai thaylou* (οὐκ ἔνι ἄρσεν καὶ θῆλυ), Jew or Greek, slave or free. These are all-inclusive categories just as Paul uses the terms in Romans 1:26–27.

15. Three French translations (La TOB, La Bible en Français Courant, and the French Jerusalem Bible), Luther's German translation, and the New King James Version all have "the lie."

16. So Brownson, *Bible, Gender, and Sexuality*, 218 and Vines, *God and the Gay Christian*, 112, who do not like Paul's "outdated" patriarchal thinking. But this is not the issue.

17. Josephus, Ap. 2.199 (Loeb translation). He uses the same term terminology as Paul, who describes the unnatural as "against nature" (*para physin*).

18. Referenced in Rollin Grams as *Plato in Twelve Volumes*, trans. Harold N. Fowler, Loeb Classical Library 9; (Cambridge, MA: Harvard University Press; London, William Heinemann Ltd., 1925).

19. See Rollin Grams, "'Nature' and 'Against Nature' in Romans 1:26-27: A Study in the Primary Sources," *Bible and Mission*, last modified December 4, 2016, https://bibleandmission.blogspot.com/2016/12/nature-and-against-nature-in-romans-126.html. With an excellent knowledge of the ancient classical texts, Grams cites Aristotle's use of natural and unnatural in his discussion of the universe and physics. In his work, *On the Heavens*, Aristotle discusses the movement of bodies 'according to nature' (*kata physin*) and 'against nature' (*para physin*) using these terms 38 times.

20. Vines, *God and the Gay Christian*, 109. See also Brownson, *Bible, Gender, and Sexuality*, 204–22.

21. The use of "nature" and "natural" in this context fits with Paul's other uses of these terms, which always refer to what is constitutionally and naturally determined to be, not to changeable customs. In Romans 2:14, for example—just a few verses beyond 1:26–7—Paul speaks of "Gentiles, who do not have the law, [but] by *nature* do what the law requires." Gentiles, created in God's image—like all human beings—cannot avoid a sense of the moral order. These Gentiles are "*physically* [literally *by nature*] uncircumcised" (Rom. 2:27). Elsewhere, using the image of an olive tree, Paul states, regarding Israel, "For if God did not spare the *natural* branches [the Jews], neither will he spare you" [the Gentiles] (Rom. 11:21; Gal. 2:15; 4:8; Eph. 2:3). This use of the term "nature" as a creational given is more than proven for the term in Romans 1:26–7. The context, as we shall show at length in the last chapter, is the description and then the rejection of God the Creator—the refusal by pagans "to worship and serve *the Creator* who is blessed forever" (Rom. 1:25). This refusal to recognize God as Creator is strictly and immediately, in the next verse, tied to homosexual practice, as Romans 1:26 states so clearly: "For this reason."

22. Gushee, *Changing Our Minds*, 89.
23. Wilson, *Letter to My Congregation*, 69, admits that this is a problem.
24. Wilson, "Starve the Gay Controversy."
25. Vines, *God and the Gay Christian*, 103.
26. Walter Wink, "Biblical Perspectives on Homosexuality," *Reconciling Works*, https://reconcilingworks.org/images/stories/downloads/resources/003_Homosexuality_and_the_Bible-Wink.pdf. Originally published in Christian Century, November 7, 1979, p. 1082. Wink is professor at Auburn Theological Seminary, New York City. There is another modern theory that no sexual orientation is fixed. See Ambrosino, "I'm gay—But I wasn't born this way." Says Ambrosino, "The line between heterosexuality and homosexuality isn't just blurry, as some take Kinsey's research to imply—it's an invention, a myth, and an outdated one."
27. Postma, "Wolterstorff: Biblical Justice and Same-Sex Marriage." This is surprising reasoning from an expert in Calvinism, since the basis of Calvinist theology is a healthy understanding of the doctrine of creation, a foundational notion at the heart of Romans 1:18–32.
28. Vines, *God and the Gay Christian*, 128.
29. John L. Allen Jr., "Interview with Anglican Bishop N.T. Wright of Durham, England," *National Catholic Reporter* (21 May, 2004). http://www.nationalcatholicreporter.org/word/wright.htm. Cited by Kevin DeYoung, "Not that kind of homosexuality?" *The Gospel Coalition*, last modified November 13, 2014, https://www.thegospelcoalition.org/blogs/kevin-deyoung/not-that-kind-of-homosexuality/.
30. Gagnon, *The Bible and Homosexual Practice*, 350.
31. Gagnon, *The Bible and Homosexual Practice*, 352.
32. Cited in Gagnon, *The Bible and Homosexual Practice*, 352.
33. See Bernadette Brooten, a self-identified lesbian professor at Harvard, author of *Love Between Women: Early Christian Responses to Female Homoeroticism* (University of Chicago Press, 1996), and pro-homosexual scholar, William Loader, *Sexuality in the New Testament* (2010) or his much larger *The New Testament on Sexuality* (2012), and Robert A.J. Gagnon "Why San Francisco's Biggest Megachurch Is Wrong About Sex." *First Things*, last modified March 7, 2015. http://www.firstthings.com/web-exclusives/2015/03/why-san-franciscos-biggest-megachurch-is-wrong-about-sex.
34. Robert A.J. Gagnon, "Does Jack Rogers's Book 'Explode the Myths' about the Bible and Homosexuality and 'Heal the Church'?" *RobGagnon.net*, last modified June 3, 2006, http://www.robgagnon.net/articles/Rogers-BookReviewed3.pdf.
35. Hays, *Moral Vision of the New Testament*, 386.
36. See Jones, *Stolen Identity*, 17–23.

37. Jones, *Stolen Identity*, 33. Citation from the ancient Gnostic text, *Hypostasis of the Archons*, 95:8ff.

38. Robert Reilly, *Making Gay Okay: How Rationalizing Homosexual Behavior is Changing Everything* (San Francisco: Ignatius Press, 2014), 39, 41.

39. William Love's statement has been taken down, but here is a news report about his statement: "Episcopal Bishop Goes Against Church Leaders, Bans Same-Sex Marriages," *NBC News*, last modified November 12, 2018, https://www.nbcnews.com/news/us-news/episcopal-bishop-goes-against-church-leaders-bans-same-sex-marriages-n935491.

40. As the title of his latest book indicates: *Still Christian: Following Jesus out of American Evangelicalism*. However, the rejection of the historic Christian interpretation of Scripture always leads to "Christian" liberalism, followed in short order by interfaith communion, and the disappearance or evisceration of the term "Christian."

41. 1 John 5:21.

42. Blocher, *In the Beginning*, 210.

CPSIA information can be obtained
at www.ICGtesting.com
Printed in the USA
BVHW091122211220
596048BV00004B/4